the
ULTIMATE
guide to the
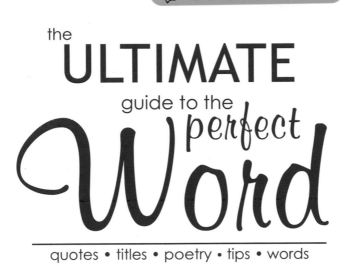
perfect
Word

quotes • titles • poetry • tips • words

by
Linda LaTourelle

BLUE GRASS
publishing
Mayfield, Kentucky

For information write:
Blue Grass Publishing
PO Box 634
Mayfield, KY 42066 USA
service@theultimateword.com
www.theultimateword.com

ISBN: 0-9745339-0-4

Library of Congress Catalog Card Number: 2003096334
1st ed.
Mayfield, KY : Blue Grass Pub., 2003

Blue Grass Publishers has made every effort to give proper ownership credit for all poems and quotes used within this book. In the event of a question arising from the use of a poem or quote, we regret any error made and will be pleased to make the necessary correction in future editions of this book. All scripture was taken from King James Version of the Bible.

Cover Design: Todd Jones, Tennessee
CK Fraternity font used with permission by Creating Keepsakes
Proudly printed in the United States of America

10 9 8 7 6 5 4 3 2 1

the
ULTIMATE
guide to the

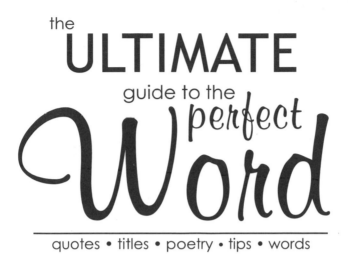

perfect

Word

quotes • titles • poetry • tips • words

Acknowledgements

acknowledgement\ak-nol'ij-m*u*nt\ n. The state or quality of being recognized or acknowledged; an expression of thanks or a token of appreciation

On the next few pages I want to give credit where credit is due. It is with the utmost sincerity I share the following words–

> dedicate\Ded"i*cate\, v. To address or inscribe (a literary work, for example) to another as a mark of respect or affection.

First of all, I want to thank the Lord for blessing me with the abilities to create this book. He opened so many doors (but that's a story for the future) and allowed His grace to flow. May His Glory shine through it all.

It is with so much love that I dedicate this book to my family. My dear husband and our two beautiful daughters have traveled the road of long days and nights above and beyond the call of duty. It has been a great learning experience for all of us and a wonderful opportunity for homeschooling in the real world. My life is so blessed because of your love for me. We are on this journey together, writing our tale day by day, year by year. I am so thankful to be sharing my life with this you. You are a blessing from above. I know this has been a difficult time with all the work, but I thank each of you, from the bottom of my heart, for all your help, love and patience with this vision I have held for so long for our family. Your encouragement has kept me focused. May you reap incredible blessings because of your constant love and devotion. You are an amazing family...My love for you is forever and always.

—*Linda (Mom)*

You are the sun in my winter sky, you are the hello in my goodbye. You are the stars shining down on me, you are everything I had hoped you would be. You are the arms wrapped around a hug, you are the pull when I need a little tug. You are the lips that feel my gentle touch. You are the one who loves me so much. You are the one who I come to for love. You are my angels sent from above. I need your love, I need you, too, because more than anyone else I am the I in I Love You.

gratitude\Grat"i*tude\, n. a feeling of thankfulness and appreciation; "he was overwhelmed with
gratitude for their help"...

Anna Faye. I want you to know that this book would not
be a reality were it not for your unconditional love, support and faith in me. It is incredible that someone would
love the way you do. There truly are no words to express my sincerest gratitude for the incredible kindness
you have shown. I thank you for so many things, but
most of all for being who you are—an awesome example
of a godly woman. I am humbled to call you my friend. May
you be so very blessed.

Todd Jones. All I can say is such altruism for a total stranger
can only be the result of a man after God's own heart. What
an awesome testimony of how God works when we give
him the reigns. That you and I should connect by one phone
call is amazing. That you should design a cover with such a
total insight into what I wanted without even expressing it—
that's divine. I am so thankful for such unbelievable kindness.
Please know that "thank you" doesn't even begin to tell you
what you have done. May blessings overflow.

Lisa. Well, little sister. What can I say? Look what God has
done. You know it all started because of your imagination
and has endured because of your encouragement. I have
been forever changed because of the confidence you
have shown in me since this project began. I am overwhelmed at how God has used this to give birth to something much more than a book—He has lovingly opened
new doors for the relationships we share as sisters (all of us).
For me that is such an awesome blessing. I have been so
overjoyed to feel the love and kudos as this book came to
be. May you be blessed by this book and may it be only the
beginning of so much more for all of us, together as sisters
and family. I thank you from the bottom of my heart for your
cheerful countenance and constant love.

"Gratitude is the fairest blossom which
springs from the soul." ~Henry Ward Beecher

8

■■■■■■■■■■■■■■■■■■■■■■■■■■■■

> Thanks\thanks\ pl.n. Grateful feelings or thoughts; gratitude: a heart full of thanks. An expression of gratitude: gave thanks to God; a note of thanks to a contributor

I want to extend very a special thank you to the many people who have helped with the various aspects of this book.

There are some people deserving of a special thanks for their contributions in ideas, editing, typing, editorial critique and more... Hannah, Lara Dan, Pam, Brandy, Darcy and Lisa, thank you for your late hours and loving assistance with typing and editing in preparation for printing. My heartfelt thanks to Tony Crouch of West KY Web Design (*www.wkywebs.com*). He worked so quickly to get my website up and running and looking good. I appreciate him so much. Thanks, Tony! A huge thank you to Josh for the tremendous help with all the technical things that sometimes were so overwhelming. You made it so simple! Blessings to Creating Keepsakes for use of one of their fonts and also to Doug at Inspire Graphics (*www.inspiregraphics.com*) for help with the fonts and Michele Conley for use of her cute swirl font. (*www.mcaf.com/mcfontsy*) Thank you all so much. I love you all. May you be blessed abundantly for your giving.

And to my parents...Thank you for your
unconditional love and support...
I love you more than you know!

No act of kindness, no matter how small,
is ever wasted. -Aesop

Table of Contents

Table of Contents

Table of Contents

Table of Contents

Table of Contents

L ife is a scrapbook of young and old in which our precious stories are told. When time moves on and our memories fail this book 'twill be sweetest tale. We can turn the pages of times gone by and see how the days and years did fly. A cherished child or faithful friend treasured everyday until the end. Blessings and miracles so rich with love these are our gifts from God above. -Linda LaTourelle

© 2003

Let the journey begin...

> **Journaling:** The process of compiling a written record of (usually personal) experiences and observations. Think of this... You are a writing part of history as you document your family stories.

Have you ever heard the saying— "Don't try eating the whole elephant at once"? Little bites make it easier to chew. Everyday, set aside a few minutes for journaling. LOOK—Spend just 15 minutes per day journaling and at the end of one year you will have written for 91 hours. See how fast it adds up! That's lots of writing with very little effort! Start today!

JOURNALING TIPS

Journaling is a journey–it's the heartbeat of your work! Yet, Scrapbookers and Rubberstampers often feel like it's the least important and most difficult part. Through these pages, I want to show you that journaling truly is the quintessential ingredient of your work. Now tell me, what can be easier than writing "who, what, where, why and when" about the events in your pictures? With one-word descriptions you can touch on the focal points of your designs. However, there's more...

Just think of journaling as afternoon tea with your best friend, joyfully engaged in a spirited chat. As with your chat time, writing is a time for you to explore and express thoughts, facts, feelings and ideas about a particular event or situation relating to the photos or perhaps even your life. Document in basic format (bullet journaling) or try your hand with more complex memoirs (paragraphs encompassing the descriptions above). Journaling is the perfect way to re-capture the moment and express to all who view your album the story behind the photos, as well as the heart of the author–usually you (or perhaps a family member).

Journaling is <u>the</u> <u>most</u> <u>important</u> embellishment for your pages and projects. Without your words, the pictures just become something nice to look at, but putting a pen to paper changes the entire emphasis of the page. It now becomes uniquely yours. The best part is that journaling is an avenue to a wealth of recollections that will hold the memory in your heart forever.

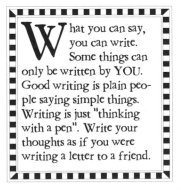

What you can say, you can write. Some things can only be written by YOU. Good writing is plain people saying simple things. Writing is just "thinking with a pen". Write your thoughts as if you were writing a letter to a friend.

JOURNALING TOOLS

- The Ultimate Guide to the Perfect Word–is definitely a must have for an abundance of quotes and phrases that will enrich your projects

- Pens...lots of them, different colors, thicknesses, shapes, types, metallic, watercolor, charcoal, etc.

- Templates...there are an abundance of journaling templates on the market to create cute little sections on your pages. Use them to do fun designs on cards that you create, too.

- Keep a pocket size thesaurus and dictionary with all your journaling tools. I am always referring to the thesaurus so I don't keep repeating myself. It also helps to get the creative juices flowing and expands your vocabulary at the same time.

- Paper...varying sizes, colors, textures, shapes, thicks and thins

- Chalks...these are wonderful to add soft touches to your journaling

- Scissors...all different shapes to create a variety of looks

- Paper cutter...mini size works for most cutting

- Accordion folder...keeps papers organized

- Notebook to list favorite quotes or jot down ideas and thoughts that come to you.

- Rubberstamps, Die cuts, Eraser, White Out, etc.

■■■■■■■■■■■■■■■■■■■■■■■■■■

JOURNALING DO'S

◎ Make your journal time a cozy time, just for you. Perhaps a cup of tea or hot chocolate. Some very soft piano music in the background. A comfy chair with a table next to it for your tools.

◎ Journaling time can actually be very therapeutic

◎ Find a quiet place to sit and journal. Noise and distractions aren't always conducive to creating a good train of thought

◎ If you get stuck on what to write:
  ~refer to the tips in my book
  ~try journaling for a different photo
  ~take a break and sip some tea
  ~write a word or two and go back later

◎ Ask other family members to share memories about the event depicted in the photograph

◎ If you've been jotting down thoughts every now and then, like when you're waiting somewhere, then you can refer back to that.

◎ Try to remember that when you go somewhere and you're taking pictures, it's a good idea to take a few notes. I have to, because I have days when I can't remember what I ate for breakfast at 8:00 and it's only 11:00. It's like my mind gets lost in the fog. *There's a quote about that... check it out!

■■■■■■■■■■■■■■■■■■■■■■■■■■

JOURNALING TIPS

◉ When you write, share your thoughts as though you were sitting and chatting with a friend about the event. This gives a feeling of freedom and makes it easier to express yourself in your journaling.

◉ Save catalogs from companies that sell items that are personalized, or specific to occasions such as holidays, birthdays, events, etc. They can open up new ideas.

◉ Try to add a small bit of journaling to each of the pictures pages, just so you don't have to read the whole story if you don't want to.

◉ Use a clear ruler (like quilters use) with a soft lead pencil to mark areas on your pages for journaling.

◉ Words of wisdom from you are your truth

◉ Use sticky notes or a paper clip to attach your notes and ideas for journaling to the page until you have time to finish it.

◉ When you develop your pictures, be sure to date them. While events are still fresh, jot down your thoughts. Make notes of cute things your child said or did, feelings you had, or things that occurred that aren't as evident in the photos. This will help to jog your memory later.

◉ Get some help! Ask family members to make a note of the top five things they remember or felt were special to the event. This way you will have their perspective, not just yours. It adds a new dimension to your journaling.

◉ Make short outlines of the event. Using the who, what, when, where & why will simplify and make it easier later.

⊚ **Make** lists of words to describe the photo. Adjectives about something can help to give us a pretty good mental picture of what was happening in the picture.

⊚ By doing simple things as lists, one word descriptions, letters, etc. you are building skills needed to become better at journaling. People often think of journaling as a chore, but in reality it is truly a gift you give to yourself. Why? Because when you look back as time goes by, you will see a picture of something much deeper than the photographs on your pages. You will see yourself reflected in your thoughts. And even better, so will others. Journaling helps to capture the essence of who we are in a way that often isn't as evident in verbal contact.

⊚ Give the gift of yourself...write from your heart... right from the start.

⊚ When writing about a picture of a person, do a bulleted list of all the great qualities this person exemplifies.

⊚ Write about a birth of your first child. Relive just that day, from morning until night (or night 'til morn). Share all the anticipation, pain, joy and awesomeness.

⊚ There are no rules in journaling. Write as simple as facts or embellish your pages with more personal info about you and your family. What a blessing to future generations to discover there were similarities between them and you. Only you can share such thoughts.

JOURNALING TIPS

◎ Always remember that "who, what, where, when and why" make for quick captions on your photos when you don't have time to journal much.

◎ Carry a small pad (3" x 4") in your purse, so that when you're in situations where you have to wait for periods of time you can jot down any thoughts about things you've recently photographed. Wait times are wasted times, so why not make it fun and purposeful for your scrapbooking.

◎ If you are concerned about what you're going to write, simply put it on separate pieces of paper and then mount those to decorative paper and put the finished pieces on your pages or projects.

◎ Journaling can be done in many fancy shapes using templates that are available for purchase. Or get creative, frame your pictures with squiggly lines lightly drawn with pencil and journal on them.

◎ Look at advertising in magazines to study color combinations, both of ink and paper. Professional designers are great teachers, their work can help inspire your creativity.

◎ Use plain paper to practice what you want to write

◎ Color your pages with words. You can embellish your pages with words that will add flair and personality to your pages. Just like positioning other decorations on pages, journaling in your own handwriting (or other family members) adds a unique touch that will be cherished forever

Think back to English 101 when you learned about adjectives and adverbs. Remember, an adjective modifies a noun (person, place or thing), while an adverb modifies verbs, adjectives and adverbs. It tells where, when, how, how often and to what extent. These kinds of words can really jazz up a simple page significantly to draw attention to the reader. Such words bring to life events in a delightfully memorable and often more vividly, realistic way. Here are some examples of adjectives for the word happy and adverbs for the word walking.

Happy: blessed, blest, blissful, blithe, can't complain, captivated, cheerful, chipper, chirpy, content, contented, convivial, delighted, ecstatic, elated, exultant, flying high, gay, glad, gleeful, gratified, hopped up, intoxicated, jolly, joyful, joyous, jubilant, laughing, light, lively, looking good, merry, mirthful, overjoyed, peaceful, peppy, perky, playful, pleasant, pleased, satisfied, sparkling, sunny, thrilled, tickled, tickled pink, up, upbeat

Walking: quietly, noisily, roughly, happily, joyfully, secretly, meanly, quickly, patiently, rambunctiously, before, after, slowly, sometime, swiftly, there, yesterday, almost, too, so, really, briskly, lazily

◎ What's in a word? Feelings, thoughts, etc.
◎ Everyone has a story that others want to hear
◎ Find quotes/poems to fit the theme
◎ Silence is the only failure. Don't fail to write now
◎ So you flunked English 101...write anyway!
◎ The strongest memory is weaker than the palest ink.
◎ There's no wrong way to write what's in you.

Only you can tell the story of you. No one in the world knows you better. Through your album you can choose how much or how little of yourself to reveal to others. Remember the past can be joyful and it can at times bring pain. But all of the emotions you feel are yours to express in your words, in your way. You own it all!

◎ Write letters to your spouse, children, parents, grandparents, friends. Keep a copy as a memento to reflect on as the years go by. Letter writing by hand or e-mail makes no difference. Most important of all—when you get a return letter from them, be sure to save it in some form in your album. When children are grown these writings become priceless treasures that bring you home to their heart. And don't forget the value they give upon original receipt.

◎ Paint a picture with your words. As you look at your photos what colors, sounds, smells, feelings, etc. does it evoke? Express yourself just as though you were there all over again. Whatever you feel in your hearts eye—write it down. Your family will be blessed over and over again because you took the time.

◎ There are a lot of fun "alphabet" stickers on the market that make for eye-catching titles.

◎ Lists are great! Jot down top ten lists of your favorite things about family members, friends, events, milestones, etc. This is a perfect tool to evoke memories when you want to journal in length.

Write to capture what you'll soon forget

Try an interview...pretend you're a reporter trying to eek out a Pulitzer worthy story. Start with the facts and then embellish with the creme de la creme. Give it all you've got with tantalizing tidbits and delectable details. Hook your reader with a good opening line such as "The Adventure Begins..." or "On this day in history...". Ideas like this will enchant your reader, and truly be a blessing on those times you sit with your child or whomever, perusing your album and recounting the event. As you do this, precious memories will flood your soul. You will be sharing the times over and over again. Remember a picture tells a thousand words! Your words along with that picture could write a book...or close to it! Have fun and remember, these are your memories to relive and share, so let 'em flow—joyfully!

By doing simple things as lists, one word descriptions, letters, etc. you are building skills needed to become better at journaling. People often think of journaling as a chore, but in reality it is truly a gift you give to yourself. Why? Because when you look back as time goes by, you will see a picture of something much deeper than the photographs on your pages. You will see yourself reflected in your thoughts. And even better, so will others. Journaling helps to capture the essence of who we are in a way that often isn't as evident in verbal contact. Give the gift of yourself—write from your heart—right from the start.

What is a picture without words?

■■■■■■■■■■■■■■■■■■■■■■■■■■■■■■■

Think of journaling like writing a letter to an old friend. Pick a topic and just start writing. In your writing, pretend you are telling the reader about an event. Describe all the details of it. Remember to use all your senses. Sometimes if you sit quietly and close your eyes the memories will become vivid. Keep a pen in your hand and paper on your lap. As you think, just jot down single words or better yet all the details you can bring to mind. You can write with your eyes closed (don't worry about neatness now, you can clean that up later), this is your rough draft. Just relax and try to remember everything about the event from the time you left until you came home. Remember the who, what, when, where and why as you think. Sometimes these little cues will help to jog your memory and allow you to remember more.

On a day like today, let me stop to reminisce and pray. May my heart recall the gifts of love bestowed on me from far above. The years have vanished, so swiftly they did fly. As I recollect the joys and sorrows in my minds eye, I know how truly blessed I've been, even though I didn't see it then. -LaTourelle

Little words of kindness
little acts of love
bring a bit of heaven from above

The Journey

As you journey on through life today take time for the little things. It seems as if we are so conditioned to need the big things that we overlook the most wonderful blessings of all. It is in simplicity that we see the beauty around us everyday, a baby's smile, an elder's tear, the birds and bees, your spouses hug. There are lessons to be learned for each of us. Though the paths we trod take us on our own separate journeys, the purpose is the same as it has been since time began. We are called to love one another in word, thought and deed. Each of us is special and blessed in our own ways. Yet, we are all alike with hands to reach out to help, arms to embrace with hugs, mouths to speak with encouragement and hearts to love unconditionally. May it be discovered on this journey that we are all in need of love on a daily basis regardless of our position, race, religion or any other difference. Let us take today to see how one person at a time we might change the world. May we never be too busy to realize that someday might never come for some and that there are needs to fill right now.

What kind of legacy
do you want to leave for your family?

■■■■■■■■■■■■■■■■■■■■■■■■■■■■

On the following pages are questions that only you can answer as you journal on your pages or in a book where you have chosen to write your life stories. These questions are designed to elicit moments from your past. The way in which you answer these questions as you journal will be a treasure to those who read it now and for generations to come. The culmination of your answers gives your readers a portrait of you and your life's experiences. The questions are in no particular order, so feel free to pick and choose.

As you journal the wonderful stories behind your photos, perhaps you can keep some of these questions in mind or seeing them will help you to see more in your photos now when you scrapbook.

The heart can see what the camera cannot capture.
These are the memories so rare. ‑Linda LaTourelle

MAGNIFICENT MEMORIES

- Who was the first person to talk to you about God? What was your reaction.

- How far was your elementary, junior high and high school from where you lived? How did you get there?

- What was your first job? What did you make?

- What was your first car like? Did you buy it?

- Who was your favorite teacher and why?

- Did you collect things when you were a child?

- Do you collect things now as an adult?

- Age when you moved away from home?

- Have you ever owned your own home? Where and when? What was it like?

- What is the strangest thing you've ever experienced? Were you alone or with others?

- What was a memorable family tradition at Thanksgiving?

- What childhood memory first comes to mind when you think about each of these and how do you respond to those thoughts? Spring, Summer, Winter and Fall

- Were you ever in a Christmas Program? Was it fun? Tell the story of what it was like.

MAGNIFICENT MEMORIES

- ◎ Write about your ancestors, what stories have you heard about them?

- ◎ Write about your religious life as a child or an adult

- ◎ Describe in your journaling what is popular now. (Cars, music, technology, etc.)

- ◎ List the really big memories before you turned thirteen, happy or sad.

- ◎ Share your favorites: books, movies, tv, events, etc.

- ◎ What one person has had the most impact on you as a person? On your career? On raising your kids?

- ◎ When, where and how did you and your spouse meet?

- ◎ School Days, Rule Days, Good Old-Fashioned School Days...What did you like? Dislike?

- ◎ And the rest of the family...(Aunts, Uncles, Cousins)

- ◎ Grandparents–how have they shaped your life?

- ◎ Who is the most important person in your life & why?

- ◎ What does the best of times (and worst) mean to you?

- ◎ Describe your best friend in preschool, elementary, middle, high school, college and now.

- ◎ Describe your spiritual beliefs

- ◎ Did you ever go on a hayride or bob for apples?

MAGNIFICENT MEMORIES

◉ Describe your childhood home. Describe your home now.

◉ What is your favorite job and your least favorite? Why?

◉ What were your favorite subjects in school?

◉ Do you have any hobbies that you love to do?

◉ Where is the best place you have lived?

◉ How are your children like you? How are they different?

◉ Who was your first love? How old were you both?

◉ Have you been brokenhearted? Have you broken someone's heart?

◉ Where was your favorite vacation spot?

◉ What is the most outrageous, daring, silly, adventurous thing you've ever done? Write about each one.

◉ What was the happiest day of your life? What was the saddest

◉ What are the best memories of your brother/sister? What are the worst?

◉ What are the best memories of your husband/wife? What are the worst?

◉ Who is your favorite author and why?

MAGNIFICENT MEMORIES

◎ What is your favorite job and your least favorite? Why?

◎ Do you have any hobbies that you love to do?

◎ What was your favorite pastime as a child? Did you like to do it alone or with someone?

◎ Who gave you your name and why?

◎ Did you have a family nickname? Who gave it?

◎ Were you baptized or dedicated as an infant? Where, when, who was there?

◎ What are your earliest memories of church?

◎ Did you pray at bedtime when you were a child? Alone or with someone?

◎ Where did your father go to work everyday? What did he do?

◎ List three special memories about each of your brothers and/or sisters.

◎ How did your mother spend her day when you were a child? How does she spend it now?

◎ Describe what your family living room when you were a child?

◎ What is your most treasured possession and why?

◎ How did you celebrate each holiday? Go into detail describing your family traditions. Do you have those same traditions now with your family?

MAGNIFICENT MEMORIES

◎ Describe your first love. How old were you?

◎ What scent or sound immediately takes you back to your childhood?

◎ What was your favorite meal when you were a child?

◎ Did you ever have a special hideaway or treehouse or fort where you hung with your friends?

◎ Do you remember the fads when you were in school? Grade school and on up?

◎ Who was your best friend in school?

◎ Who was your best friend when you left home?

◎ Who is your best friend now?

◎ What's your favorite girls night out?

◎ What was your favorite guys night out?

◎ What did you and your friends do when you were in high school on a Friday night?

◎ What is the funniest memory of your mother?

◎ What is the funniest memory of your father?

◎ Did you ever go on a blind date?

◎ How did your parents meet each other? Was it love at first sight?

MAGNIFICENT MEMORIES

◉ Describe your grandparents home when you were a child. Did you visit them often?

◉ Share a memory of your grandparents or an older person you were close to or loved.

◉ Did you ever get a really memorable valentine? From who?

◉ Did you have a favorite pet as a kid? Name?

◉ Did you have to do chores growing up?

◉ Did you get an allowance as a kid?

◉ Have you ever been in a play? When, What, Where?

◉ Have you kept any Christmas treasures from year to year? What special meaning to they hold?

◉ Did you have a special stocking or ornament? What did it look like?

◉ What is your favorite Christmas Carol?

◉ What is your most memorable Christmas present? That your received? That you gave?

◉ Describe the family dynamics at holiday time.

◉ What one word best describes your life? Home? Job? Children? Husband? Family? Personality? Now explain why.

MAGNIFICENT MEMORIES

◉ Where were your parents born? Grandparents?

◉ Do you know anything about your heritage? What country did your ancestors originate from?

◉ Did you play sports? Do your children?

◉ Do you play an instrument or sing?

◉ Are you artistic? If so, what medium do you like to create in?

◉ What does your husband do at his work?

◉ Have you moved around much? Locally, national, or international?

◉ Try doing a family tree with birthdays, weddings, anniversaries and other important dates.

◉ Have you or anyone in your family ever had 15 minutes of fame (or more)?

◉ Have you traveled to anywhere exotic?

◉ How old were you and your husband when your first child was born?

◉ How are the in-laws?

◉ How many brothers and sisters do you have? Your spouse have?

◉ If your children are grown write about them.

FEELING WORDS

The following are lists of words that will help you in get creative as you journal. When you are looking for a little more embellishment you may find it helpful to refer to these words. Happy Journaling...

HAPPY
brisk
calm
carefree
cheerful
cheery
comfortable
complacent
contented
ecstatic
elated
enthusiastic
excited
exhilarated
festive
generous
grateful
hilarious
inspired
jolly
joyful
jubilant
lighthearted
merry
optimistic
peaceful
playful
pleased
relaxed
restful
satisfied
serene

sparkling
spirited
surprised
thrilled
vivacious

EAGER
anxious
ardent
avid
desirous
enthusiastic
excited
intent
keen
zealous

SAD
blah
choked up
concerned
depressed
disappointed
discontented
discouraged
dismal
dull
embarrassed
gloomy
heavy-hearted
melancholy
moody

quiet
somber
sorrowful
sulky
sullen
sympathetic
unhappy
useless
worthless

HURT
aching
afflicted
cold
crushed
despair
heartbroken
injured
isolated
lonely
offended
pained upset
Worried

ANGRY
annoyed
awkward
belligerent
bewildered
bitter
boiling
confused

FEELING WORDS

ANGRY
enraged
frustrated
fuming
furious
grumpy
indignant
inflamed
infuriated
irate
irritated
offended
provoked
stubborn
sulky

FEARLESS
bold
brave
confident
courageous
determined
encouraged
heroic
impulsive
independent
loyal
proud
reassured
secure

INTEREST
absorbed
concerned
creative

curious
engrossed
excited
fascinated
inquiring
inquisitive
intrigued
sincere

DOUBTFUL
defeated
distrustful
dubious
evasive
helpless
hesitant
hopeless
indecisive
perplexed
powerless
questioning
skeptical
suspicious
unbelieving
uncertain
wavering

PHYSICAL
alive
breathless
empty
feisty
hollow
immobilized
nauseated
paralyzed

repulsed
sluggish
stretched
strong
sweaty
taut
tense
tired
uptight
weak
weary

AFFECTION
aggressive
appealing
caring
close
crazy about
dear
demonstrative
devoted
doting
fond
friendly
huggy
loving
mushy
partial
passionate
seductive
sexy
sympathetic
tender
warm

■■■■■■■■■■■■■■■■■■■■■■■■■■■■■■

FEELING WORDS

LOVING
admiring
affectionate
amiable
amorous
appreciative
benevolent
dear
devoted
enamored
erotic
faithful
fervent
generous
impassioned
infatuated
kind
liking
loyal
mushy
passionate
respectful
reverent
romantic
sensual
sentimental
tender
thoughtful
valuing
warm-hearted
worshipful
zealous

AFRAID
alarmed
anxious

apprehensive
cautious
fearful
fidgety
frightened
hesitant
hysterical
impatient
insecure
nervous
panicky
shaky
terrified
timid
tragic

SEE
behold
glare
glimpse
inspect
look at
note
notice
observe
peek
peer
recognize
scan
scrutinize
sight
spot
spy
watch

SMELL
aroma
bouquet
detect
discover
essence
find
flavor
fragrance
odor
odorous
perfume
scent
sniff
spice
stink
whiff

TASTE
appetite
bitter
chew
chomp
kick
lick
nibble
palate
partake
punch
sample
savor
sip
smooth
sour
spicy
stomach

■■■■■■■■■■■■■■■■■■■■■■■■■■■

FEELING WORDS

TASTE
sweet
test
zest
zing

hearken
apprehend
audible
awareness
gather
give ear to
glean
hearken
learn
listen
perceive
receive
take in
understand

TOUCH
brush
caress
communicate
cuddle
embrace
feel
grip
grope
handle
hug
kissing
paw
pet
pinch

poke
rub
scratch
squeeze
stroke

FEELING
ambiance
appreciated
comprehend
discern
elation
encounter
endure
enjoy
excited
exhilarated
experience
impression
jubilation
mood
observe
romantic
sense
sensitive
unbelieving
vibes

PASSION
adoration
anger
craving
desiring
devotion
ecstasy
fired-up

fury
intense
jazzed
joyful
lust
stormy
temper
wild
zeal

Your favorites:

_____

_____

_____

_____

_____

_____

_____

_____

_____

_____

_____

_____

_____

■■■■■■■■■■■■■■■■■■■■■■■■■■■■■

JOURNALING TIPS

◎ A hundred years from now, someone will look at your album or journal and wonder what century it was created. No date may be a bit frustrating for the reader. Give all your pages a date and place.

◎ A theme album could be fun! The trip of a lifetime or just the family vacation you remember most. Divide the album into years if you don't have sufficient documentation. Do an album full of your family's annual vacations. Let your titles be bold. Seek out quotes that relate to the times.

◎ As you read through the quotes in my book, there will be some that strike a note in you. The words will bring to mind a memory. Record that particular quote or phrase and then jot down what it was that evoked those feelings.

◎ Be sure to capture any current events shaping history right now. Describe your thoughts or opinions.

◎ Compose a letter to loved one or friend. Ask questions or chat about a common event. Hang on to their response and then respond to it in your album next to a picture of relevance.

◎ Consider recording addresses and calendars as another way of documenting history.

◎ Who has been the most influential person to you thus far in your life? Good time to dedicate a page to honor that person.

■■■■■■■■■■■■■■■■■■■■■■■■■■■■

JOURNALING TIPS

◉ Describe particular milestones in your life.

◉ Describe the spiritual path you have been on and where it is leading you.

◉ Describe those special spiritual markers from your journey.

◉ DETAILS, DETAILS, DETAILS–you have so many wonderful tales to waiting to be told!

◉ Either draw a diagram of your family tree or see your local scrapbook store for preprinted ones that allow you to fill-in the blanks. Seek out the help of other family members to complete this project. Some trees are very large and can be tedious to complete

◉ FREE…You are free to write whatever you choose. Your journaling is not a test, it's a statement of your personal recollections regarding a person or event of particular value to you.

◉ Has there ever been a hymn, scripture, poem or prayer that has had significant meaning to you? Share what and why.

◉ Have a "Story Page" or title it some other name. Let the writing be the focal point on a page, embellish with simple decorations. Have your pictures displayed on the facing page with short captions.

◉ Have a family reunion. This is a great time to reminisce about your family's history. The input from others helps to bring to mind memories long forgotten. Use a mini recorder to make it easy.

Journaling Tips

◎ What's your favorite style of music to listen to?

◎ What is your favorite movie of all time?

◎ Your favorite book?

◎ In your journaling you can pass on information that other family members might find interesting. Things like pictures depicting the location where your great grandparents house once stood or a photo of the place where you and your spouse first met. Maybe if areas of your town are old and might not be around one hundred years from now, you might want photos of that, documenting the facts to preserve history.

◎ Ask your children or your spouse or even a relative such as a grandparent to write their feelings or thoughts about a particular subject.

◎ Now is the time to get grandparents to write about things in their life. They have stories to share that only they would know. These stories are part of your family history and would be a wonderful addition to any journal.

◎ For a faster and more efficient way to journal, have several page layouts completed. You can do your rough drafts of your writing on the computer. When you have enough journaling done for all the pages, print out your rough draft and find a comfy place to sit and write (actually copy) your word.

JOURNALING TIPS

◎ As you layout each page, plan out where you want your journaling to be. As a bookmark for your journaling, you can use sticky notes or those little sticky arrows that businesses use to denote where a signature needs to be written.

◎ 'If you go to a crop or just spent an evening or weekend doing power layouts, make sure you save room on each page for journaling.

◎ Like I've already pointed out, journaling is equally important as your photos, so make it a focal point, too. Leave a matted journaling box or shape for your writing.

◎ You can save space for later by lightly drawing lines on your page.

◎ For a wedding shower gift start a mini album and on each page write your favorite quote or share a special memory of you and the bride-to-be. Include pictures from the past of the two of you.

◎ Use the quotes along with your thought and create a calendar for family members as a Christmas gift that will be treasured all year. Put your favorite photos of family members to adorn it.

◎ Ask your kids to write about your last family vacation. How was it special? What was the most and the least fun? What will they remember most?

◎ Traditions...we all have them, kids, too. Write about what they are, how they began and why they are special to you.

■■■■■■■■■■■■■■■■■■■■■■■■

JOURNALING FOR A GIFT

Too often we forget the greatest gift we can give is ourselves. There are endless opportunities to do that and it's simple and best of all it's a gift of priceless value. You can make a beautiful little book to journal in as a gift.

There are books at your local library and resources online that will show you how to put together a simple little handmade book. You can embellish it with your creative genius, just like your scrapbook pages. They are such a special blessing to receive.

Some occasions for a gift of a mini-journal are:

A wedding…fill it with scripture or lyrics from the bride and groom's favorite song. Then add your blessings for a happy life.

Baby's Birth…add some quotes or parenting tips, finish it off with prayers for a joyous new life

Graduation…a good time to recall memories of the school days past. Add some quotes on success or goals and a prayer for the new journey ahead. Then give them congrats like only you can.

Birthday…Make a book of thoughtful things you will give throughout the year. Homemade muffins, a bouquet of flowers, lunch out, etc. and then a note of why that person is so special to you.

The ideas are endless and the gift will be treasured always. You'll have fun creating it, also! Go for it!

■ ■

JOURNALING FOR CARDMAKING

◉ Making cards is fun! Think of how people love to receive your handmade creations. Well, have there ever been times when you wish you'd had a card for a particular event, but just didn't have the time to put one together? If so, here's an idea. Set aside a night for card making. Make it a special time for creating, just like going to a crop. Have a fun evening of card making. You could even make it a time to get together with some friends. During that time do some power layouts of cards for all occasions. Then the next time something pops up you'll be prepared.

◉ When you make cards, leave some blank. Design the front so it would be suitable for any need.

◉ Don't forget to sign and date the back of your card creations. Most people I know that are recipients of a handmade card like to hang onto them. It's nice for them to see the date and remember when they received it.

◉ Make a set of mini gift cards. They're easy to make and fun to give as a set. Find a quote for the occasion or make them assorted. Tie a silk ribbon around them or find a cute little tin at a dollar store to package them in.

◉ Some of the inexpensive graphics programs come with templates to design your own envelopes. Or create your own template and be creative in decorating with stamps and quotes.

JOURNALING TIPS

◉ Have a folder on your desk or in a drawer that is specifically for those little mementos you want to include in you're album.

◉ Have you thought about "Dedication Pages"? Authors dedicate their books, so why not dedicate your albums? Think about the people and their stories that helped you to create the album. How have they impacted your life? What kinds of things could you write about them that would help others to know them better, say a hundred years from now.

◉ I know some people leave a space on the first or last page to list the contents of their album. Indexing simplifies it if you want to refer to a particular photograph or event.

◉ If you're like me, forgetting comes much easier than remembering. And for me the details are the most difficult to remember. Simple journaling, even captions will make it easier to recall the feelings and details of the experience years from now.

◉ Including some of your favorite mementos will add such a personal touch to your writing. You can even write about the memento, how you acquired it and how it connected with you.

◉ Journal your wedding! Everything from your courtship, to the engagement your wedding and through the honeymoon is a memory to be treasured. What a blessing, one day, for your children to view the beginning of their parent's love story

JOURNALING TIPS

◎ Journaling includes everything from a page title, to a photo's caption, to your descriptions on a page. Journaling can be done by hand, with a stencil, with your computer or even with die-cut letters.

◎ Keeping a daily journal is a great way to keep track of events. Just writing short notes, with key words can help to jog your memory when you get ready to do your pages.

◎ Occasionally there is extra space at the end of a journal. Opportunity... Write a summary of the year the album is about.

◎ Pen the lyrics to one of your favorite songs. The site http://lyrics.astraweb.com is a great place to search for favorites.

◎ Pretend you are a reporter documenting facts about yourself. Record vital statistics such as age, height, weight, hair and eye color and anything else that will give people a greater insight.

◎ Use your journaling to honor someone who has been important in your life or inspired you. What a way for you to reflect and better yet, what a blessing for that person.

◎ Do you remember your old neighborhood?

◎ What was your backyard like?

◎ Do you have any hobbies that you love to do?

◎ Remember when you were in elementary school and the teacher did silhouettes of you. It can be done very easily by taping a piece of paper to the wall. Have your child sit upright in a chair. Position the light so it shines on the child's head and creates the shadow on to the paper. The closer the light is to the child, the closer to actual size the shadow is. Adjust the light so the shadow fits the paper. Once you have the shadow like you want, use a pencil to trace the shadow onto the paper. When you're done, you can cut the silhouette out and adhere it to your page. One thought is that you can actually reduce the size in a copy machine to create smaller silhouettes. The finished silhouettes can be used on your pages or the smaller ones could be used for fun little cards for relatives. Use the silhouette to journal on about your child.

◎ Use your journaling to honor someone who has been important in your life or inspired you. What a way for you to reflect and better yet, what a blessing for that person.

◎ What are the best memories of your mother? What are the worst?

◎ What are the best memories of your father? What are the worst?

◎ Journaling includes everything from a page title, to a photo's caption, to your descriptions on a page. Journalling can be done by hand, with a stencil, with your computer or even with die-cut letters.

- Set aside a time to write your thoughts or observations. Often we accomplish more when we create some specific plan. Take a break for yourself and fill your pages with love and memories.

- Special Touch... Trace your child's hand on a page. Journal inside it. Depending on the size of their hand, you may only have room for a few keywords. Do it a couple times a year and you'll be able to see the growth of their little hands (Try a foot, too, to add a unique look).

- There are a lot of books on the market now that are a "fill-in-the-blank" type. These can be great triggers to get you going on writing.

- Try a family album that is the basics. Kind of like a family tree. Within the pages, document pertinent information such as births, marriages, anniversaries, other important dates, as well as more intimate information about their personalities. Schooling, professions, children, events in their lives—these are the things that will be precious memories.

- Try your hand at recording a statement of purpose. What are your plans and dreams and goals? Think how interesting it will be to reflect on these years down the road.

- When we write, too often we just write about the event. For me, I would rather know about the people in the pictures. Who were they, what were their ages at the time, chronicle information of a more personal nature.

⊚ Either draw a diagram of your family tree or see your local scrapbook store for preprinted ones that allow you to fill-in the blanks. Seek out the help of other family members to complete this project. Some trees are very large and can be tedious to complete

⊚ What funny or sad stories can you remember or have been told about your family as a whole or individual members and/or extended family?

⊚ Draw floor plans of your your childhood home and the home you own now.

⊚ Just a reminder again...DATE all your work. It's wonderful to have all the documentation, but one hundred years from now, people may wonder when things happened. It helps depict what life was like in that particular day and time.

⊚ Go into detail about your spouse and your family. Tell about their schooling, college, careers, interests, hobbies and anything else that people would find interesting.

⊚ One important note is that all this journaling will be a blessing to have on those times your future family is full of questions about the past. With these wonderfully journaled albums you're creating you will have many of the anwers to their questions right at your fingertips.

⊚ Whatever paper you are using to decorate your pages with, make sure it is archival quality.

Quotes

Phrases

Titles

and

More

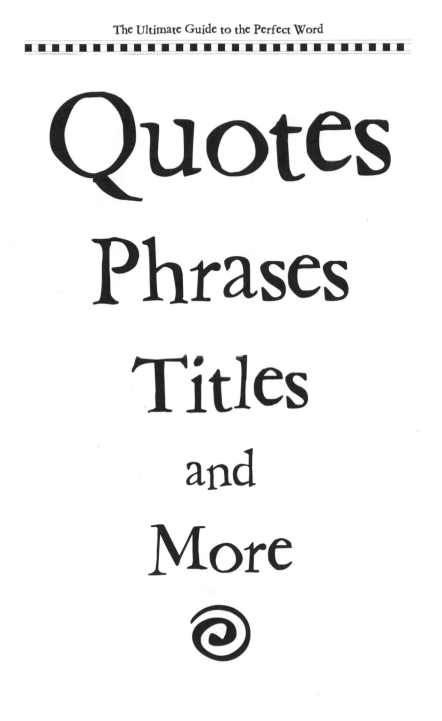

■■■■■■■■■■■■■■■■■■■■■■■■■■■■

ACCOMPLISHMENTS

◉ Start by doing what's necessary, then what's possible, and suddenly you are doing the impossible. - Francis of Assisi

◉ The world is an incredible unfulfilled tapestry. And only you can fulfill the tiny space that is yours.

◉ Throughout the centuries there were men who took first steps down new roads armed with nothing but their own vision. -Ayn Rand

◉ It is by what we ourselves have done, and not by what others have done for us, that we shall be remembered in after ages. -Francis Wyland

◉ Victory belongs to the most persevering. -Napoleon

◉ Do not follow where the path may lead. Go instead where there is no path and leave a trail. -Ralph Waldo Emerson

◉ Let your life lightly dance on the edges of Time like dew on the tip of a leaf. -Tagore

◉ No day like today to get started

◉ Journaling: The process of compiling a written record of (usually personal) experiences and observations. Think of this... You are a part of history as you document your family stories.

ACCOMPLISHMENTS

◎ Shoot for the moon, even if you miss you'll be among the stars

◎ Victory belongs to the most persevering. -Napoleon

◎ Don't bother just to be better than your contemporaries or predecessors. Try to be better than yourself. -William Faulkner

◎ It is by what we ourselves have done, and not by what others have done for us, that we shall be remembered in after ages. -Francis Wyland

◎ Let us not be content to wait and see what will happen, but give us the determination to make the right things happen. -Peter Marshall

◎ Our main business is not to see what lies dimly in the distance but to do what lies clearly at hand. -Thomas Carlyle

◎ The right man is the one who seizes the moment. -Johann Wolfgang von Goethe

◎ We would accomplish so much more if we thought of the possibilities

◎ Most of the important things in the world have been accomplished by people who have kept on trying when there seemed to be no hope at all. -Dale Carnegie

◎ Shoot for the moon, even if you miss you'll be among the stars

ACCOMPLISHMENTS

◎ We would accomplish so much more if we thought of the possibilities

◎ Our greatest battles are within our own minds. - Jameson Frank

◎ The greatest achievements are those that benefit others -Denis Waitley

◎ To accomplish great things we must not only act but also dream, not only plan but also believe. - Anatole

◎ Success is 1% inspiration–99% perspiration

◎ What funny or sad stories can you remember or have been told about your family and extended family?

◎ Each person's work is always a portrait of himself. -Samuel Johnson

◎ Believe that problems do have answers, that they can be overcome, and that you can solve them. - Norman Vincent Peale

◎ Act the way you'd like to be and soon you'll be the way you act. - Dr. George Crane

◎ Man's quest is always for sufficient self-confidence to be himself.

◎ Getting things accomplished isn't nearly as important as taking time for love. -Janette Oke

ADOPTION

◎ We didn't give your life to you, but God knew what to do. He planned it out so long ago, He knew just what you'd need. He found us sadly longing so for a baby that was sweet. Then when the time was right He opened all the doors to bring you home that night And bless our life with joy. -Linda LaTourelle

◎ A Family Is Made with Love

◎ A is for Adoption!

◎ The way my family came together. Did you know that adoption is forever?

◎ Always remember, we looked far and wide, and then we chose you

◎ Born of my heart

◎ Especially picked by your MOM and DAD!

◎ For us to have each other Is like a dream come true!

◎ I prayed for this child, and the LORD has granted me what I asked of him. -1 Sam1:27

◎ Sent from up above and filled our life with Love

◎ Truly a gift from God

◎ Today is the first day of our new family, filled with love forever more

◎ No matter whether birth or choice, a home is blessed from above. When caring parents claim their child, a family is formed by love

ADOPTION

- I think we're a happier family than if we were all kings and queens. We're so lucky we all found each other. That's what being adopted means. - Espeland & Waniek

- My Forever Family

- You grew not under my heart but in it.

- Oh Happy Day!

- Our family tree has been improved. Adoption made this so. For love, much more than blood lines, Makes us thrive and grow.

- With anxious hearts and open arms, we sought you everywhere. You, dear child, are a gift from God, the answer to our prayer.

- Blessed is this Day!

- Miracles from Heaven

- Our own little Miracle

- Hand-picked sweetly

- Today's the day

- Welcome to our World

- God has a perfect plan to make a family unit

- Home is where you are loved unconditionally

- Isn't God awesome—He knew that we would make a perfect family and so He brought you home to us!

AGE

When you are old and grey and full of sleep, and nodding by the fire, take down this book, and slowly read, and dream of the soft look your eyes had once, and of their shadows deep; how many loved your moments of glad grace, and loved your beauty with love false or true, but one man loved the pilgrim soul in you, and loved the sorrows of your changing face; and bending down beside the glowing bars, murmur, a little sadly, how Love fled and paced upon the mountains overhead and hid his face amid a crowd of stars   -Yeats

◎ Age is Just a Number. Mine is Unlisted.

◎ All These Years and Still Young at Heart

◎ As we grow old the beauty steals inward. -Emerson

◎ Born in the USA...long ago

◎ Count your life by smiles, not tears. Count your age by friends, not years.

◎ Don't worry about wrinkles they're just antique smiles

◎ When I grow I want to be a little boy. -Joseph Heller

◎ Gray hair is God's graffiti -Bill Cosby

AGE

⊚ I'm not as old as I used to be

⊚ Ever stop to think... And forget to start again?

⊚ First, I was a good BOY, Then, I became a nice KID, I was then a great GUY, Later, I grew up to be a fine MAN, Now, I'm just an old geeze

⊚ Forever Young

⊚ Funny, I don't remember being absent minded...

⊚ Geezer—formerly known as Stud Muffin

⊚ Growing old is mandatory; growing up is optional

⊚ How old would you be if you didn't know how old you was? -Satchel Paige

⊚ I finally got my head together; now my body is falling apart.

⊚ I'm 39 1/2–That's my final answer

⊚ I'm at the Age When The Gray-Haired Person I Help Across The Street Is My Spouse

⊚ I'm entering the metallic years-silver in my hair, gold in my teeth and lead in my bottom

⊚ I'm not old-I'm a recycled teenager

⊚ I love everything that's old, old friends, old books, old wine

⊚ Time himself is bald -Shakespeare

AGE

- I'm not old...I've just been young a very long time

- In my next life, I'm going to have more memory installed.

- In youth we learn; in age we understand. -Eschenbach

- Love is not a matter of counting the years...but making the years count. -Michelle St. Amand

- Over the Hill Gang

- Over what hill? I don't remember any hill

- The best classroom in the world is at the feet of an elderly person.

- The Old Folks at Home

- The older I get, the better I used to be

- You don't quit playing when you get old, you get old when you quit playing.

- To keep the heart unwrinkled, to be hopeful, kindly, cheerful, reverent-that is to triumph over old age. - Thomas Aldrich

- An old man loved is winter with flowers. -German Proverb

- You know you are getting old when your pacemaker opens the garage door

- No wise man ever wished to be younger. - Jonathan

AGE

- You're getting old when you get the same sensation from a rocking chair that you once got from a roller coaster.
- When We're Young at Heart
- Young at heart–slightly older in other places
- You're never too old to learn.
- You're not old...you're chronologically gifted
- You're only young once but you can be immature forever
- My wild oats have turned into prunes and All Bran
- Getting better all the time
- Old and lovin' it
- Aged like fine wine
- Grumpy old men
- You know you're getting old when the candles cost

AIRPLANE

- Da Bird
- Jet Settin'
- Flyin' High
- Up, up and away
- Fly the Friendly Skies
- From Here to Eternity
- Leavin' on a Jet Plane
- Free as a bird
- Cloud jumpin'
- Sleeping the flight away
- We're flyin' high now
- Mile High
- On Cloud Nine
- Cotton Candy?
- Peanuts? Some lunch!
- Comin' down the runway
- Take off...Here we go!
- Off we go into the wild blue...
- Lost our luggage...ugh!
- Last plane to Knoxville???

ALBUM TITLES

- Happy Days
- How time Flies
- As time goes by
- I remember when
- Days of Our Lives
- Our Family Tree
- Precious Memories
- Our Legacy
- Bits of Yesterday
- Generation Gap
- Dear Ancestor
- Legacy of Love
- Remember when...
- Memories and Milestones
- Seems like Yesterday
- Somewhere in Time
- The Way We Were
- The Wonder Years
- This is Your Life
- Those were the days
- Through the Years
- A Time to Remember
- Treasured Memories
- Generation to Generation
- Thanks for the Memories
- It Was the Best of Times
- It's a Wonderful Life
- Once upon a Lifetime
- Up Close and Personal
- A Legacy/Lifetime of Love
- It's a Mad, Mad, Mad, World
- Dedicated to the One I Love
- I thank God for every remembrance of you
- Memories are like keepsakes, always treasured
- We do not remember days, we remember moments
- Yesterday, Today and Tomorrow
- A Walk Down Memory Lane
- Our Family History/ Heritage

Obeautiful for spacious skies for amber waves of grain, for purple mountain majesties above thy fruited plain. America! America! God shed His grace on thee and crown thy good with brotherhood from sea to shining sea.

-Katharine Lee Bates

AMERICA

I pledge allegiance to the flag of the United States of America, and to the Republic for which it stands. One nation under God, indivisible, with liberty and justice for all.

I'm proud to be an A m e r i - c a n , where at least I know I'm free, and I won't forget the men who died, who gave that right to me and I'll proudly stand next to him to defend her still today, cuz there aint no doubt I love this land, God

AMERICA THE BEAUTIFUL

We the people...

United We Stand

Born in the USA

In God We Trust

Stars and Stripes

Let Freedom Ring

Made in America

A Star-Spangled Day

All American Boy/Girl

America Remembers

Remember our Heroes

Sweet Land of Liberty

This Land is Your Land

Every Heart Beats True

You're a Grand Old Flag

As American as Apple Pie

From the Heart of America

Proud to Be an American

Home, Home on the Range

Forever in Peace may it Wave

God bless America, land that I love

Three Cheers for the Red, White, and Blue

■ ■

AMUSEMENT PARKS

◎ Fairy tales do come true

◎ A Pirate's Life for Me

◎ A Thrill a Minute

◎ Coaster Fanatics

◎ Feel the Magic

◎ Acting Goofy

◎ I don't wanna grow up

◎ Let the Adventure Begin

◎ Look, Ma, No Hands!

◎ Mad Hatter Tea Party

◎ Magical Moments

◎ Splash Down!

◎ The Happiest Place...

◎ The Thrill of it All

◎ Under the sea

◎ Wet and Wild

◎ Ride the painted ponies

◎ Cotton Candy, Corn on the Cob & Cuddlin', Oh My!

◎ We're going down, don't throw up!

ANGELS

- ◎ Angel flyin' so close to my heart

- ◎ Angels-guardians of our souls

- ◎ Angels have wings to carry your prayers to God

- ◎ Angels may not come when you call them, but they'll always be there when you need them

- ◎ Angels dance

- ◎ Angels on duty

- ◎ Angels sent from up above,

- ◎ Please protect the ones we love

- ◎ Be not forgetful to entertain strangers, for thereby some have entertained angels unaware

- ◎ Friends are like angels, without any wings. Blessing our lives, With the most precious things

- ◎ My guardian has a tough job

- ◎ Night fall, stars appear, evening angels gather near

- ◎ Best friends—guardian angels in disguise

- ◎ Sun shines, birds sing, garden angel's flowers bring

- ◎ Tenderly Touched by an Angel's Wing

- ◎ The song of a robin is an angels voice in the garden

ANGELS

◎ We are each of us angels with only one wing, and we can only fly by embracing one another -de Crescenzo

◎ When we invite an angel into our inner sanctuary, we create a home for love

◎ Wherever you go, what ever you do, May your guardian angel watch over you

◎ Sun shines, birds sing, garden angels flowers bring

◎ I believe in Angels

◎ Angels fly because they take themselves lightly   -G K Chesterton

◎ Every time a bell rings, an angel gets its wings Good friends are angels on Earth

◎ Good friends are like angels you don't have to see them to know they are there

◎ Angels Follow You Everywhere

◎ An Angel's heart is filled with love

◎ Angels sent from up above, please protect the ones we love

◎ An Angel isas an Angel does

◎ When in doubt, look up!

◎ When in doubt ~wing it

◎ Snowflakes are angel kisses from above

ALPHABET

<u>A</u> ustin the Antelope

<u>B</u> ailey the Baboon

<u>C</u> heryln the Chinchilla

<u>D</u> arby the Duck

<u>E</u> lijah the Elephant

<u>F</u> aye the Flamingo

<u>G</u> eorge the Giraffe

<u>H</u> annah the Herring

<u>I</u> an the Iguana

J acob the Jellyfish

<u>K</u> aylee the Kitten

<u>L</u> ara the Lioness

<u>M</u> abel the Manatee

<u>N</u> atalie the Needlefish

<u>O</u> livia the Ostrich

<u>P</u> etunia the Panda

Q uintera the Queen Bee

<u>R</u> yan the Rhinoceros

<u>S</u> am the Swan

<u>T</u> odd the Tiger

<u>U</u> lysses the Urchin

<u>V</u> ictoria the Viper

<u>W</u> aldon the Walrus

<u>X</u> andy the Exotic

<u>Y</u> etty the Yak

Z oe the Zebra

Pick your child's initial and create a cute animal page

ANIMALS

- A Breed Above
- All creatures great and small, the Lord God made them all
- Animal Crackers
- Best of Breed
- Butterfly Kisses
- Every Birdy Welcome
- Ewe are loved
- Go Fish
- Hogs and Kisses
- Horsin' Around
- I'm in the MOO-d for love
- Kitten Kaboodle
- Land Snakes Alive
- Leap Frog
- Leapin' Lizards
- Pony Express
- Mice are Nice
- Monkey Business
- One Fish, Two Fish, Red Fish, Blue Fish
- Paws-itively Fun
- My Little Pony
- Pets "R" us
- Pick of the Litter
- Puppy Love
- Some Bunny loves you
- Something to Crow About
- Spoiled Rotten
- Stubborn as a mule
- Whale of a Good Time
- Wild Thing, I think I love you
- You quack me up!
- Hog wild for you
- Cat's Pajamas
- We Love our Pets
- City Zoo
- Best of Show
- Pick of the Litter
- Feed the Birds
- Just Ducky
- So Tweet
- Proud as a Peacock
- Lovebirds
- Duck Duck Goose
- Birds of a Feather

ANNIVERSARY

⊚ For hearing my thoughts, understanding my dreams and being my friend, for filling my life with joy and loving me without end

⊚ For me you have rendered all other men dull and all other lives uninteresting.

⊚ Grow old along with me, the best is yet to be

⊚ Happiness is being married to your best friend.

⊚ He was the ocean and I was the sand

⊚ If, out of time, I could pick one moment and keep it shining, always new, of all the days that I have lived, I'd pick the moment I met you

⊚ Always and forever

⊚ An Everlasting Love

⊚ Heart And Soul

⊚ Happy Anniversary

⊚ For Sentimental Reasons

⊚ I'll Love You For Always

⊚ Isn't It Romantic

⊚ All I ever need is you

⊚ I Got You Babe and I love you

⊚ You're my first, my last, my awesomeness

ANNIVERSARY

◉ On our anniversary I want to thank you for being with me for better or worse, for richer or poorer, in sickness and in health, through everything

◉ The Night We Were Wed

◉ Sentimental Journey

◉ That's the Glory Of Love

◉ The Very Thought Of You

◉ The Way You Look Tonight

◉ You're the Cream in My Coffee

◉ Years of Wedded Bliss

◉ Through the years It's better everyday-As long as it's okay I'll stay with you Through the years

◉ True love never grows old

◉ Two Make a Home

◉ Where your treasure is, there will your heart be

◉ The most precious possession that ever comes to a man in this world is a woman!

◉ What a difference you've made in my life

◉ Still crazy after all these years

◉ Let the good times roll on

◉ There'll never be anyone else but you

◉ May I have this dance for the rest of my life...

ANNIVERSARY

- ◎ It Had To Be You

- ◎ Just the two of us

- ◎ Never Be Anyone Else But You

- ◎ Through thickness, in joy and in home improvement

- ◎ We do not remembers days—just moments

- ◎ You are two very important things to me...
  You are my husband and my best friend
  Celebrate our love with praise to our Lord above

- ◎ Today I celebrate my love for you

- ◎ I would do it all again

- ◎ Together is the nicest place to be

- ◎ 25 years shining silver

- ◎ 50 years of golden bliss

- ◎ Happiness is being married to my soul mate

- ◎ My lover, my lover, my life

- ◎ Oh how we loved on the night we were wed

- ◎ Love is... YOU and ME together 4-ever

- ◎ A zillion-derfuls of love and marriage

- ◎ Renewing our commitment

- ◎ Love, love you do...

ANTIQUES

- Grandmas are just ancient little girls.
- Grandpas are antique little boys.
- One man's junk is another's antique
- Grandparents may be oldies...but they're goodies!
- Old as the hills, but worth a bunch
- Antique treasures found here
- Junkyard Antiques
- Antique-aholic

APPLES

- A is for Apple
- Apple Annie
- The Big Apple
- Apple of my eye
- Shiny apples, yummy pie...make me happy all the time
- Apple Dumplin' Darlin'
- As American as apple pie
- Any fool can count the seeds in an apple. Only God can count all the apples in one seed
- Comfort me with apples: for I am sick of love. -Sol. 2:5
- A word aptly spoken is like apples of gold in settings of silver. -Prov. 25:11

ARCHERY

- Straight as an arrow
- Archers shoot from the heart
- So long as the new moon returns in heaven a bent, beautiful bow, so long will the fascination of archery keep hold in the hearts of men. -Thompson
- I shot an arrow into the air
  It fell to earth I know not where
- My Quiver is full
- Aim Straight

ART & ARTISTS

We are all artists gently guided by our Master's hand, painting a vision called life. The blending of colors like joy, sorrow, wisdom and love inspire us to create a magnificent masterpiece of self.

-LaTourelle

- ◎ Imagination is the soul within. -Linda LaTourelle
- ◎ Artists paint with their heart, not their hands -LaTourelle
- ◎ The heart of the artist is a masterpiece   -LaTourelle
- ◎ I'm creative - you can't expect me to be neat too!
- ◎ Lord, grant that I may always desire more than I can accomplish. -Michaelangelo
- ◎ Murals of life as painted by _____
- ◎ Every man is an artist painting his life everyday
- ◎ He paints by the seat of his pants and his shirt and his hair.
- ◎ A picture speaks of truth -Linda LaTourelle
- ◎ Michaelangelo is my hero
- ◎ Paint your heart out
- ◎ Draw, Color, Paint–Picasso I ain't
- ◎ Blooming with expression
- ◎ Cut and Paste
- ◎ Our Little Artist
- ◎ Art and Soul
- ◎ Pint-size Picasso
- ◎ Strokes of Genius
- ◎ Artists do it with creativity
- ◎ Colour my world with love
- ◎ Creativity Runs in the Family
- ◎ A Pigment of My Imagination

▪▪▪▪▪▪▪▪▪▪▪▪▪▪▪▪▪▪▪▪▪▪▪▪

ATTITUDE

◎ Heaven is under our feet, as well as over our heads -
Thoreau

◎ That which we persist in doing becomes easier - not
that the nature of the task has changed, but our ability to do has increased. - Emerson

◎ The art of life is to know how to enjoy little and endure much. -Hazlitt

◎ We're never weaker than when we're angry. -Dr. Phil

◎ The greater the difficulty-the greater the glory. -Cicero

◎ The happiness of your life depends on the quality of
your thoughts.

◎ The human spirit is stronger than anything that can
happen to it. -C.C. Scott

◎ The really happy man is the one who enjoys the
scenery on a detour.

◎ The way I see it, if you want the rainbow, you gotta
put up with the rain. -Dolly Parton

◎ Think big thoughts but relish small pleasures. -H. Jackson
Brown

◎ Those who think they know everything are annoy-
ing to us who do!

◎ Too many people miss the silver lining because
they're expecting gold. -Maurice Setter

◎ Turn your face to the sun—the shadows fall behind

◎ Watch It! I wasn't hired for my disposition!

◎ We cannot direct the wind but we can adjust the sails

◎ Win as if you were used to it, lose as if you enjoyed it
for a change.

◎ Sometimes I'm so sweet even I can't stand it.

ATTITUDE

- You can agree with me or you can be wrong

- You can complain because roses have thorns, or you can rejoice because thorns have roses

- Oh, did you say something?

- Reach for the stars, even if you have to stand on a cactus. - Longacre

- Some days there won't be a song in your heart. Sing anyway. -Emory Austin

- My answers are right. Your questions are wrong!

- What lies behind us and what lies before us are tiny matters compared to what lies within us. -OW Holmes

- Light tomorrow with today. -Elizabeth Barrett Browning

- Decide that you want it more than you are afraid of it. -Bill Cosby

- In the middle of difficulty lies opportunity. -Einstein

- Do not wish to be anything but what you are and try to be that perfectly. -Francis De Sales

- Remember, today is the tomorrow you worried about yesterday. -Dale Carnegie

- Did you ever think you were the weird one?

- Expect nothing, live frugally on surprise -Alice Walker

- I have never met a man so ignorant that I couldn't learn something from him. -Galileo

- I never really look for anything. What God throws my way comes. I wake up in the morning and whichever way God turns my feet, I go. -Pearl Bailey

- But the fruit of the spirit is...kindness." -Gal 5:22

■■■■■■■■■■■■■■■■■■■■■■■■■■■■

ATTITUDE

◎ Who wears the crown?

◎ Do your best-what else is there?

◎ Be reasonable! Do it my way!

◎ Disguised as a responsible adult

◎ It's nice to be important, but it's more important to be nice

◎ Let's get this straight right NOW-I don't have a sense of humor!

◎ Watch It! I wasn't hired for my disposition!

◎ We cannot direct the wind but we can adjust the sails

◎ Win as if you were used to it, lose as if you enjoyed it for a change.

◎ You can agree with me or you can be wrong

◎ You can complain because roses have thorns, or you can rejoice because thorns have roses

◎ Oh, did you say something?

◎ Reach for the stars, even if you have to stand on a cactus. - Longacre

◎ Some days there won't be a song in your heart. Sing anyway. -Emory Austin

◎ Sometimes I'm so sweet even I can't stand it.

◎ If we shall take the good we find, asking no questions, we shall have heaping measures. -Emerson

◎ If you're not lighting any candles, don't complain about the dark

◎ I'm up and dressed, what more do you want?

◎ Impossible is a word only to be found in the dictionary of fools. -Napoleon

ATTITUDE

◎ Whatever!
◎ Spoiled Brat
◎ Deal With It
◎ Ask me if I care
◎ Who's the Boss?
◎ Tell me why I care
◎ Attitude? Who Me?
◎ Fussy Little Princess
◎ Whatever!
◎ Spoiled Brat
◎ Deal With It
◎ Ask me if I care
◎ Who's the Boss?
◎ Tell me why I care
◎ Attitude? Who Me?
◎ Attitudes are contagious
◎ You are what you believe
◎ Our favorite attitude should be gratitude
◎ Did you ever think you were the weird one?
◎ If you're already walking on thin ice, you might as well dance. -Gill Atkinson

Enjoy the little things, for one day
you may look back and realize they
were the big things. -Robert Brault

AUNT

- Always Understanding and Naturally Terrific

- Aunt is just another word for love

- Aunt's are Awesome

- Far or near Aunt's are special all the year

AUTUMN

- October Fest

- Harvest Moon

- A is for Autumn

- A Crop of Good Friends

- Indian Summer

- Harvest Festival Fun

- Kaleidoscope of Colors

- Summer's over School's begun

- Merrily sing the harvest home

- And they went out into the fields, and gathered their vineyards, and trode the grapes and made merry, and went into the house of their God, and did eat and drink. –Judges 9:27

- Earth is here so kind, that just tickle her with a hoe and she laughs with a harvest. -Douglas Jerrold

- We Rake, We Pile-We Jump

AUTUMN

◉ The rosy apple's bobbing Upon the mimic sea-- Tis tricksy and elusive, And glides away from me. -R. Munkittrick

◉ The vineyards are blazing with the blush of fall--this harvest has been the most blessed of all. -LaTourelle

◉ Fabulous Fall

◉ Softly float the leaves of Fall

◉ Crisp, apple red days and cozy nights.

◉ No spring nor summer beauty hath such grace as I have seen in one autumnal face -John Donne

◉ Pumpkins in the cornfields Gold among the brown Leaves of rust and scarlet Trembling slowly down Birds that travel southward Lovely time to play Nothing is as pleasant As an autumn day!

◉ Everyone must take time to sit and watch the leaves turn. -Elizabeth Lawrence

◉ Gather the gifts of earth with equal hand; henceforth ye too may share the birthright soil, the corn, drink the wine & all the harvest home. -E. Stedman

◉ Hi-Ho, Hi-Ho, It's Off to Rake we Go!

◉ I walked on paths of crisp, dry leaves after, that flamed with color and crackled with laughter.

◉ No spring nor summer beauty hath such grace

◉ Nod to the sun. Summer is over, Fall has begun!

AUTUMN

◎ Raise the song of Harvest home! -Henry Alford

◎ We live for the bounties of fall, but the harvest of friendship is blessed above all

◎ When Autumn Leaves Are Falling...

◎ Autumn's Palette

◎ Changing Seasons

BABY LOVE

A- Anticipation
B- Baby Bottles
C- Congratulations
D- Dad
E- Excitement
F- Family
G-Grandparents
H- Happy
I- Impish
J-Joy
K-Keepsakes
L- Love
M- Mom

N- Nicknames
O-Outings
P- Pets
Q- Questions
R-Reflections
S- School
T- Toys
U- Ultrasound
V- Vacations
W-Wonderderfu
X-Xtraspecial Baby
Y- Your family
Z-zzz- Lullaby

■■■■■■■■■■■■■■■■■■■■■■■■■■

As I stood and watched you sleeping, the moonlight kissed your face. My heart is overwhelmed with your beauty and your grace. How precious and so delicate is your tiny little hand. And the sweetness of your lips and eyes is nothing less than grand. Your spirit and your softness tenderly sets my heart aglow, with a love so deep and infinite that only a mother could know. So tonight I count my blessings for my darling, baby dear, for surely God did hear my heart and answered every prayer.   -Linda LaTourelle ©2003

You rose into my life like a promised sunrise, brightening my days with the light in your eyes
Maya Angelou

◆

Roses 'round the door, baby on the floor, who could ask for anything more

◆

Precious baby I look in you eyes and wonder how such innocence can be so wise

◆

Sugar and Spice and everything nice, that's what little girls are made of

◆

Twinkle twinkle little star, do you know how loved you are?

BABY

Baby powder, baths, diaper pins and more. Rattles and teddy's and dolls you adore. These are the little things that brighten each day. Snuggles and rockin' and sweet kisses, too, what else would your mother choose for you. Love is all she knows and love is all she'll give. Treasure every moment every day she lives.

-Linda LaTourelle ©

◉ 10 tiny fingers ready to play. 10 tiny toes dancing away. 2 tiny hands to hold from the start and 1 precious smile that touches your heart. -Linda LaTourelle ©

◉ A baby is: a kiss, a coo, a giggle and grin and love for you

◉ A baby is: love, kisses, joy, sunshine, smiles, sweetness...

◉ Baby face, you've got the cutest little baby face!

◉ Baby's Daily Agenda : eat, nap, play, eat, nap, play...

◉ Before you were born: I dreamed of you, I imagined you, I prayed for you. Now that you're here: I hope for you, I love you and I thank God for you. -Linda LaTourelle

◉ I'm swingin', I'm jumpin', I'm climbin'. I'm growin'

■■■■■■■■■■■■■■■■■■■■■■■■■

BABY

- They placed you in our arms and all our dreams came true

- The Sunshine of My life

- Queen of Daddy's Heart

- Baby Mine

- Rock-a-bye Baby

- Party - My Crib–2 A.M.

- With my good looks...

- Blessed Assurance, Mamma is here. Sweet love to give for her baby dear. Linda LaTourelle

- Born in the USA today!

- Bundle of joy sent from above, glorious treasure to treasure and love

- Children are a gift from God

- Cute things I say and Do

- Peek-a-pretty baby

- Daddy's Little Princess

- Peek-a-boo Playmates

- From small beginnings come great things

- Getting to know you. Getting to know all about you. You are my precious, you are the best.

■■■■■■■■■■■■■■■■■■■■■■■■■■■■■■

BABY

◎ Have you ever held a baby, a baby, a baby, a baby like this?

◎ Here Come the Tears

◎ I believe in Miracles... You're the reason!

◎ I will give thanks to Thee, for I am fearfully and wonderfully made. -Psalm 139:14

◎ Little boys are awesome blessings, filled with imagination and fun. Their charm is magic and energy abounding until the day is done. -Linda LaTourelle ©

◎ I'm Just a Baby - What's Your Excuse?

◎ Little girls are precious gifts, wrapped in love serene. Their dresses tied with sashes, their future tied with dreams.

◎ Miracle on 34th Street (Change it to your street)

◎ Baby's Milestones

◎ Mirror, mirror on the wall, Who's the cutest baby of them all

◎ Snips and snails and puppy dogs tails; that what little boys are made of.

◎ Whining and Dining

◎ Snuggle, cuddle, baby bunting

◎ Cutie Patootie

BABY

◉ The wonder of a miracle from which this love began. There's so much love in the touch of a child's hand

◉ My little hands play patty-cake they peek-a-boo and wave...They catch me while I learn to walk and splash me as I bathe...My little hands reach up to you for hugs before I sleep...and fold together when I pray the Lord my soul to keep

◉ Dear God. Thank you for the baby brother, but what I prayed for was a puppy

◉ You were our first miracle. You were the genesis of a marriage, the fulfillment of love, the promise of our infinity...You were the beginning. -Erma Bombeck

◉ A mother's children are portraits of herself.

◉ When the first baby laughed for the first time, the laugh broke into a thousand pieces and they all went skipping about, and that was the beginning of fairies. And now when every new baby is born its first laugh becomes a fairy. -James Barrie

◉ To see a newborn is to forget our own egos, to realize how little we do to affect the mystery of creation. -Samuels

◉ To hold you in our hand is to hold a miracle so grand

◉ Babies are cuddling, cooing, laughing and pooing. to share

BABY NICKNAMES

Bug	Rosebud
Peanut	Stinker
Boogie Baby	Papa's Buddy
Grandma's Joy	Kissable Kid
Lil' Slugger	Little Bubba
Mommy's Jewel	Mr. Huggable
Daddy's Lil' Dude	Precious Cargo
Sweet Pea	Lil' Darlin'

BABY SLEEPTIME

- A Lullaby Moment
- Close your little sleepy eyes . . .
- Down for the Count
- Dreamland Express
- Golden Slumbers
- Good Night, Moon
- Night, night sleep tight, don't let the bed bugs bite.
- Having a child fall asleep in your arms is one of the most peaceful feelings in the world.
- In the Wee Small Hours of the Morning
- Mr. Sandman
- Now I lay me down to sleep
- Recharging
- Shhh... baby is dreaming
- The Princess of Dreams
- With a butterfly kiss and a ladybug hug, sleep tight little one, like a bug in :

BABY FIRSTS

First Bath	First Smile
First Food	First Steps
First Easter	First Tooth
First Outing	First Word
First Vacation	First Haircut
First Christmas	First Crawling
First Photo	First Rolling Over

BABY FOOD

- Bottomless pit
- Chow Time
- Milk Monster
- Sweet Potato
- Sweetie Pie
- Lil' Pumpkin
- I want my bottle
- Feed Me, Feed Me
- Me Want Cookie
- Veggie Vengeance
- Look Ma, no hands!
- Isn't this finger food?
- Finger Lickin' Good!
- Peanut Butter and Jelly
- Animal Crackers In My Soup
- Mommy's Little Mess Maker
- Food Fight-guess who lost!
- Yummy, Yummy, Yummy
- Eat it? I Can't even pronounce it
- I Got Veggies In My Tummy
- Quick, hide the broccoli and peas
- Hard to be neat when you're learning to eat

BABY

- The best thing to spend on kids is time

- My fair baby

- The many faces of _____

- The noblest job of all is being a parent

- Who's Spoilin' Who?

- Shake, Rattle, and Roll

- Yes Sir, that's my Baby!

- Someday when I'm all grown up, you're what I want to be.

- Sweet Pea: Water often with tender love care Grows fast!

- Thank Heaven for little babies, they grow up in a most delightful way

- My child you touched my soul right from the start and showed me how to love in a way I never knew. I know it was for you I have yearned all these years. In one moment my life was changed forever and if I live to forever there can never be anyone who will fill my heart with such a joy and love. -LaTourelle

- Dancing in on angel feet straight from Heaven's brightest star

BAKING

- A is for Apple Pie
- Baking Beauty
- C is for Cookie
- Cookie Monster
- Dough, Re, Me
- Deedle, deedle Dumplin'
- Everyone loves to be kneaded
- Got cookies?
- Have your cake and eat it, too
- Home baked love
- Just like Mom used to bake
- Lovin' from the oven
- Mamma's Kitchen
- Mom's Apple Pie
- Pat-a-cake, Pat-a-cake, Baker's Man
- Sweet aroma
- That little old baker, Mom
- Cinnamon & Spice Yummy and Nice
- That Little Old Baker...Mom (or whoever)
- Pies and Cookies and Cakes, Oh, My
- Blue Ribbon Baker
- Baked with Tender Loving Care

BALLET

- A Pointe in Time
- Ballet Beauty
- Ballet never becomes easy, it only becomes possible. Agnes DeMille
- Ballet teachers keep their students on their toes.
- Ballet Togs
- Beautiful Ballerina
- Dancing on Air
- Graceful Beauty
- Holding on to the Air
- Little Ballerinas
- Prima Ballerina
- The Art of Ballet
- Tiny Dancer
- Toe shoes and tutus
- TuTu Cute
- Dancin' Queen
- En Pointe
- Twinkle Toes
- Tiny Dancer
- Tap Dogs
- First Recital

■■■■■■■■■■■■■■■■■■■■■■■■■■■

BALLET

◉ Ballet is a dance executed by the human soul. -Pushkin

◉ Dance is the hidden language of the soul. -Martha Graham

◉ Dance what you love. -LaTourelle

◉ Dancing appears glamorous, easy, delightful. But the path to paradise of the achievement is not easier than any other. There is fatigue so great that the body cries, even in its sleep. There are times of complete frustration, there are daily small deaths. -Martha Graham

◉ Fine dancing, I believe like virtue, must be it's own reward. -Jane Austin

◉ Great dancers are not great because of their technique, they are great because of their passion.

◉ I'd rather learn from one bird how to sing, than to teach ten thousand stars how not to dance. -E.E. Cummings

◉ If ballet was easy, then everyone would be doing it.

◉ It takes an athelete to dance, but an artist to be a dancer. -Shanna LaFleur

◉ Learning to walk will set you free. Learning to dance gives you the greatest freedom of all: to express your whole self, the person you are. -Hayden

◉ Why do I dance?.....Why do I breathe?

◉ You can dance anywhere, even if only in your heart.

BAND MUSIC

Early in the morning I hear on your piano you (at least, I guess it's you) proceed to learn to play. Mostly little minds should take and tackle their piano while the birds are singing in the morning of the day.   -
Robert Louis Stephenson

◎ Clef-hangers

◎ Fit as a fiddle

◎ Always Twirling

◎ Ebony and Ivory

◎ Pickin' and grinnin'

◎ Mr. Tambourine Man

◎ Music From The Heart

Jam Session

76 Trombones

I've Got Rhythm

Live and in concert

Strike Up The Band

Practice Makes Perfect

◎ A harp is just a nude piano.

◎ Pretty good isn't good enough

◎ It's Still Rock and Roll to Me

◎ The Drum Major is...the Leader of the Pack

◎ I'm Just A Singer In A Rock and Roll Band

◎ Marching to the beat of my own drum

◎ There are two golden rules for an orchestra: start together and finish together. The public doesn't give a damn what goes on in between. -Sir Thomas Beecham

◎ A painter paints pictures on canvas. But musicians paint their pictures on silence.   -Leopold Stokowski

◎ Blow trumpet, for the world is white with May-Tennyson

BAPTISM

- A Child of God
- Saved by Grace
- Washed my sins away

Adopted by God
Jesus Loves Me
White as Snow

BARBEQUE (GRILLIN')

- Chillin' 'n Grillin'
- Grill or Chill
- Road Kill

Boy meets Grill
Grilling King
Where's the beef?

- It is a far, far better barbecue that I have now, than I have ever had before
- To BBQ or not to BBQ, that is the question
- It is better to have burnt and lost, then never to have barbecued at all

BASEBALL

- A Grand Slam

- If winning isn't everything, why do they keep score?
  -Vince Lombardi

- A hot dog at the ball park is better than steak at the Ritz. -Humphrey Bogart

- Baseball is life. The rest is just details. -Sporting News

- Buy me some peanuts and cracker jacks. I don't care if I ever get back.

- Casey at the Bat

- I may not be the bestest pitcher in the world, but I sure out-cutes 'em. -Satchel Paige

BASEBALL

◉ In a league all your own

◉ It ain't over 'til it's over–Yogi Berra

◉ Root Root Root for the Home Team

◉ The best sound I ever heard in my life was a ball hit
   with a bat. -Ted Williams

◉ The Ol' Ball Game

◉ There are three things you can do in a baseball game.
   You can win, or you can lose, or it can rain. -Stengel

◉ We Are the Champions

◉ Whoever wants to know the heart and mind of America had better learn baseball. -Jacques Barzun

◉ World Series Here We Come

◉ I think I was the best baseball player I ever saw.
                                         -Willie Mays

◉ I think there are some players born to play ball.
                                      - Joe DiMaggio

BASKETBALL

- ◉ Hoopla

- ◉ Hot Shots

- ◉ Court Side

- ◉ Slam Dunk

- ◉ H-O-R-S-E

- ◉ Zero Gravity

- ◉ The Hoopster

- ◉ Taste of Victory

- ◉ White Men Can Jump

- ◉ The main ingredient of stardom is the rest of the team.

- ◉ Any American boy can be a basketball star if he grows up, up, up. Around the Rim

- ◉ There are four seasons: Winter, Spring, Summer and Basketball

- ◉ Score

- ◉ Charge 'em

BATHS

B eauty sat bathing by a spring, where fairest shades did hide her; The winds blew calm, the birds did sing, the cool streams ran beside her.

- Bath Time is Splash Time
- Bathing Beauty
- Bubble Bath Fun
- Clean as a Whistle
- Little Mermaid
- Making a big splash
- Me & Rubber Ducky
- Scrubbily bubbily
- Tiny Bubbles
- Bath time, Splash time
- Bubbles and bubbles galore
- Splish Splash We're Taking A Bath
- Baby Loves Bathtime
- Spit Shiny Clean

■ ■

BE YOURSELF

◎ If you cannot be a poet, be the poem. -David Carradine

◎ It takes courage to grow up and become who you really are. -e.e. cummings

◎ How many cares one loses when one decides not to be something, but to be someone. -"Coco" Chanel

◎ If God had wanted me otherwise, He would have created me otherwise. -Johann von Goethe

◎ Be what you are. This is the first step toward becoming better than you are. -Julius Charles Hare

◎ Be who you are and say what you feel, because those who mind don't matter and those who matter don't mind. -Dr. Seuss

◎ Wherever you go, go with all your heart. -Confucius

◎ You were born an original

BEARS

◎ Bear Hugs

◎ Beary Cute

◎ Beary Sweet

◎ Beary Precious

◎ Grin and bear it

◎ Bears Live Here

◎ Beary Best Friends

◎ The Bear Necessities

◎ Happy Bearthday!

BEARS

◉ Don't feed the Bears!

◉ BEARY Special, Cute, etc.

◉ Hugs make life bear-able

◉ Love Bears All Things

◉ This bears my hug to you.

◉ This is a home for Bears...

◉ Have a beary happy day.

◉ A Beary Special Boy/Girl

◉ Little Hearts Never Fear When Teddy Bear Is Near

◉ A room without a bear is like a face without a smile.

◉ I wish I was a teddy bear...everybody loves them, nobody cares if they're fat or old

◉ You have a beary special place in my heart.

◉ You make life BEAR-able.

◉ Nothing satisfies like a good bear hug.

◉ Lions and Tigers and Bears, Oh My!

◉ Beauty is in the eyes of the bear-holder...

◉ Beware of Greeks Bearing Gifts

◉ There's no bear like an old bear

◉ A washed bear is not a happy bear

◉ When everyone else has let you down there's always Mr. Bear to hug you and kiss you and always be there

BEAUTY

- What a Doll
- 100% adorable
- American Beauty
- Baubles and Bangles
- Beauty and the Beast
- Call Me Irresistible
- Color Me Beautiful
- Dressing Up
- Fashion Frenzy
- I Feel Pretty
- Lady in Red
- Ooh La La!
- Pretty Baby
- Pretty Woman
- Sitting Pretty
- Picture Perfect
- Isn't She Lovely?
- Puttin' on the Ritz
- I Enjoy Being a Girl
- Model in the Making
- Pretty is as Pretty Does
- Pretty Maids All in a Row
- Here's looking at you kid
- Funny Face, I Love You!
- Blooming Into a Woman
- Five Foot Two, Eyes of Blue
- Can't take my eyes off of you
- A face only a mother can love
- Mirror, Mirror, On the Wall
- Time may be a great healer, but it's a lousy beautician
- You can take no credit for beauty at sixteen. But if you are beautiful at sixty, it will be your soul's own doing. -Marie Stopes
- As we grow old, the beauty steals inward. -Emerson

100

BEAUTY

◉ A man should hear a little music, read a little poetry, and see a fine picture every day of his life, in order that worldly cares may not obliterate the sense of the beautiful which God has implanted in the human soul. -Johann Wolfgang von Goethe

◉ Anyone who keeps the ability to see beauty never grows old. -Franaz

◉ Man looks at the outward appearance, but the LORD looks at the heart. -1Sam. 16:7

BEES, BUGS & BUTTERFLIES

◉ Ants in your pants
◉ Be My Luv Bug
◉ Bee Happy
◉ Bee My Baby Tonight
◉ Bee-utiful
◉ Bug Collectin'
◉ Busy as a Bee
◉ Cute as a Bug
◉ Good night, sleep tight, don't let the bed bugs bite.
◉ Here's the Buzz
◉ Honey of a Day
◉ Ladybug, Ladybug Fly Away Home
◉ Love Bugs
◉ Our Bee-utiful Daughter/Son
◉ Snug as a Bug
◉ Social Butteflry
◉ Spelling Bee
◉ The Flu Bug
◉ You can never tell with bees. - Winnie the Pooh

■ ■

BEES, BUGS & BUTTERFLIES

◎ Butterflies are self propelled flowers -Heinlein

◎ Butterflies count not months but moments and still have time enough.

◎ Flowers and butterflies drift in colour: illuminating spring

◎ If nothing ever changed, there'd be no butterflies.

◎ Love is like a butterfly, it goes where it pleases and it pleases wherever it go

◎ Lady Bug, Lady Bug Fly Away Home

◎ Shoo Fly Don't Bother Me

◎ Busy as a Bee

◎ I'm Buggy for Bugs

◎ It's a Bugs Life

◎ The Latest Buzzz!

◎ Love Them Bugs

◎ What's the Buzzz?

◎ Bugs under glass . Buggin' Out

◎ Bugs Catcher . Cootie Bug

◎ Don't Worry, Bee Happy. - Bobby McFarran

◎ Luv Bugs . The Flu Bug

◎ June Bugs . A Bugs Life

◎ The Ants Go Marching One By One

◎ Snuggle Bugs . Snug as a Bug in a Rug

BEST FRIENDS

- Let us be grateful to people who make us happy, they are the charming gardeners who make our souls blossom. -Marcel Proust

- Life without a best friend is like the sky without sun

- Nothing is closer to heaven than a best friend.

- One of the greatest things about being a teenager is the sharing, the closeness and the great times you have with your friends

- Piglet sidled up to Pooh from behind. "Pooh!" he whispered. "Yes, Piglet?" "Nothing," said Piglet, taking Pooh's paw. "I just wanted to be sure of you. -A.A. Milne

- Soul-mates are people who bring out the best in you. They are not perfect but are always perfect for you.

- The best kind of friend is the one you could sit on a porch with, never saying a word, and walk away feeling like that was the best conversation you've had.

- There is no distance too far between best friends, for friendship gives wings to the heart.

- Are we going to be friends forever? Asked Piglet. Even longer, Pooh answered. -Milne

- You'll always be my best friend. You know too much

- Best friends are we, my sister and me.

BEST FRIENDS

I n the sweetness of friendship let there be laughter, and sharing of pleasures
-Gibran

◎ A best friend is a sister destiny forgot to give you

◎ A best friend is somebody who knows every last thing about you, yet still manages to like you anyway

◎ A best friend knows exactly what you are saying, even if you're not talking.

◎ A true friend reaches for your hand and touches your heart

◎ Ah, how good it feels! The hand of an old friend.- Longfellow

◎ Best friends are always together in spirit and in truth

◎ Best Friends are kisses blown to us by angels.

◎ Best friends are relatives you make for yourself.

◎ Friends are like stars…you don't always see them, but you know they're always there. -Hulali Lut

◎ If I could reach up and hold a star for every time you made me smile, the entire evening sky would be in the palm of my hand."

◎ If you're alone, I'll be your shadow. If you want to cry, I'll be your shoulder. If you want a hug, I'll be your pillow. If you need to be happy, I'll be your smile. But anytime you need a best friend, I'll just be me.

BEST FRIENDS

◎ I believe that best friends are quiet angels to lift our wings when we forget how to fly.

◎ Bestest Friend's Forever

◎ A single rose can be my garden... a single friend, my world. -Buscaglia

◎ Best Friends

◎ Forever Friends

◎ Best Buds

◎ Friends to the End

◎ The best things in life aren't things, they're friends.

◎ The secret to joy is to have a best friend

◎ Old friends are the best friends

◎ It is one of the blessings of old friends that you can afford to be stupid with them. -Emerson

◎ Let us be grateful to people who make us happy, they are the charming gardeners who make our souls blossom. -Marcel Proust

◎ Life without a best friend is like the sky without sun

◎ While everybody else shakes my hand, you my heart. -A. A. Milne

◎ You're the best of all the rest, because of you I'm truly blessed. I love you so

■■■■■■■■■■■■■■■■■■■■■■■■■■■■■■

BICYCLE

◎ A bicycle built for two

◎ A woman needs a man like a fish needs a bicycle

◎ And awaaay she goes!

◎ Born to Bike

◎ First set of wheels

◎ Go speed racer

◎ I'm a big kid now!

◎ Look Mom, no hands!

◎ If you don't like my driving, get off the sidewalk

◎ I'm peddling as fast as I can

◎ Look Ma, no training wheels

◎ Pedal Practice

◎ Steady as he/she goes

◎ The wheels on my bike go round and round

◎ Bicycle Marathon

◎ Future Triathalon Winner

◎ I brake for ice cream

◎ Biker Babe

◎ Biking Buddies

BIRDS

- Be kind to your web-footed friends
- Bird's Eye View
- Birds of a Feather
- Blue Bird of Happiness
- Duck Duck Goose
- Eating Like a Bird
- Feed the birds
- Just Ducky
- Something to Crow About
- Sun shines, birds sing, garden angels flowers bring
- You quack me up!
- A little birdie told me...

BIRTH

- A Brand New Life
- A wee bit of Heaven drifted down from above, a handful of happiness, a heart full of love. -Rice
- Ah, Sweet Mystery of Life
- And then there was you
- Blessings and Miracles
- From small beginnings come great things.
- Heaven Sent
- His/Her Name is Wonderful
- In the beginning
- Labor of Love
- Look Who the Stork Brought
- Love At First Sight
- Love is a baby to love

BIRTH

◎ Miracle on (your) Street

◎ We have increased the size of our house by two feet!

◎ Welcome to the World, Little One

◎ We've waited so long for this special day, for a child of our own to be sent our way

◎ What a difference you've made in my life

◎ When a baby is born, so is a mother

◎ When they placed you in our arms, you slipped into our hearts.

◎ With every little baby's birth, a bit of stardust falls to earth

◎ You are my special angel sent from heaven above

◎ Because of you our family is complete

◎ Life is a miracle with you

◎ A Miracle Happened Today

◎ Our Dream Came True

◎ Ready or not, here I come

◎ Sweet Beginnings

◎ First Time Ever I Saw Your Face

◎ The Story Begins

BIRTHDAY ADULT

A birthday is just the first day of another 365-day journey around the sun. Enjoy the trip!

- ◉ King/Queen for a Day
- ◉ Nifty Fifty
- ◉ Oh, No! It's the Big -!
- ◉ Older and Wiser
- ◉ 39 and Holding
- ◉ Let Them Eat Cake
- ◉ Let's Party!
- ◉ Lordy Lordy Look Who's Forty
- ◉ So many candles . . . so little cake
- ◉ After fifty it's patch, patch, patch
- ◉ Birthdays are good for you; the more you have, the longer you live.
- ◉ Happy Birthday to a treasured friend
- ◉ Youth has no age. -Picasso
- ◉ You know you are getting old when the candles cost more than the cake. -Bob Hope
- ◉ You're not old...you're chronologically gifted
- ◉ Born in the USA a looooooong time ago
- ◉ There was a star danced, and under that was I born. - Shakespeare
- ◉ Forty is the old age of youth; fifty is the youth of old age
- ◉ Over the hill? I don't remember any hill.

BIRTHDAY ADULT

◎ I don't believe in aging. I believe in forever altering ones aspect to the sun. - Virginia Woolf

◎ It takes a long time to become young. -Pablo Picasso

◎ Just remember, once you're over the hill you begin to pick up speed. - Charles Schultz

◎ For all the advances in medicine, there is still no cure for the common birthday. -John Glenn

◎ If things get better with age, then you are approaching Magnificent.

BIRTHDAY KIDS

◎ Surprise!

◎ Silly Sixes

◎ Party Girl

◎ 16 Candles

◎ I wish for...

◎ Nine is fine

◎ Make a Wish

◎ Simply Seven

◎ Sweet Sixteen

◎ Time for Cake

◎ Party Animals

◎ Ready, Set, Blow

◎ Thrilling Threes

◎ M'm! m'm? Good

◎ You take the cake!

◎ Happy Bearth-Day

◎ Today Is Your Day

◎ They grow up so fast

◎ Happy Birthday to you

◎ We're havin' fun now

◎ Just what I've always wanted

◎ A pinch to grow an inch

◎ One year older-cuter too

◎ GREAT to be EIGHT!

◎ So many candles–so little cake

◎ Have a Beary special day

◎ Present Time

◎ Birthday Bash

◎ Fantastic Four

◎ A Perfect Ten

◎ Presents and Cake and Friends What Fun!

■■■■■■■■■■■■■■■■■■■■■■■■■■■■

BIRTHDAY ONE

Joyfully giggling and sparkling with glee, my one year old daughter smiles softly at me. Just looking at her it's easy to see how she'll capture your heart and bless you completely. -LaTourelle ©

☉ One-derful

☉ The big One

☉ Fun being one

☉ One is Wonderful

☉ It's fun to be one

☉ Bearly one year old

☉ Our son is "One"-derful!

☉ Oh my, baby's turning ONE

☉ Isn't it fun... _____ is one!

☉ A little cake and lots of fun

☉ Birthday Party Number One

☉ My one year old daughter giggles with joy and sparkles with glee, she's sweetness and sunshine as she looks at me. One moment with her and she'll steal your heart. What a blessing she's been right from the start. Hugs and kisses, dresses and bows, she's a miracle baby every moment she grows.

-LaTourelle

■■■■■■■■■■■■■■■■■■■■■■■■

BIRTHDAY 2 & 3

◉ Look Who's Two!

◉ Terrific twos

◉ Warning: I am Two

◉ Bippity Boo Baby's Two

◉ Peek a Boo Look Who's Two

◉ Zippity Do, Today I'm Two

◉ Now See Who's 2

◉ Look who's 2 - so much to do

◉ Wow, Now I'm 3

◉ Look at me - I'm 3

◉ Sing with glee cuz I am 3

◉ Come and See, Today I'm 3

BLESSINGS AND PRAYERS

May you always have work for your hands to do. May your pockets hold always a coin or two. May the sun shine bright on your windowpane. May the rainbow be certain to follow each rain.

◉ And help us, this and every day, to live more nearly as we pray. ~John Keble

◉ Let me walk beside you, in the sunlight or the rain, let me share your joys and triumphs or your times of pain.

BLESSINGS AND PRAYERS

◉ May you always have - Walls for the winds, A roof for the rain, Tea beside the fire, Laughter to cheery you, Those you love near you, And all that your heart may desire

◉ Two hands clasped in prayer can do more than a hundred working.

◉ Prayer is exhaling the spirit of man and inhaling the spirit of God. -Edwin Keble

◉ Who rises from prayer a better man, his prayer is answered. -George Meredith

BLUE JEANS

◉ Blue Jeans and Bare Feet
◉ Blue Blue my world is Blue
◉ Don't you love the patches
◉ Worn by time, faded by love
◉ Forever in Blue Jeans -Diamond
◉ Blue is my world when I'm without you.

BOATS, SHIPS & SAILING

◉ Sail On
◉ Ship Shape
◉ Calm Waters
◉ Ahoy, Matey
◉ Shore Party
◉ South Pacific
◉ Island Paradise
◉ The Love Boat

BOATS, SHIPS & SAILING

- Red sky at night, sailor's delight. Red sky in morning, sailors take warning

- God bless this ship and all who sail in her

- The Anchor Holds

- The best ships are friendships

- Why I love snorkeling...scuba diving...

- My body is here but my heart has gone sailing

- If you want to swim you gotta get out of the boat

- Down by the pond sailing my little boat. What did I do, my creation won't float? Oh well, I'll lie and dream of when I grow big. Someday I'll sail the sea on my own rig.

- Sailing, sailing over the ocean blue...

- The blue of the ocean, the grey of the sky. the drum beat of waves, a ship sailing by...

- Take a boat ride on the bay, feel the touch of ocean spray, catch the breeze flowing through your hair, look around to see God everywhere. -LaTourelle

- Steady as she goes

- Red Sails In The Sunset

- Come sail with me out on the sea and we will sing of love

BODY

- Twinkle Little Toes
- Dimple Darlin'
- Mr. Thumbkin
- Pinky Petunia
- Hands & Feet
- Sweet Cheeks
- Funny Face
- Ebony Eyes
- Baby Blues
- Tiny toes
- Bed Head
- Kissy Face
- Baby Face

BOO BOO'S

- Mommy kiss it?
- make it better
- A Time to Heal
- Boo Boo time
- Bumps and Bruises
- On the Mend
- Owie Wowie...Ouch
- Waaaaaaaaaa...
- Stitch by Stitch
- The Healing Touch
- Kiss the hurt away
- Sign My Cast

BOOKS

- In books lies the soul of the whole past time. - Carlyle

- A truly great book should be read in youth, again in maturity and once more in old age-Robertson Davies

- As a boy I was saved from a life of ignorance by my library. -James Michner

- From candlelight to early bedtime, I read. -Jefferson

- A bookstore is one of the only pieces of physical evidence we have that people are still thinking

- Very young children eat their books, literally devouring their contents

- Book lovers never go to bed alone

- The love of learning, the sequestered nooks, and the all the sweet serenity of books. -Longfellow

BOWLERS

◉ Old Bowlers never die they just end up in the gutter

◉ Bowling is a Ball

◉ Gutter Ball

◉ Heaven seems a little closer at the bowling ally.

◉ Hitting the Lanes

◉ Strike

◉ Ten in the pit

◉ Bowler's Prayer: Spare us Lord.

◉ Bowlers always have time to spare !

BOXING

◉ I Coulda been a Con-tenda -Marlan Brando

◉ A Fighting Chance

◉ And in this Corner

◉ Down for the Count

◉ Face to Face

◉ On The Ropes

◉ Take Down

◉ The Contender

◉ The Main Event

◉ Wrestle Mania

BOYFRIEND

◉ My boyfriends back

◉ Boy Meets Girl

◉ What a Babe!

◉ Let me call you sweetheart

◉ Totally cool dude

◉ Where the boys are

◉ Wonder Boy

◉ A boy is . . .

◉ A boy is a magical creature--you can lock him out of your workshop, but you can't lock him out of your heart. -Allan Beck

◉ Boys and their toys

◉ Boys are beyond the range of anybody's sure understanding, at least when they are between the ages of 18 months and 90 years. -James Thurber

◉ No girls allowed

◉ Boys will be boys, and so will a lot of middle-aged men. -Kin Hubbard

◉ Daddy's little boy

◉ First set of wheels

◉ It's a Guy Thing

BOYS

◎ Oh Boy! It's a Boy!

◎ 100% Boy

◎ Boys'R'us

◎ Just Like Dad

◎ Little slugger

◎ Men At Work

◎ Wonder Boy

◎ About a boy

◎ So handsome!

◎ Little Boy Blue

◎ Just me & my Pa

◎ No Girls Allowed

◎ Just one of the guys

◎ Life's filled with wonder and always a joy, When you share life with your little boy.

◎ Like Father, Like Son

◎ Little boys are angels too!

◎ Mom's "Son"flowers

◎ My _____ Sons

◎ Of all the blessings God sends from above, the one most precious is a baby boy to love.

◎ The glory of the nation rests in the character of her men. And character comes from boyhood. Thus every boy is a challenge to his elders. -Herbert Hoover

◎ Popsicle kisses and big bear hugs, Little boy trains and jars full of bugs.

BOYS

◉ The Son Also Rises

◉ Our little man

◉ Daddy's little boy

◉ I wanna be just like Daddy

◉ Action Hero

◉ Daddy is my hero

◉ There is nothing like the blessing Of a bouncing, baby boy He will fill your home with energy And touch your heart with joy. He'll hug you and bug you And try you within But each precious memory You'll treasure again and again. -Linda LaTourelle

◉ There is nothing so aggravating as a fresh boy who is too old to ignore and too young to kick. -Kin Hubbard

◉ Trust with dirt on its face, Beauty with a cut on its finger, Wisdom with bubble gum in its hair, and the Hope of the future with A frog in its pocket.

◉ What are Little Boys Made of?

◉ When you can't do anything else to a boy, you can make him wash his face. -Ed Howe

◉ Thank heaven for little boys

◉ Snips and snails and puppy dogs tails; that what little boys are made of.

◉ Thank God I'm a Country Boy

BOYS

⊚ All Boy

⊚ Hug a boy!

⊚ The Joys of Boys

⊚ Bouncing Baby Boy

⊚ Boys and their toys

⊚ It's a Boy's Life

⊚ Mommy's little boy

⊚ My Three Sons

⊚ All American Boy

⊚ Genuine Boy

⊚ Dad's Sidekick

⊚ I'm a Big Boy Now

⊚ A brand new baby boy, to fill our lives and hearts with joy

⊚ Blue jeans and sling shots Toads, whistles and worms

⊚ Boys will be boys, and so will a lot of middle-aged men -Kin Hubbard

⊚ Mud puddles, need I say more?

⊚ The Boy from New York City

⊚ Boy Meets World Boy

⊚ One small son to hug good night, one small son to grow up right, one small son with love to give, one small son to have fun with

⊚ Cool Dude

⊚ Way to Go Sport

⊚ It's A Boy Thing

⊚ Father & Son Duet

⊚ Boy O Boy

⊚ Dad's Caddy

⊚ Dad Driving Partner

⊚ Our Little Man

⊚ Boy after His Dad's Own Heart

⊚ Boys Just Want to Have Fun

BROTHERS

- #1 Brother
- Baby Brother
- Big Brother
- Stinky Bro
- Oh Brother!
- My brother did it
- Brother, Brother
- Brotherly Love
- The Brother Club
- Brothers are forever
- Brothers are the Best
- Brothers in Arms
- I Love My Brother
- My Brother, My buddy. . .
- Big brother is watching you
- Am I my brother's keeper?
- My brother's such a noisy kid
- My brother-is one drool dude
- I'm smiling because you're my brother and I'm laughing cuz there's nothing you can do about it
- A brother is a little bit of childhood that can never be lost.
- Brother's—Oh, brother!
- Me and my big Brother
- He's the Big Brother
- He's the Little Brother
- _____been promoted to Big Brother
- A Brother is a Special Friend
- Am I my brother's keeper?
- Being Brothers is the best (sisters, etc. Use Bee accents)
- Big brother is watching you
- What's up Bro'?
- Brotherhood

BROTHERS

◉ My brother taught me everything I really need to know

◉ The best thing about having a brother, I always had a friend

◉ In all the world there just ain't no other like my brother

◉ There's No Buddy Like a Brother

◉ Brother's Rule, Sister's Drool

◉ My brothers such a pest He tells me what to do. I wish he was a sister I do, I do, I do.

◉ Brothers are worms in the garden of life

◉ Forever my Brother, always my Friend

◉ He Ain't Heavy-He's My Brother

◉ My brothers are strong handsome and wonderful

◉ Brothers are a Special Hug From God!

◉ Brothers from the start, Friends from the heart

◉ Brothers make the best friends

◉ Brotherly Ties

◉ Brother's are Fine-Especially Mine

BUBBLES

◉ Bubble Trouble

◉ Bubbles, bubbles everywhere

◉ Bubbly Bubbles

◉ May your day bubble over with fun

◉ Tubs full of bubbles and bedtime tales

◉ You make me feel like dancing on bubbles

◉ Tiny Bubbles

◉ Bubble Bathing Beauty

◉ Blow them bubbles

■■■■■■■■■■■■■■■■■■■■■■■■■■■

BUILDING

- The Money Pit
- Building Memories
- If I had a hammer...
- Bang, bang, zzzz, $$$

This Old House

Home Improvement

Under Construction

A Moving Experience

- It's really the cat's house - we just pay the mortgage.

- Adventures of Building a New Home

- Hospitality is making your guests feel at home, even if you wish they were

- A man builds a fine house; and now he has a master, and a task for life: he is to furnish, watch, show it, and keep it in repair, the rest of his days. -Emerson

- House, n. A hollow edifice erected for the habitation of man, rat, mouse, beetle, cockroach, fly, mosquito, flea, bacillus, and microbe.

- I am grateful for the lawn that needs mowing, windows that need cleaning, and floors that need waxing because it means I have a home.

- The fellow that owns his own home is always just coming out of a hardware store. -Frank Hubbard

- There's nothing to match curling up with a good book when there's a repair job to be done around the house. -Joe Ryan

- One only needs two tools in life: One to make things go and duck tape to make them stop. -G.M. Weilacher

- A big enough hammer fixes anything

- Caution: Men at Work . Wrecking Crew

CAMERA

◎ Superstar   Mug Shots

◎ Say Cheese   What a ham!

◎ Strike a pose!   Capture the Memory

◎ Caught on film   Kodak Moment

◎ Intimate Portrait   Pretty as a picture

◎ A picture perfect day

◎ Budding photographer

◎ Picture-Perfect Memories

◎ Lights, camera, action

◎ Smile, you're on candid camera

◎ Mom's got the camera again

◎ You ought to be in pictures

◎ A Picture Paints A Thousand Words

CAMPING & HIKING

◎ A Blanket of Stars

◎ A Cabin in the Woods

◎ A Hiking we will go...

◎ Ah, Wilderness!

◎ Around the Fire

◎ Calm Waters

◎ Campfire Cookin'

◎ Campfire Story Teller

◎ Climb Every Mountain

◎ Creepy Crawlers

◎ Cuddly Campers

◎ Down by the riverside

◎ Explorer Extraordinaire

CAMPING & HIKING

- Ghost Stories
- Happy campers
- Happy Trails to You
- Home Sweet Tent
- I'm in Bug Trouble
- Lakeside Adventures
- Let's go camping
- Lovin' the Outdoors
- On the Trail
- Where's my real bed
- Outdoor Adventures
- The Great Outdoors
- The Big Hike
- The simple life
- Trail Blazers
- Rugged outdoors man
- Sleeping Under the Stars
- S'more Great Moments
- Roastin' Marshmallows
- Where the wild things are...
- My idea of roughing it is when room service is late!
- I love camping...in my motorhome

CANDY, COOKIES & CAKE

- Sweet Shoppe
- Baby Cakes
- Candyland Life is Sweet
- Sugar Shack, Sugar Sugar
- Cookie Crumbs
- Cookie Monster
- Sweet Endings
- Holiday Treats
- How Sweet It Is
- Here's the Scoop
- You Take the Cake
- Sweets for the Sweet
- Caught With a Hand in the Cookie Jar
- Who took the cookie from the cookie jar?

CARS & TRUCKS

- Pit Stop
- Auto Racing
- Full Throttle
- Garage Guru
- Junkyard Wars
- Classy Chassis
- On Track
- One lap to go!
- Breakneck Speed
- Race to the finish
- The Checkered Flag

- Tools of the Trade
- Wrench Warfare
- Mr. Goodwrench
- Go Fast! Turn Left!
- A Man and His Truck
- Red Light, Green Light
- On the road again...
- Baby let me drive your car
- Start your engines!

CASTLES

- My knight in shining armour
- Building Sand Castles
- Castles in the Sky
- The Ivory Tower
- Damsel in Distress
- My Home is My Castle

CATS

◉ Every Life Should Have Nine Cats

◉ We Are Siamese, If You Please

◉ When you have a cat, Everyday is Purr-fect

◉ This house owned by one spoiled rotten cat

◉ It's really the cat's house - we just pay the mortgage.

◉ A dog is a dog , but a cat is a purrrrson

◉ Dogs think they're Human and Cats think they're GOD!

◉ Cats always know just how you're feeling... They don't care, but they know.

◉ If there is one spot of sun spilling onto the floor, a cat will find it and soak it up. - Jean Asper McIntosh

◉ Sittin' pretty with my kitty

◉ Blessed are the PURR at heart

◉ Cats are designated friends.

◉ I'm Not Rude, I've Got Cat-i-tude

◉ Dogs have masters -Cats have staff

◉ Cats Are Angels with Fur

◉ Home is Where the Cat Is

◉ Cool Cats

◉ Curious Kitty

◉ Cat Nappin'

◉ CAT-astrophe

◉ Kitty, Kitty

◉ A Little Cat Nap

◉ Love that Cat

◉ The Cat's Meow

◉ Purr-fectly Sweet

◉ The Cheshire Cat

◉ Cat's in the Cradle

◉ My Cat Kneads Me

◉ Meow Meow Meow

◉ Kitten Kaboodle

◉ Will Work for Tuna

◉ Love me—Love my cat

CELEBRATIONS

- A Night to Remember
- A Time to Celebrate
- Celebrate Good Times
- Celebrate!
- Cheers!
- Having a Party
- Here's to You
- I'm So Excited
- It's a Date
- It's My Party and I'll Cry if I Want to
- Midnight at the Oasis
- Oh, What a Night!
- Party Girl
- Party Hearty
- Party of the Century
- Party 'Til the Cows Come Home
- Saturday Night Fever
- Some Enchanted Evening
- The Night Is Still Young
- The Party Place
- We're Havin' Some Fun Now
- Where's the Party?
- It's Saturday night and I just got paid...
- Let's Party
- The Midnight Hour
- Paint the Town

■■■■■■■■■■■■■■■■■■■■■■■■■■■■

CHEERLEADING

- Pep Rally
- Go, Team, Go
- We Got Spirit
- Jump, Shout, Yell!
- Stand Up and Cheer
- Cheer them to a WIN!
- Pom-poms and Ponytails
- Cheerleaders are simply a jump above the rest
- Go BLUE (school colors)
- Go, Fight, Win-Lets Go
- I don't play the field - I rule the sidelines.
- Wimps lift weights, cheerleaders lift people.
- You make the touchdown, we'll make the noise!
- It's hard to be humble when you can jump, stunt, and tumble!
- A good cheerleader is not measured by the height of her jumps but by the span of her spirit

CHERISH

- Priceless
- Love of my Life
- Cherish is the word...
- To Cherish From This Day Forward
- You're nothing short of my everything - Ralph Block
- Hold that which you cherish tenderly.

CHILD

- Child's batteries recharging
- Each child is a unique and unrepeatable miracle
- It is a wise child that knows his own father -Homer
- Patience is the mother of a beautiful child.
- See child's name... See child's name Play!!
- The jewel of the air is the sun; the jewel of the house is the child.
- The laughter of a child is the light of a home
- The more I encourage my child to think for himself, the more he will care what I think.
- The only crown I ask, Dear Lord to wear is this, that I may teach a little child.
- 10-Karat Child
- Bless this Child
- I Am a Child of God
- Train up a child Prov. 22:6
- Inside the Mind of a Child
- The things I teach my child today will shape all of his tomorrows
- The world shines bright with endless possibilities each time a child is born.
- A child can ask many questions that a wise man cannot answer.
- A child fills a place in your heart you never knew was empty

CHILD

A hundred years from now it will not matter what my bank account was, the sort of house I lived in, or the kind of car I drove . . . but the world may be different because I was important in the life of a child.

- ◎ Cutie Pie
- ◎ Stinky!
- ◎ But Mom!
- ◎ Rock Star
- ◎ Barefootin
- ◎ Daddy did it
- ◎ Busy as a Bee
- ◎ Tough Tot
- ◎ Wunderkin!
- ◎ Tough as nails
- ◎ Bundle of Love

- ◎ Crocodile Tears
- ◎ Cute as a Bug
- ◎ All my children
- ◎ All About Me
- ◎ All Gods children
- ◎ #1 Kid of the Year
- ◎ It runs in the family
- ◎ I'm A Big Kid Now
- ◎ Bottomless pit
- ◎ It's Tool Time!
- ◎ Just Me and My Dad!

- ◎ One Fish, Two Fish, Red Fish, Blue Fish
- ◎ It's the Little Things in Life That Matter
- ◎ Its the smile that keeps me outta trouble!
- ◎ Say it Loud! We're Cute and We're Proud!
- ◎ Give me a little hand to hold in mine.
- ◎ Give me a little voice to teach to pray.
- ◎ Going to Grandma and Grandpa'a house
- ◎ Attention all kids, NO is a complete sentence

CHILD

- Kids Will be Kids
- Kids Zone
- King of the Sandbox
- Let the Fun Begin
- Let's go fly a kite
- I Love to Laugh
- Little Bubba
- Little Lambikins
- Look what I can do!
- Look who's talking
- Miss Cuddle Puss
- Model Children
- Motor Mouth
- Mr. Huggable
- Heart Tugs!
- Hello, little one!
- Precious Treasures
- Preschool Blues
- President in training
- Pretending is Fun
- Put Me In Coach!
- Reach for the Stars!
- The Little Rascals
- The little riders
- The Little Streaker
- The Littlest Angel
- Ring around the Rosie
- Practice makes perfect
- Some Bunny loves you
- Rookie of the Year
- Born to Cause Trouble
- Peek a boo! I see you!
- Toddler Two Step
- They call me trouble
- Toddler Tidal Wave
- Sidewalk Chalk Art
- Helping hands
- Gorgeous Girl
- Retro Rocker
- Mamma knows best
- Our Little Acorn
- Our Little All Star
- Our little angel
- Giggles and Grins
- Our Star Swimmer
- Caught in the act
- First Set of Wheels
- I love to dance or...
- Funny Face, I Love You
- Cute Things I Say & Do
- Caution Kids Crossing
- I'm Rollin' in the Snow
- Sweet and Simple
- Shake your sillies out
- So many toys
- So many choices
- I'm Swingin' in the Sun
- I Love Mommy/ Daddy

CHILD

There is a garden in every childhood, an enchanted place where colors are brighter, the air softer, and the morning more fragrant than ever again.   -Elizabeth Lawrence

I'm Walkin' in the Rain

Children are life's treasures

Father/Mother's little helper

(Childs name) Daily News

Make up? What make up?

____ pounds Of Terror

My Many Colored Days

Piggy Back rides are best

The Young and the Restless

Don't ya love my dimples?

Color My World With Love

Take time for the little things

Make Room for Daddy

I'll rise, but refuse to shine

Which way to Hollywood

Twinkling With Mischief

Jesus Loves the Little children

☺

CHILD

◉ Before I got married I had six theories about bringing up children; now I have six children and no theories. -John Wilmot

◉ Children are a gift from God -Ps 127

◉ Children are the flowers in the garden of life

◉ Children are the hands by which we take hold of heaven. -Henry Ward Beecher

◉ Children have never been very good at listening to their elders, but they have never failed to imitate them. -James Baldwin

◉ From the Moment I saw you I knew it would be a Grand Adventure!

◉ Special is as special does

◉ He/She will fill our lives with sunshine- and our hearts with love.

◉ I don't care how poor a man is; if he has family, he's rich. -Colonel Potter

◉ I will give thanks to Thee, for I am fearfully and wonderfully made. -Psalm 139:14

◉ A mother holds her children's hands for a while, their hearts forever

◉ Precious and priceless, loveable too, the worlds sweetest miracle is sweet little you

◉ If nothing is going well, call your grandmother.

◉ It's the little blessings that help us to see just how lovely life can be.

Children put a twinkle in your eyes and a smile in your heart

◉ Sugar and spice and everything nice, that's what little girls are made

◉ There are only two lasting bequests we can leave our children, one is roots, the other, wings. -H. Carter

◉ If children grew up according to early indications, we should have nothing but geniuses. -Goethe

◉ Cleaning your house while the kids are still growing is like shoveling the walk before it stops snowing

◉ For this child I prayed and the Lord has given me my petition which I asked of Him. -1 Sam 1:27

◉ When you're close to the ground there's more dirt to be found

◉ Beloved children have many names.

◉ Blessed are the children...for theirs is a world of wonder

◉ Boys will be boys, and so will a lot of middle-aged men -Kin Hubbard

◉ I'll have fun, fun, fun 'til my daddy takes my bicycle away

◉ Childhood is the most beautiful of all life's seasons

◉ I Scream, you scream, we all scream for Ice Cream!

CHILDREN'S PRAYERS

⊚ To God, who kept me through the night and waked me with the morning light

⊚ Be present at our table, Lord, be here and everywhere adored These morsels bless, and grant that we may feast in Paradise with Thee

⊚ He prayeth best, who loveth best all things both great and small; for the dear God who loveth us, He made and loveth all -Coleridge

⊚ For the song of bird and hum of bee, for all things fair we hear or see, Father in heaven, we thank thee

⊚ God, make my life a little light within the world to glow; a little flame that burneth bright wherever I may go

⊚ Good night, good night says the fire fly's light, sweet dreams my child may you sleep so tight

⊚ For health and food, for love and friends, for everything Thy goodness send, Father in heaven, we thank Thee. -Emerso

⊚ Now I lay me down to sleep, I pray Thee, Lord, thy child to keep; Thy love guard me through the night and wake me with the morning light.

⊚ Now, before I run to play, let me not forget to pray

CHOCOLATE.

S crapbooking is my passion, but chocolate comes in a very close second!

- ◎ Chocolate is the answer - no matter what the question is!
- ◎ A day without you is like a day without chocolate
- ◎ If the world was fair, a VCR would program itself, chocolate would not be fattening and men would give birth to babies
- ◎ Pamper yourself-indulge in chocolate morn, noon & nite
- ◎ A grandma is admired for her wisdom, patience, understanding and her chocolate chip cookies
- ◎ Coffee, chocolate, men... Some things are just better rich
- ◎ Research shows twenty out of any nine people eat chocolate
- ◎ All I really need is love, but a little chocolate now and then doesn't hurt!
- ◎ Chocolate is the food group they don't tell you about!
- ◎ When the going gets tough, the tough get chocolate
- ◎ Make mine chocolate
- ◎ Chocolate is my life
- ◎ I love you as much as chocolate itself!
- ◎ I never met a chocolate I didn't like.
- ◎ Chocoholic's Anonymous drop out
- ◎ Forget love! I'd rather fall in chocolate!
- ◎ Friends are the chocolate chips of life
- ◎ Life...Liberty...and the pursuit of chocolate
- ◎ I'd give up chocolate, but I'm no quitter
- ◎ Do Not Disturb: Chocolate fantasy in progress
- ◎ Warning! Chocoholic in Residence
- ◎ The way to a woman's heart-Chocolate!

CHOCOLATE...
Need I say more?

CHRISTMAS

- I Believe
- Cool Yule
- Santa Express
- Oh Holy Night
- Jingle Bells
- Silent Night
- Deck them halls
- Be jolly, by golly
- Happy Holly Days
- Claus & Company
- Babes in Toyland
- Christmas Blessings
- Faith, Hope & Love
- 'Tis the Season
- You'd better not pout!
- Christmas Morning Magic
- Holly Jolly Christmas
- Home for the Holidays
- Homespun Christmas
- I believe in Santa.
- Gingerbread Boys!
- Santa's Little Helper(s)
- Storybook Christmas

■■■■■■■■■■■■■■■■■■■■■■■■■■■■

CHRISTMAS

Our hearts grow tender with childhood memories and love of kindred, and we are better throughout the year for having, in spirit, become a child again at Christmas-time.
                                        -Laura Ingalls Wilder

◉ Unto Us a Child is Born

◉ Trimming our Tree

◉ Wrapping Up the Holidays

◉ To Gramma's House We Go

◉ Will work for milk and cookies.

◉ Don't get your tinsel in a tangle!

◉ Love is the light of Christmas

◉ In search of the perfect Tree

◉ Girls and Boys love Toyland

◉ Cookin' up a merry christmas.

◉ Who needs Santa-I have Nana!

◉ Santa Claus is coming to town

◉ May your Christmas be Beary and Bright

◉ The Best Gift of All

◉ The Magic of Christmas

◉ The Night Before Christmas

CHRISTMAS

- Rockin' around the Christmas tree

- Twinkle, Sparkle Christmas Star

- Peace on earth goodwill to men

- I will honor Christmas in my heart, and try to keep it all the year. -Charles Dickens

- Christmas began in the heart of God. It is complete only when it reaches the heart of man

- God grant you the light in Christmas, which is faith

- Jesus is the reason for the season
  Jolly Old St. Nicholas

- Laughing All the Way

- Merry Chris Moose

- Naughty or Nice

- Oh Christmas Tree

- Have a Holly Jolly Christmas

- The Greatest Story Ever Told

- For Christmas comes but once a year.

- Have a twinkle, jingle, ringy ding Christmas

- It's Beginning to Look a Lot Like Christmas

- Have you been naughty or nice?

- Have yourself a Merry Little Christmas

- Christ is the Heart and Soul of Christmas

■■■■■■■■■■■■■■■■■■■■■■■■

The rooms were very still while the pages were softly turned and the winter sunshine crept in to touch the bright heads and serious faces with a Christmas greeting. -Louisa May Alcott

◎ Here we go a caroling, a caroling we go

◎ Holiday hugs and mistletoe kisses.

◎ Then and Now, the true gifts of Christmas are Peace, Joy and Love

◎ There's no place on earth like a kitchen at Christmas!

◎ Tiny Tots with their eyes all aglow will find it hard to sleep tonight. -Mel Torme

◎ 'Twas the night before Christmas, when all through the house, not a creature was stirring - not even a mouse: The stockings were hung by the chimney with care, in hopes that St. Nicholas soon would be there. -Clement C. Moore

◎ Candles and stars And Christmas tree lights twinkle and glow In the velvet night

◎ Dear Santa, Here's some cookies, take my brother and leave the gifts

◎ Yes (childs name) there is a Santa Claus!

◎ While visions of sugar plums danced in their heads.

◎ Don't go under the mistletoe with anyone else but me.

◎ Dear Santa, I want it all and I want it now!

◎ Jesus is the reason for the season

CHRISTMAS

◎ Even when it's cold outside our memories keep us warm

◎ We'll keep our Christmas merry still -Sir Walter Scott

◎ Heap on the wood!-the wind is chill; But let it whistle as it will,

◎ No matter what I get for Christmas you're all I really need

◎ Christmas Cheer Recipe...Combine loads of good wishes, heartfuls of love and armfuls of hugs. Sprinkle with laughter and garnish with mistletoe. Top off with presents Serves everyone!

◎ Christmas cookies and happy hearts this is how the holiday starts

◎ Come sit at my table and share with me, warm ginger-bread cookies and cinnamon tea

◎ What if Christmas, perhaps, means a little bit more
                                        -Dr. Seuss

◎ The ornaments of our home are the friends that gather there.

◎ 'Twas the night before Christmas . . .

◎ I'm Dreaming of a White Christmas

◎ It Came Upon A Midnight Clear

◎ Family is the best part of Christmas

◎ Follow the star, He knows where you are

◎ Chestnuts roasting on an open fire

CHRISTMAS

The merry family gatherings--
The old, the very young; The strangely lovely way they harmonize in carols sung. For Christmas is tradition time-- Traditions that recall The precious memories down the years, The sameness of them all. -Marshall

◉ And the angel said unto them, Fear not! For, behold, I bring you tidings of great joy, Which shall be to all people. For unto you is born this day in the city of David A Saviour, which is Christ the Lord. And this shall be a sign unto you: Ye shall find the babe wrapped in swaddling clothes, lying in a manger. Luke 2:10-12

◉ Every mother's child is gonna spy, to see if reindeer really know how to fly. -Mel Torme

◉ Hark the herald angels sing, Glory to the new-born king. Peace on earth, and mercy mild, God and sinners reconciled! -Wesley

◉ I heard the bells of Christmas Day; their old familiar carols play--peace on earth, good-will to men!
- Longfellow

CHURCH

◉ Without faith it is impossible to please God

◉ Be more concerned what God thinks about you than what people think about you

◉ Breathe in God's spirit-- exhale God's love

◉ Choices have consequences

◉ Count your blessings, not your problems

◉ Faith is daring the soul to go beyond what the eyes can see

◉ Fill a place-- not just a space

◉ For a healthy heart, exercise your faith

◉ Get a life ! John 3:16

◉ God answers prayer--- not advice

◉ God does not promise a comfortable journey, only a safe landing

◉ God gives special grace for each trial we face

◉ God loves you whether you like it or not

◉ Going to church does not make you a Christian anymore than going to McDonalds makes you a hamburger

◉ Having a sharp tongue may cut your own throat

◉ He who is content with little, possesses much

◉ Live life so that the preacher won't have to lie at the funeral

◉ Life is short-- pray hard!

CHURCH

◎ Hello God! Today I will be your "waiter" How can I be of service? –IS 40:31

◎ Helping others is the best way to help yourself

◎ Hurting people need comfort not sermons

◎ If God is for us, tell me, who can be against us?

◎ If you find yourself with time on your hands--- put 'em together and pray

◎ If you have a kind thought, share it now!

◎ If you see someone without a smile, give them yours

◎ If you walk with the Lord, you'll never be out of step

◎ If you want to cast a big shadow   stand in God's light!

◎ If you'll stand for Jesus He'll stand for you!

◎ If you're living your life like there is no God, you'd better be right!

◎ If you're too busy to pray, you're too busy

◎ In this life it's not what you have but Who you have that counts!

◎ Is there room for Him at your inn?

◎ Jesus will calm the storm-- or calm you in the storm

◎ Making a living is not the same as making a life

◎ You will never posses that which you're not willing to profess

◎ Your life may be all that some know of the Bible

CHURCH

- Morning praise will make your days
- T G I F - Today God Is First
- The first step to hearing God is listen Jn 6:5-13
- There is no right way to do a wrong thing
- Those who follow Christ lead the way for others
- Your words are the windows to your heart
- Trust God's authority, not man's majority
- We're called to stand out! Not blend in!
- What does it take for God to get our attention?
- What WOULD Jesus Do?
- When you don't witness, you just did
- Where He guides-- He provides!
- Wisdom doesn't 'come with age' - it 'comes with the walk -Ps 27:11

CIRCLE

- Circle of Life
- Dancing in Circles
- If you love someone put there name in a circle not a heart because hearts break but circles go on forever
- And the circle it goes round and round

CIRCUS

◉ Clowning Around
◉ Dumbo's Circus
◉ Under the Big Top
◉ Lions and tigers and bears, oh my!

CLOUDS

◉ Head in the clouds
◉ Walking on cloud nine
◉ Every cloud has a silver lining

COFFEE

◉ Java Jungle
◉ I love you a latte.
◉ Make Mine Mocha
◉ Is there life before coffee?
◉ You're the cream in my coffee.
◉ Instant human: Just add coffee.
◉ Man does not live by coffee alone. Have a Danish.
◉ I don't have a problem with caffeine. I have a problem without caffeine!
◉ There's too much blood in my caffeine-stream.
◉ I don't do mornings....until I've had my coffee.
◉ Sleep is a poor substitute for coffee.

COLLEGE

◉ Dorm...Sweet Dorm
◉ I is a college student.
◉ There's no place like my dorm room
◉ Where's Mom Now that I need Her ?

COLORS

◉ Color me happy

◉ Color me beautiful

◉ Pink Flamingo

◉ Pink Lemonade

◉ Ebony and Ivory

◉ Tie a yellow ribbon

◉ The yellow brick road

◉ Roses are red...my fav!

◉ Color my world with love

◉ All the colors of the rainbow

◉ If the shoe fits...buy every color

◉ When I Am Old I Shall Wear Purple

◉ Blue is the color of my true loves eyes

COMPUTER

◉ A chat has nine lives.

◉ A web-surfer and his leisure time are soon parted

◉ My favorite site: www.home.com

◉ To err is human, to really foul things up requires a computer.

◉ Virtual reality is its own reward.

◉ You can't teach a new mouse old clicks.

◉ Want to make your computer go really fast? Throw it out a window

◉ Computers have lots of memory but no imagination

◉ Give a person a fish and you feed them for a day; teach that person to use the Internet and they won't bother you for weeks

◉ Computer programmers know how to use their hardware

◉ Pentium wise; pen and paper foolish.

◉ The geek shall inherit the earth

◉ Computer programmers don't byte, only nibble a bit

COOKING

- Baked with Love

- Baking Beauties

- Kitchen Goddess

- Finger lickin' good

- Cookin' Up a Storm

- I kiss better than I cook...

- Home on the Range

- Breakfast of Champions

- My favorite recipe...eat out

- Hey good lookin'-what's cookin'?

- Kitchen closed - until help arrives

- If yer lookin' for home cookin'...Go home

- Mama made the house smell so sweet with the love in her homemade bread.

- A messy kitchen is a happy kitchen and this kitchen is delirious.

- My husband and I share work in the kitchen - I cook and he eats.

- The only reason I have a kitchen is that it came with my house

- The way to a man's heart is through his stomach.

- The way to a woman's heart is through the door of a good restaurant. -Elliot Joseph

COOL TALK

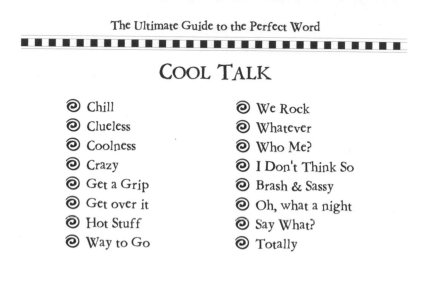

- Chill
- Clueless
- Coolness
- Crazy
- Get a Grip
- Get over it
- Hot Stuff
- Way to Go
- We Rock
- Whatever
- Who Me?
- I Don't Think So
- Brash & Sassy
- Oh, what a night
- Say What?
- Totally

COUNT

- Count your age by friends, not by years.

- Count your blessing, not your troubles.

- Count your blessings, name them one by one

- Count your days by garden hours, don't remember clouds at all.

- Count your garden by the flowers, never by the leaves that fall.

- Count your many blessings, see what God has done!

- Count your nights by stars, not shadows.

- Count your years with smiles, not tears.

COUNTRY

- Back In The Saddle Again
- Country Bumpkin
- County Livin' is the Life for Me
- Cowboys Don't take baths... We just dust off.
- Cowboys, Cowlicks And Cuddles
- Cowtown Cuties
- Down On The Farm
- Giddy Up
- How the West Was Fun
- Howdy Ya'll
- I feel the country calling me
- I was country when country wasn't cool
- Lil' Buckaroo or Lil' Cowpoke
- Mama's don't let your baby's grow up to be cowboys
- Raised on Country Sunshine.
- Ride'm Cowboy
- Thank God I'm a Country Boy/Girl
- The Lady Takes the Cowboy Every Time
- There's a little cowboy in all of us, a little frontier. Louis L'Amour
- Wanted...
- Wild Wild West

COUPLES

◎ Sweet Hearts

◎ Lovebirds

◎ The Odd Couple

◎ He Said, She Said

◎ Just the Two of Us

◎ For Me and My Gal

◎ Happy Two-gether

◎ We're Two of a Kind

◎ Made for Each Other

◎ Together Hand in Hand

◎ A Match Made in Heaven

◎ Sugar and Cream

COUSINS

◎ Kissing Cousins

◎ Kooky Kousins

◎ A Herd of "Cow-sins"

◎ Cousins are Cool

◎ Crazy about my cousins

◎ Cousins are those childhood playmates who grow up to be forever friends.

◎ Crazy is a relative term in my family

CRAFTING

- Crafty Lady
- Sew Crafty
- Crazy for craftin'
- The Bead Mistress
- Beadin' and Braidin'
- She's a crafty mama
- Don't lie…just embellish
- _____, get your craft gun
- Creative minds are rarely tidy.
- Little hands make big masterpieces
- Won't somebody clay with me?
- A creative mess is better than tidy idleness.
- I'm creative - you can't expect me to be neat too!
- People that are organized are just too lazy to get up and look for it!
- My husband lets me have all the craft supplies I can hide

CUTE

- Cutie Pie
- Cute as can be
- Cute as a Bug
- Cute as a Button
- Cute, cute, cute!
- Cute but Dangerous
- Cute Things I Say and Do
- I should be in a commercial for cute
- They oughta put me in the movies

CRYING

Laugh and the world laughs with you...Cry and you get your way!

- ◎ Tear Jerker
- ◎ Cry Baby Cry
- ◎ As Tears Go By
- ◎ Big Boys Do Cry
- ◎ Crocodile Tears
- ◎ No Whine Zone
- ◎ You better not pout
- ◎ My Achy Breaky Heart
- ◎ After All These Tears
- ◎ Heaven knows we need never be ashamed of our tears, for they are rain upon the blinding dust of earth, overlying our hard hearts. - Dickens
- ◎ Teardrops Fall Like Raindrops
- ◎ It's my party and I'll cry if I want to...

DAD

A father is neither an anchor to hold us back, nor a sail to take us there, but a guiding light whose love shows us the way

- ◎ #1 Dad
- ◎ Hop on Pop
- ◎ Daddy O
- ◎ Daddy's Girl
- ◎ Just like Dad
- ◎ Dear Ol' Dad
- ◎ My Dad Rules!
- ◎ We Love Dad
- ◎ Daddy and me
- ◎ Like Father-like Son
- ◎ Don't Wake Daddy
- ◎ Daddy's Little Angel
- ◎ Daddy's little helper
- ◎ World's Best Dad
- ◎ Just me and my Dad
- ◎ Go Daddy Go
- ◎ Father Knows Best
- ◎ His Father's Son

A father is someone you look up to no matter how tall you grow.

◉ Our Dad has a heart of gold

◉ Father is a special word for love

◉ Like Father- Like Daughter/Son

◉ Dad always takes first place

◉ My Dad's the King of my Castle

◉ When Dad Says 'No', Ask Grandpa

◉ When Daddy ain't happy-look out

◉ Great Fathers Get Promoted to Grandfathers

◉ My father didn't tell me how to live; he lived, and let me watch him do it. -Kelland

◉ The most important thing a father can do for his children is to love their mother. -Theodore Hesburgh

◉ The world's greatest Dad belongs to me

◉ Father of the Year

◉ Daddy's Little Man

◉ Daddy's Little Prince/Princess

◉ Father's Little Dividend

◉ Fathers are a work of heart

◉ My Daddy hung the moon

◉ My Heart belongs to Daddy

◉ No One Can Fill Your Shoes

DANCE

- Tappin'
- Dance Fever
- Let's Dance
- All That Jazz
- Dance With Me
- Dancing Queen
- Do A Little Dance
- Do The Locomotion
- Do You Wanna Dance?
- Dressed to Dance
- Fancy Footwork
- Dance To The Music
- Save the Last Dance For Me
- Puttin' on the Ritz
- Let's Do the Twist
- Twinkle Toes
- Put on your dancin' shoes
- Let's Dance
- Oh How We Danced
- Dancin' on Daddy's Toes
- Waltzin' the Night Away
- Two-Step
- Tango & Rumba With Me
- Something In The Way She Moves

A Daughter is...a joy bringer, a heart warmer, a memory maker, a Daughter is Love.

- A Daughter Like You is a Very Precious Gift

- You're the end of my rainbow, my pot of gold

- You're Daddy's little girl, to have and hold

- A daughter may outgrow your lap...but she will never outgrow your heart.

- As is the mother, so is her daughter. -Ezek 16:44

- Chance made you my daughter... Love made you my friend.

- Daughters are little girls that grow up to be your best friends

- Daughters are Special... Especially Mine

- You were once my little girl & now my shining star

- You're the sparkle in my eyes, the twinkle in my toes and the kiss on my heart

- Isn't She Lovely

- A daughter is a joy forever

- Daughter you are Love

- My Darling Daughter

- A Girl's Best Friend Is Her Mother

- A son is a son until he takes a wife, but a daughter's a daughter for the rest of her life

- Giggles and curls, ribbons and bows- she's so adorable from her head to her toes!

- Mothers and Daughters are closest when daughters become mothers

- You're the sparkle in my eyes, the twinkle in my toes, the song in my soul and the kiss on my heart

- You have a smile that lights up the world

■■■■■■■■■■■■■■■■■■■■■■■■■■■

DIET

◎ A waist is a terrible thing to mind

◎ Lord, if I can't be skinny, let all my friends be fat

◎ If we are what we eat, then I'm easy, fast & cheap

◎ A balanced diet is a cookie in each hand

◎ Thou shalt not weigh more than thy refrigerator

◎ Starvation diet...No chocolate for 24 hours!

DIFFICULTY

◎ Difficulties are just another reason to work harder

◎ In the middle of every difficulty lies opportunity -
Einstein

◎ Obstacles are those frightful things you see when
you take your eyes off your goal. -Henry Ford

DIRT

◎ Caked with mud   ◎ Down and Dirty
◎ Fun in the Mud   ◎ Mud Bath
◎ Mud Pies! 10 cents   ◎ Puddle Jumper
◎ A little dirt never hurt
◎ Mommy's Little Mud Puppy

DIVING

◎ Under the sea   ◎ Dive deep, live shallow
◎ Just dive right in   ◎ Taking the plunge

DOCTOR

◎ What's up Doc?   ◎ The Doc Stops Here

◎ I left my sponge in San Francisco

◎ I've grown accustomed to my gown

Dogs

- Bad to the Bone
- Best of Show
- Bone Voyage
- Dog Gone Cute
- A dog and his boy
- Fur-rocious Fun
- In the Dog House
- It's a Dog's Life
- It's im-paws-ible!
- Lady and the Tramp
- Let sleeping dogs lie.
- Licks of Love
- No Bones About It
- Pokey Little Pup
- Puppy Love
- See Spot Run
- Licks of Love
- A Dog's best friend is his human
- A spoiled, rotten _____ lives with me
- Dogs are just children with fur
- Dogs Leave Pawprints On You Heart
- He's not my dog, he's my best friend
- How Much is That Doggie in the Window?
- If you want the best seat in the house, you have to

When dog food is new and improved tasting, who tests it?

DOLLS

- Doll collector at heart
- Some of my best friends are dolls
- One can never have too many dolls
- Never too old to play with dolls
- Here is my dolly all tattered and torn. Everyone loves her even though she is worn. Her body is floppy and her hair is a mess, but I love her dearly, and she loves me best!

DRAMA

- Cast List
- Razzle Dazzle
- Center Stage
- Curtain Up!
- A Class Act
- A Star Is Born
- In the Spotlight
- I'm in the Company
- All the World's a Stage
- Baby Take a Bow
- Behind the Scenes
- Bowing Out
- Break a Leg
- Audition Time
- Dressing the Part
- In the Director's Chair
- Costume & Wardrobe
- Leading Lady/Man
- Lights, Camera, Action
- Little Miss Broadway
- Give My Regards to Broadway
- Another Opening, Another Show
- An Actor's Life for Me

DREAMS

- Dreamboat
- California Dreamin'
- Daydream Believer
- All I have to do is dream...
- A Kiss To Build A Dream On
- Dare to dream
- Life is But a Dream
- When You Wish Upon a Star, Your Dreams Come True
- You see things; and you say 'Why?'; But I dream things that never were; and I say 'Why not?' - George Bernard Shaw
- Mr. Sandman, Bring Me a Dream
- A Dream Is a Wish Your Heart Makes
- The moment of enlightenment is when a person's dreams of possibilities become images of probabilities.

DRESS UP

- All dressed up and ready to go
- Take a bow baby
- Coat of many colors
- Dressed In My Best
- Dressing Up
- Fashion Frenzy
- Forever in Blue Jeans
- Handbags & Gladrags
- Itsy Bitsy Teeny Weeny Yellow Polka Dot Bikini
- Material Girl
- Miss Fancy Pants
- Ooh La La
- Princess on Parade
- Puttin' On the Ritz
- She Wore a Yellow Ribbon
- Shoe Business
- What A Doll!
- The Red Shoes
- Living Doll
- Miss America
- Crib Couture

DRIVING

- Look Out World - Here I come (new license)!
- On the road again… and again… and again.
- Caution: Legally Blonde Driver!
- If you don't like my driving, get off the road
- How Many Roads Must A Man Travel Down Before He Admits He Is Lost?
- Mr. Hot Rod
- Hot Wheels
- My first license
- Student Driver
- Driver Wanted
- Enjoying the Ride
- Pedal Practice
- Red Light, Green Light
- The Driver's Seat
- First set of wheels
- You Drive Me Crazy
- Vroom Vroom Vroom
- Watch me Go
- Get ready to rumble
- Baby You Can Drive My Car
- Look mom, no training wheels

■■■■■■■■■■■■■■■■■■■■■■■■■■

DUCKS & ROOSTERS

- Like a duck out of water
- Loose as a goose
- She's a mother hen
- Waking up with the chickens
- Happy as a duck in water
- Roosters Crow, but Hens Deliver

DUMB

- We're one giant, inbred, dysfunctional family. - Shapiro
- Because I'm the Boss, right honey?
- Did you ever stop to think and forget to start again?
- Due to intense mind fog, all thoughts are grounded
- I'm not as dumb as I am. -Dave Schroeder
- I hope my ship comes in before my dock rots
- The difference between genius and stupidity is that genius has it's limits

Earth

- Earth Day
- Earth Angel
- Heaven on earth
- Salt of the Earth
- For thee the earth puts forth sweet flowers

EASTER

In your Easter bonnet with all the frills upon it, You'll be the grandest lady in the Easter Parade

- Hoppin' Down the Bunny Trail
- Hoppy Easter
- Hippity Hoppity... Easter's on its way
- One Cute Easter Chick
- Painting Easter Eggs
- Some bunny loves you
- The Glory of Easter
- The Greatest Story Ever Told

■■■■■■■■■■■■■■■■■■■■■■■■■■■■■■■

EASTER

- Basket Full of Goodies
- A Hunting we will go
- A Tisket, A Tasket
- A Very Bunny Day
- Bunny Love
- Carrot Patch
- Baskets and Bunnies
- Funny Bunny
- Hippity Hoppity
- Easter Parade
- Christ is Risen Today
- Coloring Eggs
- Easter Egg Hunt
- Easter Egg-citement
- Easter Parade
- Eggs-cellent
- A hunting we will go
- Here Comes Peter Cottontail
- Green Eggs and Ham
- Halleluiah, He is Risen
- Jelly Bean Time
- You're no bunny 'til somebody loves you

EDUCATION

Education is not filling a bucket, but lighting a fire. -William Yeats

- To touch the soul of another human being is to walk on holy ground. - Stephen Covey

- You see things; and you say 'Why?'; But I dream things that never were; and I say 'Why not?' - George Bernard Shaw

- If you think education is expensive, try ignorance! -Andy McIntyre

- Self-education is, I firmly believe, the only kind of education there is. -Isaac Asimov

- The aim of education should be to teach us how to think

EDUCATION

Wh12at lies behind us and what lies before us are tiny matters compared to what lies within us. -Emerson

◎ Education is what survives when what has been learnt has been forgotten. -B.F. Skinner

◎ Students don't care how much you know as a teacher until they know how much you care about them

ENCOURAGEMENT

◎ All things bright and beautiful--are my wishes for you

◎ Because you are special

◎ Heartfelt thoughts of you

◎ Hope this day puts a song in your heart

◎ I painted a star on my window, so I could wish on cloudy nights for you

◎ May your day be as bright as a flower

◎ May your sorrows be patched & your joys be quilted

◎ Of all the joys in a long and happy life, there's none so precious as the love between husband and wife

◎ Stitch your day with kindness, sew in love and hem it with prayer

◎ The best and most beautiful things in this world cannot be seen or even touched, they must be felt with the heart

◎ Write it on your heart that every day is the best day in the year -Ralph Waldo Emerson

◎ If happy thoughts were flowers I would send you a bouquet

EXERCISE

- Exercise is a dirty word. Every time I hear it, I wash my mouth out with chocolate.

- My idea of exercise is a good brisk sit. -Phyllis Diller

- Whenever I feel like exercise, I lie down until the feeling passes. -Hutchins

EYES

- Angel Eyes
- Brown-Eyed Girl
- Can't take my eyes off of you
- Close Your Sleepy Little Eyes
- Dreamy Eyes
- Five Foot Two, Eyes of Blue
- I Can See Clearly Now
- I only have eyes for you
- Jeepers Creepers
  Where'd You Get Those Peepers?
- Love At First Sight
- Pretty Little Angel Eyes
- The eyes are the windows to the soul
- When I look into your eyes
- My eyes adore you
- When Irish eyes are smiling
- Smoke Gets In Your Eyes
- Private Eyes
- Bright Eyes
- Lyin' Eyes
- Those eyes...
- Baby Blues

FAIRIES

- Freckles are fairies kisses
- Garden fairies come at dawn. Bless the owners then they're gone.
- Leave room in your garden for fairies to dance.
- When the first baby laughed, the laugh broke into thousands of pieces and they all skipped about. That was the beginning of fairies.

FAIRYTALES

- Reality is for people who lack imagination
- A little land of make believe, A place of love and no fights. A place where the laughter never ends. Full joyous days and nights.
- Fairy tales do come true☐
- They lived happily ever after
- Royal Wedding
- Into the sunset

K nights in shining armor saving damsels in distress. Castles gleaming with majesty holding treasures for the blessed. Those were the days of adventure and times of true romance. Kings and queens lived in grandure as enchanted fairytales were born.

-Linda LaTourelle

- Once upon a time...
- My knight in shining armor
- Come up here, O dusty feet! Here is fairy bread to eat. Here in my retiring room, Children, you may dine On the golden smell of broom and pine; And when you have eaten well, Fairy stories hear and tell. - Robert Louis Stevenson

FAMILY

- ◎ A family blossoms with a Mother's love
- ◎ A Family is a Circle of Love
- ◎ A family is a gift that lasts forever
- ◎ A family is a patch-work of love
- ◎ All In The Family
- ◎ Bless our nest
- ◎ Crazy is a relative term in my family
- ◎ Families are forever.
- ◎ Family Folk
- ◎ Family Frenzy
- ◎ Family Heritage
- ◎ Growing Our Future
- ◎ Happiness is Homemade
- ◎ In-laws and Out-laws
- ◎ It Runs in the Family
- ◎ Kindred Spirits
- ◎ Man, Woman & Child
- ◎ Married with children
- ◎ Yours, Mine, and Ours
- ◎ A family is a haven of rest, a sanctuary of peace and most of all a harbor of love. -Feldman
- ◎ Theory of Relativity

A family is where holidays are celebrated with feasting, birthdays are acknowledged with gifts, and thoughts of days gone by kept alive with fond remembrances. -Feldman

- ◎ Families are like quilts, lives pieced together, stitched with memories, and bound by love.
- ◎ Family ties are precious threads, no matter where we roam, They draw us close to those we love, and pull our hearts toward home.
- ◎ Having someplace to go is home. Having someone to love is family, having both is a blessing.
- ◎ I don't care how poor a man is; if he has family, he's rich.
- ◎ One in a million family
- ◎ Circle of Love
- ◎ My Family is...
- ◎ Happy Family

167

FAMILY

- ◎ The family that prays together...stays together.
- ◎ Cherish your family for they are your treasure. A storehouse of riches...wealth beyond measure
- ◎ I grew up with six brothers. That's how I learned to dance -waiting for the bathroom. -Bob Hope
- ◎ All American Family
- ◎ It's a Family Affair
- ◎ A crowded nest is still the best
- ◎ Full House
- ◎ Generation to Generation
- ◎ Kinfolk
- ◎ A Nest that's Blessed
- ◎ Together forever
- ◎ We are one in love

FAMILY CELEBRATIONS

- ◎ Family Reunion
- ◎ Holiday on Ice
- ◎ Hollydaze
- ◎ Home for the Holidays
- ◎ Homecoming
- ◎ It's All Relative
- ◎ It's Good to Be Home
- ◎ Jolly Holidays
- ◎ Kindred Spirits
- ◎ Same Time, Next Year
- ◎ We Gather Together

FAMILY TREE

- Like branches on a tree, we may grow in different directions, yet our roots remain as one.
- Our family tree is blessed with thee
- Shake your family tree and watch the nuts fall
- Ancestors—the roots from whence we came
- Out on a limb with my Family tree

FARMING

- Animal House
- At Home on the Range
- Back In the Saddle Again
- Be kind to your web-footed friends
- Bless this Barn
- Cattle Call
- Counting Sheep
- Greener Pastures
- Hay is for Horses
- High On the Hog
- Hog Heaven
- Hog Wild
- This Little Piggy
- Animal House
- At Home on the Range
- Back In the Saddle Again
- Bless this Barn
- Cattle Call
- Chicken Run
- Cow-town Cuties
- Down on the Farm
- Ewe Are Loved
- Funny Farm
- Green Acres
- EIEIO
- Horse Sense
- Lil Cowpoke
- My Little Pony
- Quite the Stud
- Wild Horses
- Wild in the Country
- Ye Old Homestead
- The Farmer in the Dell
- Farm livin' is the life for me
- Old MacDonald had a farm

FATHER

◉ Blessed indeed is the man who hears many gentle voices call him father -Lydia Child

◉ All the feeling which my father could not put into words was in his hand -Freya Stark

◉ Fatherhood is pretending the present you love most is soap-on-a-rope. -Bill Cosby

◉ It is a wise father that knows his own child. - Shakespeare

◉ It is admirable for a man to take his son fishing, but there is a special place in heaven for the father who takes his daughter shopping. -John Sinor

◉ Old as she was, she still missed her daddy sometimes. -Naylor

◉ Sometimes the poorest man leaves his children the richest inheritance. -Renkel

◉ The greatest gift I ever had came from God, and I call him Father

◉ It doesn't matter who my father was; it matters who I remember he was. -Anne Sexton

◉ To her the name of father was another name for love. -Fanny

◉ Any Man Can Be A Father, But It Takes Someone Special To Be A Daddy

◉ The most important thing that a father can do for his children is to love their mother. -Hesburg

◉ Be kind to thy father

◉ Great is the man who holds his child's heart close with utmost love and tenderness. -LaTourelle

FATHER

◎ It is a wonderful heritage to have an honest father.

◎ My father didn't tell me how to live; he lived, and let me watch him do it. -Kelland

◎ Daddy... You love us, provide for us, protect us. Your strength is what I lean on every day. We want you to know that we pray for you and thank you for loving us so much.

◎ My heart is happy, my mind is free, I had a father who talked with me. -Bigelow

◎ The Father is the one who loves

FATHER AND SON

◎ I want to be just like you

◎ Just Me and My Dad!

◎ Like Father, Like Son

◎ The Old Block

◎ My Hero, My Dad

FIREMAN

◎ Firemen are HOT stuff

◎ If you think it's tough being a Firefighter...try being a Firefighter's wife

◎ Hug a firefighter, feel warm all over

◎ What you call a hero...I call just doing my job

◎ A Hunk Of Burning Love

◎ Baby, Light My Fire

◎ Fight Fire With Fire

◎ Too Hot to Handle

◎ Fired Up

◎ Engine No _____

◎ A time chill

◎ Dalmation Dude

◎ Burning Love

◎ Hot today... here tomorrow

◎ Rescue Mangers

◎ Hot Stuff

◎ Hot fun in the _____

FISHING

⊚ Catch O' The Day

⊚ Down at the ol' fishin' hole

⊚ Fish More...Work Less

⊚ Fish Tales

⊚ Fish tremble when they hear my name

⊚ Fishing from Dawn to Dusk

⊚ Fishing: The art of casting, trolling, jigging or spinning while freezing, sweating, swatting and swearing

⊚ Give a man a fish and you can feed him for a day, teach a man to fish and you can get rid of him every weekend.

⊚ Gone Fishing-Be Back Someday

⊚ Hooked on Fishing

⊚ Life, liberty and the pursuit of fishing.

⊚ My Dads a Reel Catch (fishing tackle, rods and fish)

⊚ One old fisherman lives here with the catch of his life.

⊚ The Old Man and the Sea

⊚ The poorest day of fishing is better than the best day of working.

⊚ One fish, two fish, red fish, huge fish

⊚ To Fish or Not to Fish...What a Stupid Question

⊚ Women Want Me, Fish Fear Me

FISHING

- Old Fishermen never die . . . their bobbers just quit bouncing.

- Old Fishermen never die–they just smell that way.

- Got Fish?

- Here Fishy, Fishy, Fishy

- Hook, line and sinker

- All I need to know about life, I learned from Fishing

- An angler is a man who spends rainy days sitting around on the muddy banks of rivers doing nothing because his wife won't let him do it at home

FLOWERS

- Love is the only flower that grows and blossoms. Without the aid of the seasons.
  -Kahlil Gibran

- I loved you when love was Spring, and May, Loved you when summer deepened into June, and now when autumn yellows all the leaves...-V. Sackville-West

- Earth laughs in flowers. -Ralph Waldo Emerson

- Give me at sunrise a garden of beautiful flowers where I can walk undisturbed. -Whitman

- Flowers really do intoxicate me. -Vita Sackville-West

- Perfumes are the feelings of flowers. -Heinrich Heine

- When you have only two pennies left in the world, buy a loaf of bread with one, and a lily with the other. -Chinese Proverb

FLOWERS

◉ Can we conceive what humanity would be if it did not know the flowers? -Maurice Maeterlinck

◉ Flowers are the sweetest things God ever made, and forgot to put a soul into. -Henry Beecher

◉ Flowers are without hope. Because hope is tomorrow and flowers have no tomorrow. -Antonio Porchia

◉ Flowers have spoken to me more than I can tell in written words. They are the hieroglyphics of angels, loved by all men for the beauty of their character, though few can decipher even fragments of their meaning. -Lydia M. Child

◉ God loved flowers and created soil. Man loved flowers and created the vase

◉ I perhaps owe having become a painter to flowers. -Claude Monet

◉ The poet's darling. -William Wordsworth, "To the Daisy"

◉ The flower is the poetry of reproduction. It is an example of the eternal seductiveness of life. -Giraudoux

◉ 'Tis my faith that every flower enjoys the air it breathes! -William Wordsworth

◉ To be overcome by the fragrance of flowers is a delectable form of defeat. -Beverly Nichols

◉ Summer set lip to earth's bosom bare, And left the flushed print in a poppy there. -Francis Thompson

FLOWERS

A rose can say I Love You, Orchids can enthrall; But a weed bouquet in a chubby fist, Oh my, that says it all!

- A Family Blossoms With A Mother's Love
- A rose by any other name would smell as sweet
- A rose is a rose is a rose
- A thing of beauty is a joy forever
- April Showers Bring May Flowers
- As delicate as a flower
- Beauty is a fading flower
- Bloom where you are planted
- Bluebonnet Beauty
- Bright as flowers, be thy life's hours.
- Crazy Daisy
- Everything's coming up roses
- Flower child
- Flower Patch
- Flower power
- Flowers are the stars of the earth.
- Lone Star Splendor Blue Bonnets
- Tiptoe through the tulips
- Where the Lilies Bloom
- Life is a flower of which love is the honey.
- I'd rather have roses on my table than diamonds on my neck. -Emma Goldman
- Garden fairies come at dawn, bless the flowers then they're gone.

■ ■

FLOWER GARDEN

The kiss of the sun for pardon, the song of the birds for mirth, one is nearer to God in a garden than anywhere else on Earth

◎ My garden, My heaven

◎ Life began in a garden

◎ Take Time to Smell the Flowers

◎ The earth laughs in flowers -Emerson

◎ In the garden, my soul is sunshine

◎ Friends are flowers in the garden of life

◎ The garden is a mirror of the heart

◎ Flowers leave some of the fragrance in the hand that bestows them.

◎ He who plants a garden plants happiness

◎ Bless the flowers and the weeds, my birds and bees

◎ I plant the flowers, my dog digs the holes

◎ Kind hearts are the gardens, Kind thoughts are the roots, Kind words are the flowers, Kind deeds are the fruits.

◎ Nothing is more the child of art than a garden -Scott

◎ She who has flowers in her garden surely has flowers in her heart

◎ The rustle of the wind reminds us a Fairy is near

◎ Though an old man I am but a young gardener - Jefferson

◎ Tickle the earth with a hoe; it will laugh a harvest

FOOD

◉ A Slurpin' Good Time

◉ A Tasty Tradition

◉ A teenage boy's idea of a balanced diet is a hamburger in each hand.

◉ Any time is cookie time

◉ Carrot cake counts as a serving of vegetables.

◉ Caught With a Hand in the Cookie Jar

◉ Eat it? I can't even pronounce it!

◉ Eat, Drink, and be Merry

◉ Finger-Lickin' Good

◉ I can't believe I ate the whole thing

◉ I Cook With Wine, sometimes I Even Put It In The Food

◉ If we are what we eat I'm fast, cheap, and easy.

◉ If you want breakfast in bed, sleep in the kitchen.

◉ Just Peachy

◉ Let's Eat

◉ Life's a Bowl of Cherries

◉ Life's too short, eat more chocolate

◉ Love me-love my MESSES!

◉ Man shall not live by bread alone

◉ Messy Matilda/Marvin

◉ Mmm Good

◉ Who needs a fork?

◉ Feed me...NOW

FOOTBALL

- Backyard Football
- Football Super Star
- Half Time
- If winning isn't everything... why do we keep score?
- Inch by inch my goal is a cinch.
- Instant Replay!
- Just for Kicks
- Kick off the new season
- Let the Games Begin
- MVP
- My favorite season is Football
- No Pain, No Gain
- On the Bench
- Superbowl Here We Come
- Sweet Smell of Victory & Stinky Socks
- Team Player
- The Longest Yard
- The Rookie of the Year
- There are four seasons: Football, Hockey, Basketball, and baseball.
- Touchdown
- Way to Go!
- We Are The Champions
- We didn't loose the game, we just ran out of time
- We interrupt this marriage to bring you--football season
- When you win, nothing hurts - Joe Namath
- You Gotta Be a Football Hero

FRECKLES

- A face without freckles is like a night without stars
- Freckles are angel kisses
- Freckles are fairy's kisses
- Freckles are sun kisses

FREEDOM

- America will never be destroyed from the outside. If we falter and lose our freedoms, it will be because we destroyed our-selves. -Abraham Lincoln
- If our country is worth dying for in time of war let us re-solve that it is truly worth liv-ing for in time of peace. - Hamilton Fish
- That noise you hear is the sound of FREEDOM
- You're a grand old flag, You're a high flying flag And forever in peace may you wave. You're the emblem of, the land I love, The home of the free and the brave.

I thought how many men like him Had fallen through the years. How many died on foreign soil? How many mothers' tears? How many pilots' planes shot down? How many died at sea? How many foxholes were soldiers' graves? No,

FRIENDS

I f I had a flower for every time I thought of you, I would walk in my garden forever

- ◉ Some people come into our lives, leaving footprints on our hearts, never to be the same
- ◉ A Budding Friendship
- ◉ A friend in need is a friend indeed
- ◉ A Friend Is A Present Which You Give Yourself - Stevenson
- ◉ A friend is the one who comes in when the whole world has gone out. -Pulpit
- ◉ A friend knows the song in my heart and sings it to me when my memory fails. -Roberts
- ◉ A friend loves at all times
- ◉ A good long talk with a friend can cure almost anything
- ◉ All for one and one for all
- ◉ Are we going to be friends forever? Asked Piglet. Even longer, Pooh answered.
- ◉ Bridge Over Troubled Water
- ◉ Circle of Friends
- ◉ Forever Friends
- ◉ Friends are Angels without Wings
- ◉ Friends are God's helpers
- ◉ Friends are hugs from God
- ◉ Friends are kisses blown to us by angels

If you're alone, I'll be your shadow. If you want to cry, I'll be your shoulder. If you want a hug, I'll be your pillow. If you need to be happy, I'll be your smile. But anytime you need a friend, I'll just be me.

◉ Giggles, Secrets, and Tears, Too

◉ I felt it shelter to speak to you. -Emily Dickinson

◉ Kindred Spirits

◉ If you need me-I'm there.

◉ I Wanna Be Like You

◉ I want to make you smile,

◉ If I could reach up and hold a star for every time you've made me smile, the entire evening sky would be in the palm of my hand.

◉ If you live to be a hundred, I want to live to be a hundred minus one day, so I never have to live without you.

◉ It is one of the blessings of old friends that you can afford to be stupid with them. -Ralph Waldo Emerson

◉ Friends fill your life with joy, your soul with sunshine and your heart with love.

◉ Friendship isn't a big thing - it's a million little things.

FRIENDS

◉ The best kind of friend is the one you could sit on a porch with, never saying a word, and walk away feeling like that was the best conversation you've had

◉ Lean On Me

◉ Life Is Nothing Without Friendship

◉ Life Long Friends

◉ Many people will walk in and out of your life, - but only true friends will leave footprints in your heart.

◉ Never shall I forget the days I spent with you. Continue to be my friend as you shall always find me yours. - Beethoven

◉ Friend: Amigo, Buddy, Chum, Comrade, Crony, Pal

◉ Our Gang

◉ Planting Seeds of Friendship

◉ Right next door, or miles at, friends are always close at heart

◉ Some people make the world more special just by being in it

◉ Tweedledum and Tweedledee

◉ Two Friends, One Heart

◉ Piglet sidled up to Pooh. "Pooh!" he whispered. "Yes, Piglet?" "Nothing," said Piglet, Taking Pooh's paw. "I just wanted to be sure of you." -A. A. Milne

◉ Soul-mates are people who bring out the best in you. They are not perfect but are always perfect for you.

◉ The better part of one's life consists of his friendships. - Abraham Lincoln

◉ The Three Musketeers

◉ To the world, you may just be one person... but to one person, you might just be the world.

◉ To touch the soul of another human being is to walk on holy ground - Stephen Covey

◉ True Friends Remain In Our Hearts Forever

◉ Laugh and the world laughs with you. Cry and you cry with your girl friends. -Kuslansky

◉ We have been friends together In sunshine and in shade. - Caroline Sheridan Norton

◉ When it hurts to look back, and you're scared to look ahead, you can look beside you and your best friend will be there.

◉ When you die, if you've got five real friends, then you've had a great life.

◉ Yes'm, old friends is best, 'less you can catch a new one that's fit to make an old one out of. -Sarah Orne Jewett

◉ Your best friend is the one who brings out the best in you

FRUIT

- ◎ Brown as a berry
- ◎ Like peaches and cream
- ◎ American as apple pie
- ◎ Nutty as a fruitcake
- ◎ She's the apple of my eye
- ◎ Sweet as honey
- ◎ The apple of my eye
- ◎ Wrinkled as a prune
- ◎ Heard it through the grapevine
- ◎ When you get lemons, make lemonade

Fun Sayings

- ◎ What's Up Duck?
- ◎ I don't repeat gossip, so listen closely the first time!
- ◎ I Just Wish My Mouth Had a Backspace Key!
- ◎ I like you. You remind me of when I was young and stupid.
- ◎ When the Going Gets Tough, The Tough Use Duct Tape
- ◎ OK, Who Stopped Payment on my Reality Check?
- ◎ When the Going Gets Rough, You are Obviously in the Wrong Place
- ◎ I love to give homemade gifts... umm, which one of the kids would you like

Gardens

⊚ Adventures in Gardening

⊚ An old gardener lives here with an American Beauty

⊚ As for me and my garden...just a bit of Earth will do

⊚ Every Birdy Welcome

⊚ Garden: A thing of beauty and a job forever

⊚ God's green acre

⊚ I Fought the Lawn and the Lawn Won

⊚ If you would have a mind at peace, a heart that cannot harden, go find a door that opens wide upon a lovely garden. French Proverb

⊚ Inch by inch, row by row gonna make this garden grow!

⊚ The shortest way to heaven is through a garden gate

⊚ Our Little Gardener

GENEALOGY

⊚ Genealogists are time unravelers

⊚ I used to have a life, then I started doing genealogy

⊚ So many ancestors-so little time!

⊚ To a genealogist, EVERYTHING is relative!

⊚ Whoever said seek and ye shall find was NOT a genealogist

⊚ Isn't genealogy fun? The answer to one problem, leads to two more! Genealogists live in the past lane.

⊚ Genealogy: Chasing your own tale!

GET WELL

⊚ Sending you a bouquet of get well wishes

⊚ Wishing you sunshine, lollipops and get well

⊚ Up and running that's what we wish for you

GIRLS

Sugar and Spice and everything nice
that's what little girls are made of love

- ◉ Girls Will Be Girls
- ◉ Glamour Girl
- ◉ Pretty Baby
- ◉ I Enjoy Being a Girl
- ◉ Little Lady
- ◉ California Girl
- ◉ Cinderella Girl
- ◉ Daddy's Girl
- ◉ Daddy's Little Princess
- ◉ Diamonds are a Girl's Best Friend
- ◉ Sweet Dream Baby
- ◉ Little Surfer Girl
- ◉ Little Women
- ◉ Sweet Thang
- ◉ Drama Queen
- ◉ Funny Girl
- ◉ Thank heaven for little girls, For little girls get bigger every day. Thank heaven for little girls, They grow up in the most delightful way. That's what little girls are made of love
- ◉ She will fill our lives with sunshine-And our hearts with Love
- ◉ Giggles and curls, ribbons and bows- she's so adorable from her head to her toes!
- ◉ A Sweet new Baby Girl to Bring Happiness into our World

GIRL POWER

- #1 Girlfriend
- 100% Girl
- Ain't Misbehavin'
- Brash and Sassy
- Chicks Rule
- Chill Out
- Classic Chic
- Clueless
- Crazy
- Dream Girl
- Exclusively Feminine
- Genuine Girl
- Girl Power
- Girlfriend
- Girls just wanna have fun
- Girl's Night Out
- Girls Rule-Boys Drool
- Go Girl
- Hot Stuff
- Just a Girl
- Rockin' Girl
- Sassy
- Say What?
- That Girl!
- Too Cool
- Uptown Girl
- What a Babe!
- WOW!
- You Go Girl
- What a Girl Wants
- What a Girl Needs
- Chick Flick

GIRLS BEAUTY

- Pretty as a Picture
- Pretty in Pink
- Pretty Maids all in a Row
- Pretty Young Thing
- Pretty is as Pretty Does
- Bee-utiful
- Pretty Woman
- Beauty... is the shadow of God on the universe. ~Mistral

GIRLFRIENDS

- Junk food
- Laughing together
- Long talks
- Makeovers
- Movies
- Secrets
- Shoes
- Shopping
- Slumber Parties
- The best kind of friend is a girlfriend

GIRL SCOUTS

- Bridging
- Brownies
- Make New Friends
- On my honor...
- The Girl Scout Law
- Serve God and my country
- Want Cookies?

GIVING

- The only gift is a portion of thyself. -Ralph Waldo Emerson

- You give but little when you give of your possessions. It is when you give of yourself that you truly give. -Gibran

- There are two ways of spreading light: to be the candle or the mirror that reflects it. -Edith Wharton

- God's gifts put man's best dreams to shame. -Elizabeth Barrett Browning

- The Lord loveth a cheerful giver.

GLASSES

- Bespeckled
- It's the Shades
- Spectacular
- Sight for Sore Eyes

GOALS

- Ideals are like stars; you will not succeed in touching them with your hands, but like the seafaring man on the desert of waters, you choose them as your guides, and following them, you reach your destiny. -Carl Schurz

- Don't bother just to be better than your contemporaries or predecessors. Try to be better than yourself. -William Faulkner

- There are no shortcuts to any place worth going. -Sills

- Whatever you can do or dream you can, begin it. Boldness has genius, power, and magic in it. -von Goethe

- Obstacles are those frightful things you see when you take your eyes off your goal. -Ford

- Shoot for the moon. Even if you miss, you'll land among the stars

GOD

- Be God or let God.
- God gave us each a song
- God is the perfect poet. -Robert Browning
- God understands our prayers even when we can't find the words to say them.
- God's gifts put man's best dreams to shame. -Elizabeth Barrett Browning
- I believe in the sun even if it isn't shining. I believe in love even when I am alone. I believe in God even when He is silent.
- Prayer is when you talk to God; meditation is when you listen to God. -Diana Robinson
- Some of God's greatest gifts are unanswered prayers. -Brooks
- God is an unutterable sigh, planted in the depths of the soul. -Jean Paul Richter
- Weave in faith and God will find the thread
- God is...

GOLF

- Caddy shack
- Iron Man
- Golf Fore Ever
- Born to Golf-forced to work
- A bad day of golf is better than a good day at work
- A game in which you claim the privileges of age, and retain the playthings of childhood. -Samuel Johnson
- Give me life, liberty and the pursuit of golf balls.
- Golf is a game in which you yell FORE, shoot six, and write down five.
- Golf is not just exercise, it is an adventure, a romance . a Shakespeare play in which disaster and comedy are intertwined
- If I had to choose between my wife and my putter-I'd miss her
- If it goes right, it's a slice, If it goes left, it's a hook, If it goes straight, it's a MIRACLE!
- I'm not over the hill, just on the back nine
- Now that I'm older I can hit the ball out of sight
- Golf is a good walk spoiled - Mark Twain
- The ardent golfer would play Mount Everest if somebody put a flagstick on top -Pete Dye
- I've spent most of my life golfing... the rest I've just wasted

GOT?

- Got Dirt?
- Got Milk?
- Got Cookies?
- Got Money?
- Got Chocolate?

GRACE

- Grace and glory differ very little; the one is the seed, the other is the flower; grace is glory militant, glory is grace triumphant. -Thomas Brooks
- Grace has been defined as the outward expression of the inward harmony of the soul. - Hazlitt
- Grace is but glory begun, and glory is but grace perfected. -Edwards

GRADUATION

- Ready to Take the World on
- School Day Memories
- The Graduate
- The Road to Success
- Grad Night
- Hats Off

GRADUATION

Dare to dream, dare to try, dare to follow your heart. Opportunity is calling and graduation's the time to start. As you seek new challenges and make your dreams come true, may this graduation day be a reminder of all that you can do.

◎ Way to Go! You Made It!

◎ The Tassel Is Worth The Hassle

◎ Things turn out best for the people who make the best out of the way things turn out. -Art Linkletter

◎ We cannot direct the wind but we can adjust the sails.

◎ Wherever you go, go with all your heart. -Confucius

◎ You did it with flying colors

◎ We think of Kindergarten and our first day. Now we've reached the end we are going away

◎ Class of any year

◎ Graduation Day

◎ Hard Work Pays Off

◎ I Made It

◎ Let Your Light Shine

◎ Reach for the Stars

◎ Next Step: College

◎ Next Step: Real Life

◎ Put your future in good hands-God's hands

GRANDCHILDREN

- God gives us Grandkids to keep us young at heart
- Grandchildren are the crown of the aged
- Grandchildren are the dots that connect the lines from generation to generation
- Granny's Sweet Pea
- Grandpa's Delight
- Generation to Generation
- A grandchild is a gift from above—one to cherish & to love
- Grandkids make life Grand!
- The joy of grandchildren is measured in the heart
- My name is NO NO, but grandma calls me precious
- Great joy comes in seeing our family enter another generation
- I thought I had forgotten how to hold a baby... but my arms remember.
- If I had known grandchildren were this much fun I would have had them first
- Life is easier if you hear the steps of grandchildren walking beside you!
- Perfect love sometimes does not come til the first grandchild. -Welsh Proverb
- The handwriting on the wall means the grandchildren found the crayons.
- Grandchildren don't make a woman feel old; it's being married to a grandfather that bothers her

GRANDPARENTS

- It's such a grand thing to be a mother of a mother - that's why the world calls her grandmother

- The simplest toy is one which even the youngest child can operate...it's called a grandparent

- A grandparent is a gift from above —one to cherish, one to love

- And when I say my prayers at night I ask God to bless and hold him tight Cause when it comes to giving hugs my grandpa's arms are filled with love.

- Come Grandma, walk with me... Help me to be the best kid I can be. Take me here and take me there... Show me now how much you care. The many hours we share together... Will be the times I'll always remember forever.

- TGIF - this grandma/grandpa is fantastic

- I'm the Twinkle in my grandma's (pa's) eye

- Just Grandpa/Grandpa and Me

- Just when a mother thinks her work is done she becomes a grandmother.

- Grandparents sort of sprinkle stardust over the lives of little children. -Alex Haley

- Perfect love sometimes does not come until grandchildren are born. -Welsh Proverb

- Saw it...wanted it...told Grandma...got it!

- Shhh... here is a secret, but it is true- Everyone needs a Grandpa like YOU!

- Sitting on my grandpa's lap Reading a book or taking a nap It's the safest place to be to feel his strong arms holding me

- Through my grandmother's eyes I can see more clearly the way things used to be, the way things ought to be, and most important of all, the way things really are.

- Two proud grandparents live here

- Who needs a pony when you've got Grandpa

- Who's spoilin' who?!

- You Put the Grand in Grandma/pa

GROWING

- I'm a big kid now
- Scaling New Heights
- Up, Up, and Away
- When I get big I'll get even
- Getting Bigger Inch by Inch
- Look Who's Growing Up
- Growing by leaps and bounds

GROWING OLD

- Grow old along with me, the best is yet to be. The last of life, for which the first was made
- The years teach much which the days never knew. -Ralph Waldo Emerson
- Age is opportunity no less, than youth itself, though in another dress, and as the evening twilight fades away, the sky is filled with stars, invisible by day. -Longfellow
- When grace is joined with wrinkles, it is adorable. There is an unspeakable dawn in happy old age. -Victor Hugo
- It is not by the gray of the hair that one knows the age of the heart. -Bulwer-Lytton
- Middle age is when you choose your cereal for the fiber, not the toy
- The great thing about getting older is that you don't lose all the other ages you've been. -Madeleine L'Engle

GYMNASTICS

- Beaming
- Perfect Ten
- Up in the Air
- Zero Gravity
- On the Beam
- Tumbling Time
- Tuck and Roll
- Falling with style
- Perfect Balance
- The King/Queen of the Rings
- What goes up must come down

HAIR & HAIRCUTS

- Blondie
- Static Cling
- Carrot Top
- Crazy Hair Day
- Frizzy or Dizzy
- Glamorama Girl
- Great Do Dude!
- A Whole New Look
- Big Hair
- Curly Head
- Cuts and Curls
- Future Hair Stylist
- Goldilocks
- Hair-n-dipity
- Great Lengths
- Brand New Hair Do
- Kids Kuts and Kurls
- Blonde Ambitions He is not Balding - He is in Follicle Regression

■■■■■■■■■■■■■■■■■■■■■■■■

HAIR & HAIRCUTS
- Bad Hair Day
- Locks of Love
- Bald Hair Day
- Bald is Beautiful
- Beehive or Bubble
- Hair larious
- Hair? What hair?
- I've got BED HEAD
- Just got my ears lowered
- _____ gets a buzzz!
- R A G G M O P P Ragmop!
- Only my hairstylist knows for sure
- Shave and Haircut 2 bits
- Shear Magic
- Snip Snip Clip Chop
- The Cutting Edge
- To Dye For
- What a Doll
- Wiggin' Out

HALLOWEEN
- A Big BOOO to You
- A Bootiful Night
- A HOWLIN' Good Time
- A Spooktacular Halloween
- A Way spooky Boo day to you
- Are you a scaredy-cat?
- Bats R Us
- BBBB-BOO
- Beary Scary
- Happy haunting to you
- Frightfully Delightful

HALLOWEEN
- Bobbing for Apples
- Boo Bash
- Pumpkin Patch
- Boo from the crew
- Boo'tiful
- Costume Parade
- Carving out memories
- Cute Little Spooks
- Cutest Little Pumpkin in the Pumpkin Patch
- Disguise the Limit
- Don't be scared... It's just us
- Fangtastic!
- Forget the ghost, beware of the sugar bugs
- Guess Who
- Hallo-scream
- Halloween Party
- Happy Halloween... whatever you are!
- Happy Pumpkin Day
- Happy Trick or Treating
- A Spooktacular Halloween
- In Search of the Perfect Pumpkin
- It's the Great Pumpkin
- Jack-O-Lantern
- Just a Little Bit Corny
- Masquerade
- Spookiest spook around
- Monsters on Parade
- On the Cutting Edge (carving pumpkins)

HALLOWEEN

- Our Little Punkin'
- Pickin' Pumpkins
- Costumes, and Pumpkins, & Candy, Oh MY!
- Positively Defrightful
- Pumpkins Come and Pumpkins Go But a Jack-O-lantern steals the show
- I'm bats about you
- No Tricks... only Treats
- Silly as a Scarecrow
- Sugar High
- Sweets to Eat
- The Boo Crew
- Too Cute to Spook
- Halloween is a real treat
- Mommy's Lil' Pumpkins
- Trick or Treat! Give me something good to eat. Give me candy. Give me cake. Give me something sweet to take!
- You are so Bootiful to me

HANDS & FEET

- Sweet Little Feet
- Ten Tiny Fingers hold on tight Ten Teeny Toes wiggle with delight Two pretty eyes twinkle with glee One loving smile beaming at me

Forget not that the earth delights to feel your bare feet and the winds -Kahlil Gibran

HANDS & FEET

- Baby Steps
- Barefootin'
- Dancin' Feet
- Steppin' Out
- All Thumbs
- Sweet Little Feet
- My Little Piggies
- Alive and Kicking
- Dear little bare feet, dimpled and white, In your long nightgown wrapped for the night; Come, let me count all your queer little toes, Pink as the heart of a shell or a rose.
- Foot Loose and Fancy Free
- I Want to Hold Your Hand
- The pitter patter of little feet
- My Toes were made for Eatin'
- Put Your Hand in the Hand of the mom who made you
- These little fingers may be very small, but I can still wrap daddy around them anytime
- Sometimes you get discouraged, because I am so small and always leave my fingerprints on furniture and walls, but everyday I'm growing . . . I'll be grown up one day and all the tiny fingerprints will surely fade away. So, here's a real handprint Just so you can recall, exactly how my fingers looked when I was very small.

193

HANNUKAH

- We kindle these lights...
- Dreidle, Dreidle, Dreidle
- Festival of Lights
- One Candle More
- Lighting the Menorah
- Holy Lights
- Shalom

HAPPINESS

The happiness of life is made up of minute fractions--the little soon forgotten charities of a kiss or smile, a kind look, a heartfelt compliment, and the countless infinitesimal of pleasurable and congenial feeling. -S Coleridge

- Happiness is when what you think, what you say, and what you do are in harmony. -Gandhi

- If you want to be happy, be. -Leo Tolstoy

- My crown is called content, a crown that seldom kings enjoy. -William Shakespeare

- Three grand essentials to happiness in this life are something to do, something to love, and something to hope for. -Joseph Addison

- Happiness is Homemade

To see a world in a grain of sand and heaven in a wild flower, hold Infinity in the palm of your hand and Eternity in an hour.
-William Blake

◎ There is no duty we so much under rate as the duty of being happy. -Robert Louis Stevenson

HARVEST

◎ We live for the bounties of fall, but the harvest of friendship is blessed above all

◎ The vineyards are blazing with the blush of fall

◎ Harvest of Blessings

◎ Harvest Moon

◎ Crush the grapes and ring the bells, harvest time is here again

◎ This harvest has been the most blessed of all.
-LaTourelle

HATS

◎ Caps for Sale

◎ Hat Tricks

◎ Hat's All Folks!

◎ Hats Off to _____

◎ I Love Hats

◎ The Right Hat for Every Occasion

◎ Look Mom! All Hats!

◎ Love That Hat

◎ So Many Hats...So Little Time

◎ The Cat in the Hat

◎ The Mad Hatter

HEALTH

◎ Begin each day with a prayer to arm your soul

◎ He who has health has hope, and he wo has hope has everything. -Arab proverb

◎ They say smiles and laughter are the best medicine

◎ A cheerful countenance doeth good like medicine

◎ Pray, Play and Healthy Stay

HEART

◎ Be Still My Heart

◎ Close To My Heart

◎ Cold Hands, Warm Heart

◎ Heart of Gold

◎ Heart Smart

◎ Heart to Heart

◎ Hearts and Kisses

◎ Music of the Heart

◎ One Heart, One Mind

◎ The Key to My Heart

◎ Tweet Hearts

◎ With Loving Hearts

◎ You Make My Heart Sing

◎ You Set My Heart A-flutter

◎ You are my Heart's Desire

◎ You're My Sweet Heart

◎ Hands to Work Hearts to God

◎ This old heart of mine been broke a thousand times

HEART-I-TUDES

⊚ A rose speaks of love quietly, in a language known only to the heart

⊚ It's all in the heart-itude.

⊚ The best & most beautiful things in this world cannot be seen or even touched, they must be felt with the heart

⊚ The work of the hands brings forth the spirit of the heart.

⊚ When I count my blessings I count you twice

⊚ Kind words—they fall from lips we love, like evening dew on drooping flowers and to the desert of the heart ,they come like sweet refreshing showers

⊚ Have you had a kindness shown? Pass it on; 'Twas not given for thee alone, Pass it on; Let it travel down the years, Let it wipe another's tears, 'Til in Heaven the deed appears—Pass it on -Henry Burton

HEAVEN

⊚ Heaven sent

⊚ Heaven is in your eyes

⊚ Heaven on earth

⊚ I can only imagine what that day will be

⊚ I think of heaven as a garden where I shall find again those dear ones who have made my world

HERITAGE

◎ A life recorded is twice precious - first the experience itself and then the memory of it full and sweet when we read about it later. -Elaine Cannon

◎ A walk down memory lane

◎ Bits of yesterday

◎ Family faces are magic mirrors

◎ Generation to generation

◎ I remember when...

◎ Moments in time

◎ Once upon a lifetime

◎ Our family tree

◎ Picture perfect Memories

◎ Priceless Moments

◎ Remember when...

◎ Seems like yesterday

◎ Those were the days

◎ Through the years

◎ We do not remember days, we remember moments

◎ I thank God on every rememberence of you

◎ Memories are like keepsakes always to be treasured

◎ The most treasured heirlooms are the sweet memories of our family

◎ When someone you love becomes a memory, the memory becomes a treasure

◎ Travel through the pages of time

High School

- High School Memories
- Homecoming
- Prom Night
- Grad Night
- Spring Break
- Our Gang
- Senior
- Junior
- Sophomore
- Freshman
- Free at Last
- Going on my Senior Trip
- A night to remember
- A year to remember
- Graduation at Last
- Driving to Anywhere

HISTORY

- History is the daughter of time. -Lucien Febvre
- History paints the human heart. -Napoleon I
  History is who we are and why we are the way we are. -David McCullough
  A morsel of genuine history is a thing so rare as to be always valuable. -Thomas Jefferson

HOCKEY

- No Hockey, No Life...   Goal
- The Puck Stops Here!   Ice Wars
- Hitting the Ice   Slapshot

HOME

Mid pleasures and palaces though we may roam, Be it ever so humble, there's no place like home.

- A man's home is his castle.

- As for me and my house we will serve the Lord. -Joshua 24:15

- Bless this home, Lord and all who are within, whether it be the love of a family or the closeness of friends

- Home is the father's kingdom, the mother's world and child's paradise

- Home is where friendships are formed and families are grown; where joy is shared and true love is known; where memories are made and seeds of life are sown. This is the place... that people call HOME.

- I had rather be on my farm than be emperor of the world. -George Washington

- My Old Kentucky Home

- No matter what, no matter where It's always home when love is there.

- Casa Sweet Casa

- On the Front Porch

- Our Nest is Blessed

- Sweet Home _____

- The House That Love Built

▪▪▪▪▪▪▪▪▪▪▪▪▪▪▪▪▪▪▪▪▪▪▪▪▪▪▪▪▪▪▪▪

Give me a house To call my own, Family and friends To call it a home. The year's at spring And day's at morn; God's in his heaven, All's right with the world. –Robert Browning

◎ There is nothing half as pleasant as coming home again

HORSE RACING

◎ At the Track

◎ Daily Double

◎ Derby Day

◎ Jockey to Win

◎ Photo Finish

◎ Run for the Roses

◎ The Starting Gate

◎ The Winner's Circle

◎ Win - Place - Show

◎ Breakneck Speed

◎ Splendor in the Bluegrass

◎ No hour of life is wasted that is spent in the saddle. -Churchill

HOUSE RULES

◎ If you mess it, clean it

   If you dirty it, wash it

   If you open it, close it

   If it barks, feed it

   If it cries, change it

◎ Mom is the absolute authority (just don't tell Dad)

◎ When going somewhere, you will always take your little sister/brother with you

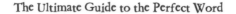

HOUSEWORK

- Oh My!
- Topsy-Turvy
- Bless this mess
- Mess? What mess?
- Martha Doesn't Live Here
- Born to shop...not to mop!
- Cleanliness is next to...impossible
- Don't Sweat the Small Stuff
- Dust was put on earth so we could measure time.
- God Made Dirt and Dirt won't hurt
- Help wanted: Please apply in kitchen
- Housework never killed anyone, but why take a chance
- Housework...just sweep the room with a glance
- I believe in miracles ... keeping this place clean is one of them.
- Cleaning the house while the kids are still growing...is like shoveling the walk while it's snowing.
- I cleaned my house yesterday Sure wish you could have seen it
- I don't do housework on days that end in "Y"
- A clean house is the sign of a broken computer
- A Little dirt never hurt
- A messy kitchen is a happy kitchen and this kitchen is delirious
- Our butler & maid resigned

■■■■■■■■■■■■■■■■■■■■■■■■■■■■■

HOUSEWORK

Inferior housekeepers are apt to be more creative. They admit to disorder in life. They like the richness of it. They are seeking some farther-reaching quality of order. -Dr. Donald Mackinnon

◉ All work and no pay makes a housewife

◉ Although you'll find our house a mess Come-in, sit down, converse. It doesn't always look like this; Some days it's even worse

◉ Beware...this home protected by killer dust bunnies.

◉ If a man's house is his castle - let him clean it

◉ If cleanliness is next to godliness...we're in big trouble

◉ My house is clean enough to be healthy & dirty enough to be happy

◉ So I'm not Super wife...Adjust!

◉ The dust bunnies are having a convention at my house.

◉ The most shocked women in the world are those who get married because they're tired of working

◉ The only place housework comes before scrapbooking is in the dictionary!

◉ There are days I'm so busy that I don't get anything done.

◉ Whenever I feel like cleaning, I lie down until the feeling goes away.

HUGS

Millions and millions of years would still not give me half enough time to describe that moment of eternity I feel when we embrace

- A grandma/grandpa is a hug waiting to happen
- Embrace me, my sweet embraceable you. -Gershwin
- Children are for hugging
- Mom makes hugs happen
- Let's go "hug" wild!
- Handle with hugs
- Bear hugs are in
- Hug collector
- 100% Huggable
- Huggable, lovable you
- Hugs make life bear-able
- Hug Dept: Always Open
- If a hug represented how much I loved you, I would hold you in my arms forever
- My favorite place to be is inside of your hugs where it's warm and loving
- Never put off until tomorrow the hug you can give today
- I wish I was a teddy bear, everybody loves them, nobody cares if they're fat and the older they get the more cuddly they become

- Hugs and kisses, stars for wishes
- A Hug a Day keeps the Monsters Away
- A hug is a handshake from the heart.
- A hug is the shortest distance between friends.
- You're so huggable you could put teddy bears out of business.
- Cookies and hugs make life bearable

HUMOR

- Blessed are they who can laugh at themselves for they shall never cease to be amused
- The man who can smile when things go wrong has probably thought of someone to blame it on.
- If you are grouchy, irritable, or just plain mean, there will be a $50 fee to put up with you

HUNTING

- A Hunting We Will Go
- Call of the Wild
- Marksmanship
- Oh, Deer
- On the Hunt
- Quick Draw McGraw
- Ready, Aim, Fire!
- Right on Target
- Road Kill Grill
- Sharpshooter
- Target Practice

I'M...

- ◉ I'm Yours
- ◉ I'm so cool!
- ◉ I'm Special
- ◉ I'm a Heartbreaker
- ◉ I'm in the Moo -od for ...
- ◉ I'm the only one like me
- ◉ I'm so busy, Mom's head is spinning

HUSBAND

- ◉ Only You
- ◉ Lucky Me
- ◉ Made for Each Other
- ◉ Magic Moments
- ◉ Close To My Heart
- ◉ I will always love you
- ◉ My Eyes Adore You
- ◉ There's Just Something About You I Love
- ◉ I This Girl's In Love with You
- ◉ To Know Him Is to Love Him
- ◉ You Had Me From Hello
- ◉ A Groovy Kind of Love
- ◉ My love for you is like a circle, it has no end
- ◉ No one is perfect until you fall in love with them.
- ◉ I don't mind the thorns if you're the rose
- ◉ Ah, sir, when I gave my heart to thee

HUSBAND HUMOR

◉ A husband is someone who takes out the trash and gives the impression he just cleaned the whole house

◉ Behind every man is a surprised mother-in-law

◉ Don't Criticize Your Wife's judgment–Look Who She Married

◉ Husband and dog missing, reward for dog

◉ Husband for Sale...remote included!

◉ I got a dog for my husband...I think it was a fair trade

◉ I love a man with dishpan hands

◉ If a mans home is his castle, let him clean it

◉ If we can send a man to the moon...why not all of them?

◉ I'm the boss of my house, my wife said so

◉ My husband lets me buy all the scrapbooking supplies I can hide.

◉ My wife says I never listen to her-at least I think that's what she said.

◉ Man is the king of his castle...but only until his queen comes home.

ILLNESS

- Chicken Pops
- Chicken Pox
- Connect the Dots
- Miserable Measles
- Mom, I Don't Feel So Good
- Saturday Night Fever
- Striped Froat
- The Healing Touch
- This Too Shall Pass

I LOVE...

- I Love Grandma, Nana, etc.
- I Love Grandpa, Papa, etc.
- I love to dance or _____
- I Love (kids favorites)
- I Love (sport, game)
- I Love (whatever)
- I Love Candy
- I Love Daddy
- I Love Mommy
- I love to laugh
- I love Jesus
- I love You

IRRESISTIBLE

- Wild Thing
- Call Me Irresistible
- Too Cute for Words
- Simply Irresistible
- Wild and Woolly
- Too Hot to Handle
- Cool Dude
- Hot Mama
- Hip Chic

JESUS

- God Has Done Great Things
- Be Still & Know that I Am God
- Jesus Loves the Little Children
- The Lord is My Strength
- Smile, God Loves You
- An Everlasting Love
- No Greater Love
- Jesus Loves Me
- Bless You

JOURNEY

- Celebrate the journey!
- Good company in a journey makes the way seem shorter.
- When preparing to travel, lay out all your clothes and all your money. Then take half the clothes and twice the money -Heller
- A man travels the world over in search of what he needs, and returns home to find it
- Heroes take journeys, confront dragons, and discover the treasure of their true selves
- The longest journey is the journey inward. -Hammarskjold
- Two roads diverged in a woods, and I. I took the one less traveled by and that has made all the difference. -Robert Frost

JOY

- Spoonful Of Sugar
- Do-Re-Mi
- Favorite Things
- Joy is in the sharing of it
- Joy comes in the morning
- The tiniest dewdrop hanging from a grass blade in the morning is big enough to reflect the sunshine and the blue of the sky

JULY 4TH

- America, We Salute You
- Little Patriot
- Red, White And Blue, Through And Through
- The American Spirit
- United We Stand

KID TALK

- I'm not stubborn
- I did that
- But Mom!
- Who Me?
- Mine

KIDS ACTION

- Born to Cause Trouble
- Just "Monkeying" Around
- Just Bee-Boppin' around
- Just Clowning around
- Just a Swingin'
- Horsin' Around
- GO GO GO!
- Go Speed Racer!!
- Hippity Hoppity Hooray
- Hop on Pop
- Jumpin' Joey

KIND WORDS

- I will always love you
- You are so special
- You are wonderful
- You look gorgeous today
- You make me feel good
- Thank you for loving me
- You're my best friend
- You make each day brighter
- I can't imagine my life apart from you
- I could not get you out of my mind today
- I prize every moment we spend together
- I appreciate all the things you have done for me
- You're my first, last, my everything

KIND WORDS FOR KIDS

- You did it
- Way to Go
- Awesome
- Totally Cool
- Superstar
- Great
- Good
- Neat
- Well Done
- Remarkable
- Fantastic
- Super Star
- Nice Work
- I Knew You Could Do It
- I'm Proud Of You

KINGS AND QUEENS

- A Knight to Remember
- A Royal Pain
- All I ask is that you treat me no differently than you would the queen.
- Being a princess is a full-time job but someone has to do it
- Crowned for the King
- Cuz I'm the Princess....that's why!
- Damsel in Distress
- I want it all and I want it delivered
- King of the Manor
- Kiss the King
- Pretty, pretty princess
- Prince Charming
- Princess of Quite Too Much
- Princess Petunia
- Queen for a Day
- Fussy Little Princess
- Queen of Daddy's Heart
- Queens of the Crop
- Royal Treatment
- The Prince of Whatever's Left
- The Queen of Everything You've Seen
- Toad Kisser
- Your Highness
- King of My Heart
- Queen Love A Lot

KISSES

Once he drew with one long kiss my whole soul thro' my lips, as sunlight drinketh dew.   -Tennyson

- ◉ A Kiss for Luck
- ◉ A Kiss is Just a Kiss
- ◉ A man had given all other bliss, And all his worldly worth for this, to waste his whole heart in one kiss Upon her perfect lips.
- ◉ A man's kiss is his signature
- ◉ Always kiss your children goodnight, even if they're already asleep.
- ◉ And the sunlight clasps the earth, And the moon-beams kiss the sea: - What are all these kissings worth, If thou kiss not me? -Shelley
- ◉ Butterfly Kisses
- ◉ First Kiss
- ◉ Gimme a Little Kiss
- ◉ Hearts and Kisses
- ◉ I believe in long, slow, deep, soft, wet kisses that last three days
- ◉ I wasn't kissing her, I was whispering in her mouth. -Chico Marx
- ◉ It's in His Kiss
- ◉ S.W.A.K.
- ◉ You have to kiss a lot of toads to find your handsome prince

KITES

- Blowing in the Wind
- Flying High
- Gone with the Wind
- Higher and Higher
- It's a Blustery Day
- Let's Go Fly a Kite
- The Kite-Eating Tree
- Up, Up, and Away
- A Great Day for Kite Flying
- May the Wind Be Always at Your Back

LAUGHTER

- Where's your tickle spot?
- He who laughs last, laughs best
- Hearty Laugh
- If you can laugh at it, you can live with it.
- Laugh and the world laughs with you - Cry and you get your way!
- Laugh and the world laughs with you. Cry and you cry with your girlfriends.
- Laughing All the Way
- Laughter is a tranquilizer with no side effects.
- Laughter is the Best Medicine
- Live Well - Laugh Often - Love Much
- The best blush to use is laughter: It puts roses in your cheeks and in your soul.
- The earth laughs in flowers.
- Gut Buster

LIFE

- The purpose of life is a life of purpose. ~Robert Byrne
- When I stand before God at the end of my life, I would hope that I would not have a single bit of talent left, and could say, "I used everything you gave me." -Erma Bombeck
- Life is a great big canvas, and you should throw all the paint on it you can. -Danny Kaye
- Be glad of life because it gives you the chance to love and to work and to play and to look up at the stars. - Henry Van Dyke
- Life is a long lesson in humility. -James M. Barrie
- Our main business is not to see what lies dimly in the distance but to do what lies clearly at hand. -Thomas Carlyle
- Let your life lightly dance on the edges of Time like dew on the tip of a leaf. - Tagore
- The true meaning of life is to plant trees, under whose shade you do not expect to sit. -Nelson Henderson
- We are the hero of our own story. -Mary McCarthy
- May you live all the days of your life
- Live for those who love you

LOVE

There's just something about that word... LOVE. Oh how it awakens one's senses with a plethora of feelings. As I read some of the intimate thoughts of these authors, poets and philosophers, I found myself reflecting on my journey in life, where I've been and the road that lies before me. Ah, sweet memories (and others, too)!

Searching for the perfect words to grace the pages of my book, I was awestruck at the passionate nature of both men and women from generations past. There has always been something so captivating about this thing called Love. Mere words simply cannot accurately describe the depth of it's meaning. Yet since time began, people have searched their souls to express Love's essence through music, word, art and so much more.

The words chosen for this book speak softly to the romantic in me. My hope is as you search for the perfect words to embellish your pages, cards or projects you will be enriched as you, too, read the enchanting thoughts conveyed within these pages. May these writings bless you with a tender and joyful recollection of all that has touched you thus far on your journey. Take what you will, drink it in and then pass it along to inspire someone along your path. I believe there is one definite purpose to life and that is to Love and be loved...may your cup ever overflow. -Linda

To melt and be like a running brook that sings its melody to the night. To know the pain of too much tenderness. To be wounded by your own understanding of love; and to bleed willingly and joyfully. To wake at dawn with a winged heart and give thanks for another day of loving; to rest at the noon hour and meditate love's ecstasy; to return home at eventide with gratitude; and then to sleep with a prayer for the beloved in your heart and a song of praise upon your lips. -Gibran

S he walks in beauty, Like the night of cloudless climes and starry skies; And all that's best of dark and bright Meet in her aspect and her eyes. -Byron

◉ Love is the whole and more than all -E.E. Cummings

◉ My bounty is as boundless as the sea, my love as deep; the more I give to thee the more I have, for both are infinite. -William Shakespeare

◉ My love for you is a journey; starting at forever, and ending at never.

◉ Once in awhile, right in the middle of an ordinary life, love gives us a fairy tale.

◉ The best feelings are those that have no words to describe them -Hammersley

◉ The heart has its reasons that reason knows nothing of -Blaise Pascal

◉ Let the world stop turning, Let the sun stop burning, Let them tell me love's not worth going through. If it all falls apart, I will know deep in my heart, the only dream that mattered had come true. In this life I was loved by you. -Bette Midler

◉ True love does not come by finding the perfect person, but by learning to see an imperfect person perfectly -Jason Jordan

◉ Other men have seen angels, But I have seen thee, And thou art enough. -G. Moore

◉ Love is the silent saying and saying of a single name -Mignon McLaughlin

◉ My love for you is like a circle, it has no end

H e felt now that he was not simply close to her, but that he did not know where he ended and she began. -Leo Tolstoy

- ☺ A man is not where he lives, but where he loves.

- ☺ Before I met my husband, I'd never fallen in love. I'd stepped in it a few times. -Rita Rudner

- ☺ I but know that I love thee, whatever thou art. - Moore

- ☺ I don't mind the thorns if you're the rose.

- ☺ I don't wish to be something to everyone, but I would like to be everything to you.

- ☺ I have spread my dreams under your feet; Tread softly because you tread on my dreams. -W. B. Yeats

- ☺ I need the starshine of your heavenly eyes, After the day's great sun. -Towne

- ☺ If you press me to say why I loved him, I can say no more than because he was he, and I was I. - Michel de Montaigne

- ☺ You know when you have found your prince because you not only have a smile on your face but in your heart as well

- ☺ When we first fall in love, we feel that we know all there is to know about life, and perhaps we are right

- ☺ When you realize you want to spend the rest of your life with somebody, you want the rest of your life to start right then

- ☺ We waste time looking for the perfect lover, instead of creating the perfect love. -Robbins

LOVE

If thou must love me, let it be for nought Except for love's sake only. Do not say, I love her for her smile...her look...her way Of speaking gently... for a trick of thought That falls in well with mine, and, certes, brought A sense of pleasant ease on such a day - For these things in themselves, Beloved, may Be changed, or change for thee - and love so wrought, May be unwrought so.   -Elizabeth Barrett Browning

☻ If you live to be a hundred, I want to live to be hundred minus one day,so I never have to live without you. -Pooh

☻ In our life there is a single color, as on an artist's palette, which provides the meaning of life and art. It is the color of love. -Chagall

☻ In thy face I see honor, truth and loyalty.

☻ The eyes are but a window to the soul they say and the lips the inviting door. With one soft kiss upon said lips a heart will love forever more -LaTourelle

☻ It was not into my ear you whispered, but into my heart. It was not my lips you kissed, but my soul. - Judy Garland

☻ The heart is a small thing, but desireth great matters. -Quarles

LOVE

Doubt thou the stars are fire,
Doubt the sun doth move,
Doubt truth to be a liar but never doubt
thy love

-Shakespeare

☺ A thing of beauty is a joy forever: Its loveliness increases; it will never Pass into nothingness; but still will keep a bower quiet for us, and a sleep Full of sweet dreams, and health, and quiet breathing. - John Keats

☺ He felt now that he was not simply close to her, but that he did not know where he ended and she began. -Leo Tolstoy

☺ I love you 'til the day after forever

☺ What greater thing is there for two human souls than to feel that they are joined together to strengthen each other in all labour, to minister to each other in all sorrow, to share with each other in all gladness, to be one with each other in the silent unspoken memories.

☺ There was one single moment tonight, where I looked up, your eyes captured my soul and I fell in love with you all over again.

☺ Grow Old with Me... the best is yet to be

LOVE

⊚ Sometimes we make love with our eyes. Sometimes we make love with our hands. Sometimes we make love with our bodies. Always we make love with our hearts.

⊚ So, fall asleep love, loved by me, for I know love, I am loved by thee. -Robert Browning

⊚ A happy marriage is a long conversation which always seems too short. -Mauroios

⊚ A promise made is a promise forever.

⊚ Are we not like two volumes of one book? -Valmore

⊚ Because she my friend and my wife, she has seen and brought out the best and worst of me, and she is still with me and I owe her my whole heart, soul, attention, love, and anything she desires of me. She will always be there. -Connolly

⊚ Love is what you've been through with somebody. -James Thurber

⊚ There are a million things that I don't know, but one that I surely know—I love you.

⊚ In true love the smallest distance is too great, and the greatest distance can be bridged. -Hans Nouwens

⊚ Love is being stupid together. -Paul Valery

⊚ Love is the greatest refreshment in life. -Picasso

⊚ Love is the poetry of the senses. -Honor de Balzac

⊚ Our souls have touched, my love. My only solace is - that if you become lost, a part of me will be lost with you. -Tom Brinck

■■■■■■■■■■■■■■■■■■■■■■■■■■

LOVE

How do I love thee ? Let me count the ways. I love thee to the depth and breadth and height My soul can reach, when feeling out   Elizabeth Barrett Browning

◎ For hearing my thoughts, understanding my dreams, and being my best friend. For filling my heart with joy and loving me without end... I do love you

◎ Husbands ought to love their wives as their own bodies. He who loves his wife loves himself. After all, no one ever hated his own body, but he feeds and cares for it .. For this reason a man will leave his father and mother and be united to his wife, and the two will become one flesh.

◎ Love is the thing that enables a woman to sing while she mops up the floor after her husband has walked across it in his barn boots. -H. Farmer

◎ The real soul-mate is the one you are married to - Tolkien

◎ The minute I heard my first love story, I started looking for you, not knowing how blind that was. Lovers don't finally meet somewhere. They're in each other all along. - Maulana Rumi

◎ The most precious possession that ever comes to a man in this world is a woman's heart. -J. Holland

◎ I love but thee with a love that shall not die 'til the sun grows cold and the stars grow old. -Willam Shakespeare

◎ Do you know that it would take you forever to realize the extent of my love for you.

◎ The mind has a thousand eyes, and the heart but one.- Francis W. Bourdillon

Y ou are the sun in my winter sky, you are the hello in my goodbye. You are the stars shining down on me, you are everything I had hoped you would be. You are the arms wrapped around a hug, you are the pull when I need a little tug. You are the lips that feel my gentle touch, you are the one who loves me so much. You are the one who I come to for love, you are my angel sent from above. I need your love, I need you too, because I am the I in I love you.

- Once you see into someone's soul, you're attached forever.

- On my soul your eyes are burned, lover's past forever spurned. One touch from you, my skin does tingle. How tenderly our breath is mingled. A single look and my heart swells, on my lips your kisses dwell. A thousand and a hundred score. A hundred and a thousand more

- Is it better for a woman to marry a man who loves her than a man she loves

- True love is when you're still dancing, long after the music has stopped

- Love puts the fun in together, the sad in apart, the hope in tomorrow, the joy in the heart

- Love vanquishes time. To lovers, a moment can be eternity -Mary Parrish

- There is no remedy for love but to love more.-Thoreau

- Love can hope where reason would despair -Lord Lyttelton

- And the Lord God said, It is not good that man should be alone; I will make him a

- help meet for him. -Gen. 2·18

- Thou art to me a delicious torment. -Ralph Waldo Emerson

- Love will find a way

L ove is patient, love is kind. It does not envy, it does not boast, it is not proud. It is not rude, it is not self-seeking, it is not easily angered, it keeps no record of wrongs. Love does not delight in evil but rejoices with the truth. It always protects, always trusts, always hopes, always perseveres. -1 Corinthians 13:4-7

■■■■■■■■■■■■■■■■■■■■■■■■■■■■■■■

LOVE

- An Everlasting Love
- Blue Moon
- Can't Hurry Love
- Dearly Beloved
- Embraceable You
- Fly Me To The Moon
- Hold Me, Thrill Me, Kiss Me
- It Had To Be You
- Love is Kind
- Poetry In Motion
- Love Shack
- Unforgettable
- Love Supreme
- Secret Love
- Shangri-La
- My Funny Valentine
- Love in the Afternoon
- Young At Heart
- A Groovy Kind of Love
- Somebody Loves Me
- These Foolish Things
- Truly, Madly, Deeply
- You made me love you
- I Can't Give You Anything But Love
- I Love You For Sentimental Reasons
- On The Street Where You Live
- I've Got My Love To Keep Me Warm
- Some Enchanted Evening

- I'll love you till the stars cease to shine
- Ah, love, let us be true to one another!
- Drink to me only with thine eye
- A jug of wine, a loaf of bread -- and Thou
- My Heart Reminds Me
- Roses Are Red
- Somebody Loves Me
- Stardust
- That Old Feeling

LOVE

- ◎ As Time Goes By
- ◎ Come Rain Or Come Shine
- ◎ Hey There
- ◎ I Can't Give You Anything But Love
- ◎ I Love You For Sentimental Reasons
- ◎ I Remember You
- ◎ I'm Yours
- ◎ Isn't It Romantic
- ◎ It's De-Lovely

LOVE TYPES

- ◎ An Everlasting Love
- ◎ Baby Love
- ◎ Brotherly Love
- ◎ Endless Love
- ◎ Forbidden Love
- ◎ A Groovy Kind of Love
- ◎ Heartfelt Love
- ◎ Love So Fine
- ◎ Mother's Love
- ◎ Puppy Love
- ◎ Summer Love
- ◎ Undying Love
- ◎ Teenage Crush
- ◎ My Steady
- ◎ Boyfriend/Girlfriend
- ◎ New Love
- ◎ Lost Love

LULLABY

⊚ Lullaby, oh lullaby! Flow'rs are closed and lambs are sleeping. Lullaby, oh lullaby! While the birds are silence keeping: Lullaby, oh lullaby! Sleep, my baby, fall a-sleeping. Lullaby, oh lullaby!

⊚ Hush little baby, don't say a word. Papa's going to buy you a mockingbird. And if that mockingbird don't sing Papa's going to buy you a diamond ring.

⊚ Lullaby, and goodnight. With roses be dight. With lilles bedecked is baby's wee bed. Lay thee down now and rest, may your slumber be blest. Lay thee down now and rest, may your slumber be blest.

⊚ Rock-a-bye baby, on the treetop, when the wind blows, the cradle will rock. When the bough breaks, the cradle will fall, and down will come baby, cradle and all.

⊚ Sleep my child and peace attend thee, All through the night. Guardian angels God will surround thee, All through the night. Soft the drowsy hours are creeping, Hill and dale in slumber creeping. I my loving vigil keepin, All through the night.

⊚ Hush-a-by, don't you cry, Go to sleep, little baby. When you wake, You shall have all the pretty little horses

⊚ Sleep, my baby, on my bosom, warm and cozy it will prove; Round thee mother's arms are folding. In her heart a mother's love. Sleep my darling babe in quiet, sleep on mother's gentle breast.

⊚ Sleep, pretty baby, the world awaits day with you; Morning returns to us ever too soon. Roses unfold, in their loveliness, all for you; Blossom the lilies for hope of your glance.

⊚ Sweet Baby of Mine, sleep gently and rest. Forever my love you will always be blessed. My darling I love you, my baby so fair. In you is a gift so precious and rare. I cherish and adore you with all of my heart. You were our special infant right from the start. -LaTourelle

I do believe that God above created you for me to love. He picked you out from all the rest, 'cause he knew I loved you best

MAKE BELIEVE

- If you can't believe, just make believe
- Imagination is grand
- Oh, what an imagination
- Welcome to the Land of Pretending, a place where joy is neverending
- Dream a little dream

MAKE-UP

- Lovely Lips
- Make Over
- Marvelous Makeover
- Rosy Cheeks
- Glamor Girl
- Like a Star
- Pretty Perfect
- Lovely Lady
- Makeover Magic
- Ooooo Baby!

MARRIAGE

- Being a husband is a whole-time job. -Enoch Arnold Bennett
- A good marriage is that in which each appoints the other guardian of his solitude. -Rainer Maria Rilke
- Let there be spaces in your togetherness. -Kahlil Gibran
- A successful marriage isn't finding the right person - it's being the right person
- The husband reigns but the wife governs. -English Proverb

Marriage is a door which looks out upon a beautiful view. As that door is opened and the horizon unfolds before you, know that nothing is sweeter than the warmth of one hand within another. -McCarty

- Marriage is a scrapbook filled with memories and hopes
- We interrupt this marriage for a football game!
- Give and take are the twin pillars of marriage
- The goal in marriage is not to think alike, but think together. -Carolyn Heilbrun
- Behind every great man there is a great woman. -English Proverb
- There is no more lovely, friendly and charming relationship than a good marriage. -Martin Luther
- Marriage is love walking hand in hand together. It is the realization that there is no one else in this world that you'd rather be with than the one you're married to. Marriage is being in love for the rest of your life.
- Marriage is building a castle together

223

MARRIAGE

If ever two were one, then surely we. If ever man were loved by wife, then thee. If ever wife was happy in a man; compare with me, ye woman, if you can. I prize thy love more than whole mines of gold, Or all the riches that the East doth hold. My love is such that rivers cannot quench, Nor ought but love from thee, give recompense. Thy love is such I can no way repay, the heavens reward thee manifold, I pray. The while we live, in love let's so persevere, That when we live no more, we may live ever.   -Anne Bradstreet

◉ The glory of friendship is not the outstretched hand, nor the kindly smile, nor the joy of companionship; it is the spiritual inspiration that comes to one when he discovers that someone believes in him and is willing to trust him with his friendship. -Emerson

◉ We loved with a love that was more than love. -Poe

◉ A man sees himself through the eyes of the woman he loves

◉ A good marriage is like a casserole, only those responsible for it really know what goes in it.

◉ All perfect marriages are made up of couples who accept the fact that they have an imperfect marriage. In dreams and in love there are no impossibilities -Arnay

◉ Keep me as the apple of the eye, hide me under the shadow of thy wings

◉ Love is the dawn of marriage, and marriage is the sunset of love

◉ Marriage should be like work, easy to love at best and best if it is easy to love

◉ Marriage: the state or condition of a community consisting of a master, a mistress and two slaves, making in all two. -Ambrose Bierce

◉ Love's greatest gift is its ability to make everything it touches sacred -De Angelis

◉ Marriage-a book in which the first chapter is written in poetry and the remaining chapters in prose. -Mickey

◉ No man is truly married until he understands every word his wife is NOT saying

MARTIAL ARTS

- Above The Belt
- Getting a Kick out of Karate
- Karate Kid
- Kick Back
- Kick It!

MEMORIES

- A Time to Remember
- A walk down memory lane
- Building Memories
- Days gone by
- Enjoy the little things, for one day you may look back and realize they were the big things.
- I remember when. . .
- Life is not measured by the number of breaths we take, but by the moments that take our breath away.
- Memories are the flowers in the garden of life
- Moments in time
- Odds and Ends
- Precious Memories
- Thanks for the memories!
- The Best Days of My Life
- The most treasured heirlooms are the sweet memories of our family
- The present is the point at which time touches eternity. -C.S. Lewis
- Times to Remember
- To everything there is a season...
- Unforgettable
- We shape our lives not by what we carry with us - but by what we leave behind.
- When someone you love becomes a memory, the memory becomes a treasure

MEN

- Mr. Style
- My Guy
- Rocket Man
- Quite the Stud
- The Right Stuff
- Mr. Right
- Ego-Maniac
- Suave and Debonair
- Too Sexy
- Man of the Hour
- Super Stud
- Honey Dude
- Still plays with cars
- Sportin' & Suave
- Real Men Don't Eat Quiche
- The Difference Between Men and Boys is the Size of Their Toys
- Men, can't live with them, can't live without them
- My Man
- He's da Man
- Manly Presence

■■■■■■■■■■■■■■■■■■■■■■

MEN VS. WOMEN

☺ My husband and I divorced over religious differences. He thought he was God and I didn't!

☺ Behind every man is a surprised mother- in-law

☺ Good men are like Martians, you hear a lot about them, but you've never really seen one.

☺ Husband and dog missing, reward for dog

☺ If a mans home is his castle, let him clean it

☺ If a woman can't find you handsome, let her find you handy

☺ If you don't like the way I drive, get off the sidewalk.

☺ Man of Many Vises

☺ Men make all the important decisions ... Women decide what's important.

☺ My toys! My toys! I can't do this job without my toys!

☺ Speak softly and carry a cellular phone.

☺ Still Plays with Cars

☺ When the Going Gets Tough, The Tough Use Duct Tape

☺ Women like silent men. They think they're listening. -Archard

☺ Don't imagine you can change a man - unless he's in diapers.

☺ For two people in a marriage to live together day after day is unquestionably the one miracle the Vatican has overlooked. -Bill Cosby

☺ Getting married for sex is like buying a 747 for the free peanuts. -Jeff Foxworthy

☺ Health watch: bringing her flowers is not harmful to your health

☺ If he asks what sort of books you're interested in, tell him checkbooks.

☺ Keep your eyes wide open before marriage, half shut afterwards. -Benjamin Franklin

☺ Loss of identity: Losing the remote to your significant other

☺ Love is the triumph of imagination over intelligence. -Mencken

☺ Marriage is the only war where you sleep with the enemy. -Gary Busey

☺ When four or more men get together, they talk about sports. When four or more women get together, they talk about men.

☺ Men like to barbecue. Men will cook if danger is involved

MIDLIFE

- Few women admit their age. Few men act theirs.

- Funny, I don't remember being absent minded.

- I like my bifocals, my dentures fit me fine, my hearing aid is perfect, but lord I miss my mind.

- If you're as old as you feel, how can I be alive at ?

- In mid-life your memory starts to go. In fact, the only thing you can still retain is water.

- Lying about my age is easier now that I often forget what it is.

- Middle age is when your age starts to show around your middle.

- Mid-life is when the growth of hair on our legs slows down. This gives us plenty of time to care for our newly acquired moustache.

- Real women don't have hot flashes, they have power surges.

- Setting an example for your children takes all the fun out of middle age. -William Feather

- The secret to staying young is to find an age you really like and stick with it.

- Time may be a great healer, but it's a lousy beautician.

MILITARY

- God Bless America

- Rosie the Riveter-Br-r-r-rr-r-r-!

- A force to be reckoned with

- A Wing and a Prayer

- Air Force Wife - The Toughest Job in the Air Force

- An Officer and a Gentleman

- Anchors away, my boys, anchors away

- Anchors Aweigh

- Armed to the teeth

- Coast Guard, we are for you!

- Defenders of the Skies

- G. I. _____

- Heroes of the Sea

- Home Is Where The Army Sends You

- Honor, Courage and Commitment (Navy Motto)

- Hooah! Airborne!

- Hurray for the Red, White and Blue

- I love a sailor boy and he loves me too!

- I thought of all the children, Of the mothers and the wives, Of fathers, sons and husbands With interrupted lives. I thought about a graveyard at the bottom of the sea Of unmarked graves in Arlington. No freedom isn't free.

MILITARY

- In the Army Now
- Intense Training
- Join the Navy!
- Keep America Proud
- Kiss the boys goodbye
- Lest We Forget
- Life, Liberty and the Pursuit of all who threaten it.
- Magnificent Marine
- My American Hero
- My Daddy's a Ruf-Tuf Marine
- Navy Men Walk the Talk
- Nothing can stop the U.S. Air Force!
- Off we go into the wild blue yonder climbing high into the sun; Here they come zooming to meet our thunder, At'em boys, giv'er the gun! Down we dive spouting our flames from under, off with one hell-uv-a roar! We live in fame or go down in flame, Nothing will stop the US Air Force!
- One of Uncle Sam's Toughest
- Our American Protectors
- Our Brave Little Soldier
- Over hill, over dale, we will hit the dusty trail
- Peace is our only product
- Proud Pilots
- Quarters, Sweet Quarters
- Remember Pearl Harbor
- Seabees Can Do
- Ship Ahoy
- Shore Leave
- Soldier Boy
- Stars and Stripes Forever
- Such is the life of a military wife
- Take to the Skies
- Tankers "Shoot to Kill"
- That noise you hear is the sound of freedom
- The American Way
- The Few , The Proud , The Marines
- The Fighting Seabee
- Their Finest Hour
- Then it's hi, hi, hee... in the field artillery, shout out your numbers loud and strong. For where e'er you go, you will always know that the Caissons go rolling along.
- Bravery is being the only one who knows you're afraid.
- A sailor went to sea, sea, sea
- To liberate the oppressed (Special Forces motto)
- War is my business and business is good!
- U.S. Navy Seals 'R Us
- Uncle Sam Wants YOU!
- Unsung Hero
- D-day Memories

MILITARY

- You can take the man from the Corps, but you'll never take the Corps from the man
- This nation will remain the land of the free only so long as it is the home of the brave. -Davis
- You don't win a war by dying for your country. You win a war by making the other son-of-a-bitch die for his. -General Patton
- When the pin is pulled, Mr. Grenade is not our friend
- Walking Proudly - The Airborne Walk
- We are proud to claim the title of United States Marines.
- We build, We fight (Seabee motto)
- We fight our country's battles, in the air, on land and sea
- We Salute You
- We went. . . we didn't ask why; our country called. . . and we were proud
- We will either find a way or make one
- We're in the Army now!
- What you call being a hero, I call just doing my job.
- When he's in a foreign land, Keep him safe in your loving hand
- You've Earned Your Stripes

MIRACLES

- Miracles do happen
- You are a miracle to me
- Out of difficulties grow miracles
- Don't believe in miracles -- depend on them
- I believe that mountains move one prayer at a time
- I believe in miracles I believe in signs.

MOM & MOMMA

- #1 Mom
- A Mom of All Trades
- Caution, Momma's Stressed
- Crazy Momma
- I Love You Mom
- Just me and my Mom
- Mommy's little Angel
- Mom's little helper
- Mom's Little Angel
- Mother's Love
- Mom always takes first place
- My Heart belongs to Momma
- Mother's make the world go round
- Lifestyles of the frantic and frazzled
- Momma Don't Allow no Pouting Here
- Moms are the sweetest presents
- If Mama ain't happy, ain't nobody happy

Mom & Momma

If you can keep your head when all about you are losing theirs, then you must be a Mom

◎ You can fool some of the people some of the time, but you can't fool Mom.

◎ Shhh! Mom is in time out!

◎ A real mom knows where to hunt for her missing kitchen utensils... in the sandbox

◎ Mom loves hugs and kisses and help with the dishes

◎ Mom–Manager Of Messes

◎ M is for MOM...not MAID!

◎ A wise mom gives her children two choices at mealtime...take it or leave it.

◎ Every mom knows when children say they are doing nothing, they are into mischief

Mom-ism's

◎ A little birdie told me

◎ A little soap & water never killed anybody

◎ Am I talking to wall?

◎ Answer me when I ask you a question

◎ Are you deaf or something?

◎ Are you trying to heat the outdoors?

◎ If I've told you once I've told you a thousand times

◎ If wishes were horses

◎ As long as you live under my roof, you'll do as I say

◎ Because I said so

◎ Candy is NOT a breakfast food

◎ Chew with your mouth closed

◎ Did you brush your teeth?

◎ Do you think I'm made of money?

◎ Don't ask me WHY The answer is NO

◎ Don't cross your eyes or they'll freeze that way

◎ Don't go out with a wet head, you'll catch cold

◎ Don't jump on the bed

◎ Don't make me come in there

◎ Don't make me get up

◎ Don't pick your nose

◎ Don't run in the house

◎ Don't sit too close to the television, it'll ruin your eyes

◎ Eat your vegetables, they're good for you

◎ Go ask your father

◎ Go play outside It's a beautiful day

◎ Hello, are you deaf?

◎ How many times do I have to tell you?

◎ I can't believe you did that

◎ I don't care who started it, stop it now

◎ You're the oldest You should know better

231

MOM-ISM'S

- I don't know is NOT an answer
- I just want what's best for you
- If all the kids jump off the bridge are you going to, too?
- If I want your opinion I'll ask for it
- If you're too sick to go to school, you're too sick to play outside
- I'm not running a taxi service
- Isn't it past your bedtime?
- Life isn't fair
- Look at me when I'm talking to you
- Now, say you're sorry and act like you mean it
- Some day you will thank me for this
- Someday when you have kids you'll understand
- Wait til your father gets home
- Were you born in a barn?
- What part of NO don't you understand?
- When I was a little girl

MONEY

- A Penny for Your Thoughts
- A penny saved is a penny earned.
- Baby You're a Rich Man
- Easy Money
- For Richer or Poorer
- Free For All

- Money Talks
- I have enough money to last me the rest of my life ... unless I buy something!
- Money Can't Buy Me Love
- Money doesn't grow on trees
- Money Money Money
- Money Well Spent
- Rags to Riches
- Gold Rush
- Show Me the Money
- Some people like to spend ... others like to save □and then they get married to each other.
- The Million Dollar Question

MOON

- The Man in the Moon looked out of the moon looked out of the moon and said it's time for bed sleepyhead
- Blue Moon
- By the light of the silvery moon
- Good Night Moon
- I See The Moon
- In the Misty Moonlight
- Magic Moon
- Moonlight Madness
- Moonstruck
- Once in a Blue Moon
- Reach for the Moon. If you fall short—You may land on a star
- Shadows in the Moonlight
- Shine on Harvest Moon
- You Hung the Moon

MORNING

- Early Riser
- Good Morning, Sunshine
- Hana Sunrise
- I Don't Do Mornings
- I Will Wake Up Happy
- I'll Rise But I Refuse to Shine
- I'm awake! Let's play!
- I'm far from tired
- I'm Still Sleepy
- Oh, How I Hate to Get Up in the Morning
- Rise and Shine
- The Glory of Daybreak
- This Is the Day that the Lord has Made
- Till the Morning Light
- Top of the Mornin' to Ya
- Up and at 'em
- Wake Up Little Suzy
- Wake Up Sleepyhead
- Watching the Sunrise
- Winter's Dawn

MOTHER

- A mother is someone who can take the place of everyone else, but no one in the world can take her place
- A mother is the only person on earth who can divide her love among ten children and each child still have all her love
- If mothers were flowers I'd pick you!

MOTHER

My mother kept a garden, a garden of the heart. She planted all the good things that gave my life its start. She turned me to the sunshine and encouraged me to dream, fostering and nurturing the seeds of self-esteem. And when the winds and rains came she protected me enough, but not too much because she knew I needed to grow strong and tough. Her constant good example always taught me right from wrong. Markers for my pathway that will last a lifetime long. I am my mother's garden. I am her legacy and I hope today she feels the love reflected back from me.

- And so our mothers and grandmothers have, more often than not anonymously, handed on the creative spark, the seed of the flower they themselves never hoped to see—or like a sealed letter they could not plainly read. - Alice Walker

233

MOTHER

She is their blanket to warm them on a cold winter night. She is the food that satisfies their hungry spirit. She is their shelter from the storm, their comfort in times of pain, their nursemaid to heal all hurts. She is the wind that lifts them up when they have fallen. She is encouragement that guides them forward. She is the love that brought them here. She is the heart daily praying them through. She is their Mother. -Linda LaTourelle

- As is the mother, so is her daughter -Ezekiel 16:44
- Mother—a special love
- BEST OF THE BEST
- Flowers have the sun, children have their mothers.
- God Bless You, Mom
- God couldn't be everywhere, so he created mothers.
- Grace was my mother's steps, heaven was in her eyes, in every gesture dignity and love.
- When Mom Says 'No', Ask Grandma

- A mother holds a special part of all that is treasured in the heart
- Most of all the other beautiful things in life come by twos and threes, by dozens and hundreds. Plenty of roses, stars, sunsets, rainbows, brothers and sisters, aunts and cousins, but only one mother in the whole world -Kate Douglas Wiggin
- A Mother understands what a child does not say
- A mother's work is never done
- A Mother's Heart Is as Big as the World
- A mother's love is the heart of the home
- As a mother, my job is to take care of the possible . . . and trust God with the impossible. -Ruth Bell Graham
- I hope my child looks back one day, and sees a parent who was there to pray. A parent with time to listen and share, with loving arms that show they care. The years fly by and children grow, but to be loved and desired they surely will know. -Linda LaTourelle
- If at first you don't succeed; do it the way your Mother told you to
- I love my Mother

MOTHER

- No matter how old a mother is, her children will always be her babies
- The one thing children wear out faster than shoes is parents. -John J. Plomp
- Who takes the child by the hand takes the mother by the heart. -German Proverb
- Like Mother- Like Daughter
- Before I Was A Mom
- Every mother is a working mother.
- A Mother's love is the heart of the home
- A Mother is a special kind of friend
- Mother a special word for love
- Any woman can be a mother, it takes someone special to be a Mom
- A Mother holds her children's hand for a while, their hearts forever
- If I could choose from all the mothers in the world, Mom, I'd choose you

MOTORCYCLES

- Born to Bike
- Born to Ride
- Born to ride my motorcycle...
- Breaking Away
- Dirt roads teach patience.
- Easy Rider

MOTORCYCLES

- Forced to work
- If she won't agree to be my babe...
- It's not the destination,
- it's the journey
- Live to Ride...Ride to Live
- My bike will take her place.
- Ride a Hog...Forever Free
- To ride or not to ride... THAT is a stupid question
- The ONLY way to travel

MUSIC

- Jam Session
- Jazzman
- Juke Box Saturday Night
- On a Different Note
- Live And In Concert
- Make A Joyful Noise
- Meistro...
- Mr. Tambourine Man
- Music From The Heart
- Boogie Fever
- Fit as a fiddle
- For the Love of Music
- Garage Band
- Good Vibrations
- It's Time to Play the Music
- I've Got Rhythm
- Jam Session
- Jazz it up
- Lift up your voice and sing
- Live and in concert

MUSIC

There is nothing in the world so much like prayer as music is. -W. Merrill

◉ Make a Joyful Noise

◉ Can't You Just Hear the Music?

◉ Make your own kind of music

◉ A jazz musician is a juggler who uses harmonies instead of oranges. -Benny Green

◉ And the night shall be filled with music -Longfellow

◉ Music cleanses the understanding; inspires it, and lifts it into a realm which it would not reach if it were left to itself. -Beecher

◉ Music expresses that which cannot be said and on which it is impossible to be silent. -Victor Hugo

◉ I've Got Rhythm—I've Got Music

◉ Life Is The Song, Love Is The Music

◉ Music is Love in search of a word. -Sidney Lanier

◉ Music makes the heart sing

◉ Music was my refuge. I could crawl into the space between the notes and curl my back to loneliness. -Maya Angelou

◉ Music washes away from the soul the dust of everyday life. -Berthold Auerbach

◉ Perfect Harmony

◉ Singin' the Blues

MY FAVORITES

- actor
- actress
- animal
- Bible verse
- book
- color
- dessert
- flower
- food
- holiday
- movie
- perfume
- pizza
- place to visit
- Fast food
- restaurant
- season
- singer
- smell
- song
- sport
- job
- toy
- candy
- person
- store
- season
- vacation
- vehicle
- game
- television show
- musical instrument
- flavor (chocolate/vanilla)
- type of clothes

In your album try writing these favorites. Do it for each of your family members. Give them a list and ask them to complete it. It's a great way to get to know your family.

Add other things as you think of them. Have your kids think about others. Getting the family involved makes the journaling more fun, meaningful and memorable.

Names of Jesus

And His Name Shall Be Called...

Savior ❖ Wonderful ❖ Counselor ❖ The Vine
Bread of Life ❖ Messiah ❖ Rose of Sharon
Lily of the Valley ❖ Lord ❖ Christ
Light of the World ❖ Son of God ❖ Rock
Living Stone ❖ Immanuel ❖ Capstone
Word ❖ Gift of God ❖ High Priest
The Almighty ❖ Mediator ❖ Root and the
Offspring of David ❖ Creator Intercessor
Son of Man ❖ Advocate ❖ Lamb of God
The Guarantee Shepherd of the sheep
The Way ❖ The Truth ❖ The Life ❖ Good
Shepherd ❖ Rabbi ❖ The Resurrection
The Gate ❖ Nazarene ❖ Lord of Glory
Lord of Peace ❖ Outstanding among 10,000
Master ❖ Man of Sorrows ❖ The Last Adam
Hope of Glory ❖ Lion of the Tribe of
Judah ❖ Desired of all Nations Amen
Faithful Witness ❖ Faithful and True
Mighty God ❖ Lord of All ❖ Everlasting
Father ❖ Prince of Peace ❖ Bishop of Souls
Our Passover ❖ Chief Shepherd ❖ Author &
Finisher of our faith KING of Kings
LORD of Lords ❖ Bright Morning Star
Alpha & Omega ❖ First & Last

The Beginning & the End

JESUS CHRIST

NEEDLEWORK

◉ I am a material girl. Wanna see my fabric collection?

◉ I love sewing - and I have plenty of material witnesses to prove it.

◉ I will cross that stitch when I come to it!

◉ I'm in therapy–Sewing is cheaper than a psychiatrist

◉ Itching to be Stitching

◉ Just another fiber artist, bobbin and weavin'...

◉ My husband lets me buy all the fabric I can hide

◉ One yard of fabric, like one cookie, is never enough

◉ Sew much fabric...sew little time

◉ You are 'sew' special

◉ You sew girl

◉ A family stitched together with love, seldom ravels.

◉ As ye sew, so shall ye rip...

◉ Caution: Enter this Sewing Room at your own Risk

◉ Creative Clutter is better than Idle Neatness

◉ From my hands....to your heart

◉ Hands to work...Hearts to God...

◉ Hubby calls me his "sew & sew"

NEW YEAR

- A New Year with Old Friends
- A Time to Celebrate
- Celebrate the Good Times
- Cheers to the New Year
- Hats, Confetti, Noisemakers - Must Be a New Year
- Having a Party
- A Toast: To the New Year
- In the Midnight Hour
- Kiss of the Decade
- Let's Party
- Midnight Kiss
- Ring out the Old, Ring in the New
- The Confetti Falls
- Until Further Notice, Celebrate Everything
- Up till Midnight
- Watching the Ball Drop
- Father Time
- For auld lang syne, my dear, For auld lang syne, We'll tak a cup o' kindness yet, For auld lang syne. -Robert Burns
- Sing and dance and make good cheer, let's make it last throughout the year.
- The New Year, like an Infant Heir to the whole world, was waited for, with welcomes, presents, and rejoicings. -Charles Dickens

NIGHTLIFE

- A Night on the Town
- And to All a Good Night
- Are You Afraid of the Dark?
- Hard Day's Night
- Hello Darkness My Old Friend
- Here Comes the Night
- In the Heat of the Night
- It Happened One Night
- Late Night
- Midnight Confessions
- On a Night Like This
- Saturday Night Live
- Sleepless in (your town)
- Strange Bedfellows
- Strangers in the Night
- Things that Go Bump in the Night
- Tonight Could Be the Night
- Walking After Midnight
- We've Got Tonight
- While You Were Sleeping
- Night time is really the best time to work. All the ideas are there to be yours because everyone else is asleep. - Catherine O'Hara
- I'm not afraid of the dark, it's the things in the dark I'm afraid of
- After Sundown

NURSES

- A nurse is God's angel of mercy
- I've grown accustomed to my gown
- LPN: means loving person near
- Nurses are angels in disguise
- Nurses are I. V. Leaguers
- Nurses Call the Shots
- Nurses care....with both hands and hearts
- Nurses give Intensive Care
- Nurses have a lot of patients
- Nurses have a masters degree in caring.
- On a scale of 1 -100, nurses are 98.6
- Pediatric nurses take care of the little things.
- RN means real nice.
- Nurses can take the pressure.
- Nursing is a work of Heart
- Physical Therapists Get All the Breaks

NURSERY RHYMES

- Dance to your daddy, my little baby, Dance to your daddy, my little lamb. You shall have a fish and you shall have a fin And you shall have your supper when the boat comes in.
- Lady Bug, Lady Bud Fly Away Home

NURSERY RHYMES

All day long they come and go, Pittypat and Tip-pytoe. Footprints up and down the hall, play-things scattered on the floor, finger-marks along the wall, tell-tale smudges on the door, by these pre-sents you shall know Pitty-pat and Tippytoe. -Eugene Field

- Sleep, pretty baby, the world awaits day with you; Morn-ing returns to us ever too soon. Roses unfold, in their loveliness, all for you; Blos-som the lilies for hope of your glance.

- Aye, faithful to Little Boy Blue they stand, Each in the same old place-- Awaiting the touch of a little hand, The smile of a little face; And they wonder, as waiting the long years through In the dust of that little chair, What has become of our Little Boy Blue, Since he kissed them and put them there. -Eugene Field

- One for the money, Two for the show, Three to make ready, And four to go!

NURSERY RHYMES

Wynken, Blynken, and Nod one night sailed off in a wooden shoe-sailed on a river of crystal light, into a sea of dew. "Where are you going, and what do you wish?" the old moon asked the three. "We have come to fish for the herring fish that live in this beautiful sea; nets of silver and gold have we?" said Wynken, Blynken, and Nod.

- Hush a bye baby
  Daddy is near
  Mamma so loves you
  Because you're so dear

- Here we dance round the blueberry bush, the blueberry bush, the blue berry bush. Here we dance round the blueberry bush on a frosty winter morning

- One, two,
  Buckle my shoe
  Three, four,
  Shut the door
  Five, six
  Pick up sticks
  Seven, eight,
  Lay them straight
  Nine, ten,
  Let's do it again

- There was a little girl who had a little curl right in the middle of her forehead...

- Thirty days hath September, April, June, and November; February has twenty-eight alone, all the rest have thirty-one, excepting leap-year, that's the time when February's days are twenty-nine

- Georgy Porgy, pudding and pie, kissed the girls and made them cry. When the boys came out to play, Georgy Porgy ran away.

- Monday's child is fair of face, Tuesday's child is full of grace, Wednesday's child is full of woe, Thursday's child has far to go, Friday's child is loving and giving, Saturday's child works hard for its living, but the child that's born on the Sabbath day is bonny and blithe, and good and gay.

- Rock a bye baby your cradle does gleam. Daddy's quite noble and Mamma's a queen. Sister's a darling a wears a gold ring. Brother's a prince, who'll one day be king

- O Baby of mine may you always know your Masters love where ever you go. His blessings and grace are truly divine—love him always o baby of mine

- There is nothing like the blessing of a sweet baby from above to fill your life with magic and touch your heart with love.

NURSERY RHYMES

◉ Rest, little head, on my shoulder, so; A sleepy kiss is the only fare, Drifting away from the world we go, Baby and I in the rocking chair.

◉ Have you ever heard of the Sugar-Plum Tree? 'T is a marvel of great renown! It blooms on the shore of the Lollipop sea In the garden of Shut-Eye Town... So come, little child, cuddle closer to me In your dainty white nightcap and gown, And I 'll rock you away to that Sugar-Plum Tree In the garden of Shut-Eye Town. -Eugene Field

◉ The wheels on the bus go round and round, round and round. The wheels on the bus go round and round, round and round all day long. The babies on the bus go fast asleep. The babies on the bus go fast asleep all day long.

◉ This little piggy went to market, this little piggy stayed home, this little piggy had roast beef, this little piggy had none and this little piggy cried wee-wee all the way home

◉ Pat-a-cake, pat-a-cake Baker's man! Bake me a cake as fast as you can. Pat 'em and sift 'em and throw them up high, put them in the oven for baby and I

PARADES

◉ Easter Parade

◉ Christmas Parade

◉ Floating Along

◉ Forward, March!

◉ Marching Bands

◉ Parade of Lights

◉ Pomp and Circumstance

◉ Rose Bowl Parade

◉ Thanksgiving Day Parade

◉ View from the Boulevard

◉ Bands and Horses and Floats, Oh My!

PARADISE

◉ Paradise Lost

◉ Lost in Paradise

◉ Paradise is for Lovers

◉ Surfer's Paradise

◉ Color of Paradise

◉ My Garden of Paradise

◉ Kisses from Paradise

◉ Honeymoon in Paradise

◉ Just another day in Paradise

◉ Almost Paradise

◉ Paradise is always where love dwells. -Jean Paul F. Richter

PARENT TALK TOO
(DAD-ISMS)

- A little dirt never hurt anyone ... just wipe it off.
- Big boys don't cry.
- Come here...pull my finger!
- Don't worry ... it's only blood.
- Eat your veggies. They will grow hair on your chest.
- How about never? Is never good for you?
- If I've told you once ... I've told you a thousand times.
- I'll tell you why ... Because I said so! That's why!
- Now you listen to me, Buster!
- We're not lost ... I'm just not sure where we are.
- What's so funny? Wipe that smile off your face!
- Who ever said life was supposed to be fair?
- You call that a haircut?
- You didn't beat me ... I let you win.
- You'll always be my Daddy's little princess
- Go ask your mother
- Back in my day...
- What do I look like...a bank?
- Go to your room
- You're grounded
- Give me the car keys
- You'll live by my rules.

PARENTAL WISDOM

A Hundred Years from now, it will not matter what your bank account was, the sort of house you lived in, or the kind of car you drove, but the world may be different because you were important in the life of a child.

- Don't worry that children never listen to you; worry that they are always watching you. -Robert Fulghum
- How pleasant it is for a father to sit at his childs table. It is like an aged man reclining under the shadow of an oak he had planted. -Sir Walter Scott
- In absence of love there is nothing worth fighting for.
- Love is a bouquet of dandelions
- Love is peanut butter kisses and ice cream hugs.
- Love is reading the same bedtime story for the umteenth time
- Love is watching Mr. Rogers instead of your favorite soap
- Some times we're so concerned about giving our children what we never had growing up, we neglect to give them what we did have growing up. -James Dobson

PARENTAL WISDOM

- How do you spell LOVE?

- The work will wait while you show the child a rainbow, But the rainbow won't wait while you do the work.

- No man can possibly know what life means, what the world means, what anything means until he has a child and loves it. And then the whole universe changes and nothing will ever again seem exactly as it seemed before. -Hearn

- I could tell that my parents hated me. My bath toys were a toaster and a radio. -Rodney Dangerfield

- I don't think my parents liked me. They put a live teddy bear in my crib. - Woody Allen

- The years teach much that the days never know -Emerson

- Sometimes your child can say something really small, but it fits just right into this little space in your heart

- Discipline is the bridge between goals and accomplishments -Jim Rohn

- Character is doing the right thing when no one is looking. -JC Watts

- It does not requre many words to speak the truth -Chief Joseph

PARENTING

- Parents hold their children's hands for a little while, their hearts forever.

- We never know the love of a parent until we become parents ourselves.

- Setting a good example for your children takes all the fun out of life.

- It's not an empty nest until they get their stuff out of the basement

- Be nice to your kids - they pick your nursing home.

- Limousine Driver
- Man, Woman, and Child
- Married with Children
- The Parent Trap
- Personal Chauffeur
- Proud Parents
- Taxi Driver

PARK PLAY

- Barefoot in the Park
- Inside, Outside, Upside Down
- In the Swing of Things
- A Real Swinger
- Play Date
- Saturday in the Park
- Swingin' Around
- Swings are Angels' Wings
- Up, Up, and Away
- Mom's Day at the Park
- See-Saw, Up we go

PATRIOTIC

- America, you're beautiful
- And the rocket's red glare
- Liberty, Democracy, Freedom
- I'm a Yankee Doodle Dandy
- Happy 4th of July
- Have a Star Spangled Day.
- God Bless the USA
- Stars and Stripes
- Red, white and blue
- In God We Trust
- Let Freedom Ring
- My country 'tis of thee
- This land is your land
- Today's Little Patriot
- United We Stand
- We had a Blast!
- Freedom over Fear
- United We Stand
- America Remembers
- Made in America
- Uncle Sam
- American Pride
- Old Glory
- Sweet Land of Liberty
- God Bless America
- You're a grand old flag; you're a high flying flag
- Home of the free and the brave
- Hooray for the red, white and blue
- Forever in Peace may it Wave

PETS

- Animal farm
- Quick as a bunny
- Sly as a fox
- Wise as an owl
- Quiet as a mouse
- Strong as an ox
- Busy as a bee
- Cross as a bear
- Hungry as a Bear
- Stubborn as a mule
- Happy as a lark
- Slippery as an eel
- Gentle as a lamb
- Mad as a wet hen
- Bunny Love
- Feed the birds
- Itsy bitsy spider
- Our private zoo
- Precious Pets
- The birds
- Waddle I do without you?
- Please Mom, Can we Keep him?
- Birds of feather flock together
- All animals are equal, but some are more equal than others
- A spoiled, rotten (animal name) lives with me
- Be kind to your web-footed friends

PLAYING

- ◉ Play day, play day, everyday is my way
- ◉ Play is hard Work
- ◉ Play is often talked about as if it were a relief from serious learning. But for children play is serious learning. Play is really the work of childhood. -Fred Rogers
- ◉ Play today, sleep tomorrow
- ◉ Playing Around the playground
- ◉ Playing Dirty playing in the mud
- ◉ Playing Dress up
- ◉ Playing hard
- ◉ Playing With My Toys
- ◉ I'd rather be playing
- ◉ Sleep...No Play
- ◉ A child reminds us that playtime is an essential part of our daily routine
- ◉ There's nothing like playing dress up with your best friend
- ◉ Playtime, it's my favorite time
- ◉ All play and no work is cool
- ◉ All work and no play makes for a boring life
- ◉ Playmate come out and play with me
- ◉ Play Day at the Park
- ◉ I LOVE to Play

PLEASING THOUGHTS

Finally, brethren, whatsoever things are true, whatsoever things are honest, whatsoever things are just, whatsoever things are pure, whatesoever things are lovely, whatsoever things are of good report; if there be any virtue, and if there be any praise, think on these things. -Philippians 4:8

◎ What lies behind us, and what lies before us are tiny matters, compared to what lies within us.- Ralph Waldo Emerson

◎ Accentuate the positive, eliminate the negative

◎ The sunshine that comes from your heart is warmer than any that comes from the sky

◎ These things have I spoken unto you, that MY Joy might remain in you, and that your joy might be complete - John 15.11

◎ Have a heart that never hardens, a temper that never tires and a touch that never hurts. -Dickens

◎ Share Goodness, Demonstrate Kindness, Celebrate Love

◎ Think Love, Live Joy

◎ Build a Nest of Pleasant Thoughts

◎ Joy is yours Today... Just Take It

◎ Happy is as Happy Does

PMS

- All stressed out and no one to choke
- Do NOT start with me. You will NOT win
- Don't tick me off! I'm running out of places to hide
- Guys have feelings too. But like--who cares? I have PMS
- I can go from normal to insane in just seconds.
- I have an ATTITUDE... and know how to use it!
- I have PMS and I'm all out of chocolate, need I say more?
- I only have one nerve left, and you're getting on it!
- I'm busy. You're ugly. Have a nice day
- I'm multi-talented--I can talk and make you mad at the same time.
- I'm one of those bad things that happen to good people.
- It's not PMS that's bothering me...it's YOU
- It's not PMS...it's an estrogen fog
- Next mood swing...9 minutes
- Why do people with closed minds always open their mouths?
- You have the right to remain silent, so please SHUT UP

PMS is:

- Pardon My Screaming
- Pardon My Sobbing
- Pass My Shotgun
- Pass My Sugar
- Perfectly Marvelous Stamper
- Permanent Male Stupidity
- Permanent Menstrual Syndrome
- Perpetual Munching Spree
- Positively Magnificent Scrapper
- Pouty Male Syndrome
- Pouty Mood Syndrome
- Pretty Mean Spirited
- Pretty Mean Stamper
- Psychotic Mood Shift
- Puffy Mid-Section
- Punish My Spouse
- Real women don't have hot flashes...they have power surges
- Remember my name - you'll be screaming it later.
- Sorry if I looked interested. I'm not
- The difference between a woman with PMS and a pitbull is LIPSTICK
- Warning: I have an attitude and I know how to use it.
- Whatever...
- When I have PMS...I don't have my period...I have an explanation POINT
- Pack My Suitcase
- Tonight? Dream on!

POETS/POETRY

- Poetry and painting are rooted in the same law. The work of heaven. -Su Tung-po
- Poetry is painting with words, but a painting needs no words to speak.
- True poets don't write their thoughts with a pen...They release the ink that flows From within their heart.
- Women make us poets, children make us philosophers. - Malcolm de Chazal
- A poet is a man who puts up a ladder to a star and climbs it

POLICEMEN

- Badge of Honor
- Today's Heroes
- Long arm of the Law
- Men In Blue
- Pigs are beautiful too
- POLICE STATION TOILET STOLEN...Cops have nothing to go on
- The Lady and the Officer
- The Law
- The man behind the shield
- Thin Blue Line
- You hold the key to my heart
- You make my heart skip a Beat
- All in a day's work
- Make no Mistake
- World's Greatest Policeman
- America's Heroes

POTTY

- We fought the Potty and the Potty won!
- It's my potty and I'll cry if I want to!
- My kids love to potty all the time
- A whole lot of pottying goin' on
- It's a Party in the Potty!!
- Naughty in the Potty
- He/She's a Big Kid Now
- Bye-Bye Diapers
- Big Kid Undies
- You bowl me over
- Caught in the Pot
- Grin and Swish it
- Potty Animals
- Potty Party
- You did it

PRAISE HIM

- With God All Things Are Possible
- You are precious in His sight
- Praise the Lord
- Have Faith
- Keep the Faith
- What a Blessing you Are
- Jesus loves the little children
- Delight in the Lord
- As for me and my house we will serve the Lord
- Praise His Name
- My Jesus, My Saviour

■■■■■■■■■■■■■■■■■■■■■■■■■■

PRAISES FOR A CHILD

These are just short phrases, but can be used to as a simple description for all sorts of photos or artwork. You can even create little cards using them, or put a note in a lunch or under a pillow. Use your imagination as you watch the blessing your child will receive from seeing or hearing these words as they come from your heart! As you sow, so shall ye reap! Have fun with your writing!

- ⊘ A Big Kiss
- ⊘ A Big Hug
- ⊘ A Plus Job
- ⊘ Awesome
- ⊘ Beautiful
- ⊘ Beautiful Sharing
- ⊘ Beautiful Work
- ⊘ Bingo
- ⊘ Bravo
- ⊘ Creative Job
- ⊘ Dynamic
- ⊘ Excellent
- ⊘ Exceptional
- ⊘ Fantastic

- ⊘ I like You
- ⊘ I Love You!
- ⊘ I Respect You
- ⊘ I Trust You
- ⊘ I'm Proud Of You
- ⊘ Looking Good
- ⊘ Magnificent
- ⊘ Marvelous
- ⊘ Neat
- ⊘ Nice Work
- ⊘ Nothing Can Stop You Now
- ⊘ Now You're Flying
- ⊘ Outstanding Performance
- ⊘ Phenomenal
- ⊘ Remarkable Job
- ⊘ Spectacular
- ⊘ Super
- ⊘ Super Job
- ⊘ Super Star
- ⊘ Super Work
- ⊘ Terrific
- ⊘ That's Correct
- ⊘ That's Incredible
- ⊘ Way To Go
- ⊘ Well Done
- ⊘ What A Good Listener
- ⊘ What An Imagination
- ⊘ Wow
- ⊘ You Are Exciting
- ⊘ You Are Fun
- ⊘ You Are Responsible
- ⊘ You Belong
- ⊘ You Brighten My Day
- ⊘ You Care
- ⊘ You Figured It Out

PRAISES FOR A CHILD

- You Learned It Right
- You Make Me Happy
- You Make Me Laugh
- You Mean A lot To Me
- You Tried Hard
- You're A Darling
- You're A Good Friend
- You're A Joy
- You're A Real Trooper
- You're A Treasure
- You're A Winner
- You're Beautiful
- You're Catching On Now
- You're Fantastic
- You're Growing Up
- You're Important
- You're Incredible
- You're On Target
- You're On Top Of It
- You're On Your Way
- You're Perfect
- You're Precious
- You're Sensational
- You're Special
- You're Spectacular
- You're The Best
- You're Unique
- You're Wonderful
- You've Got A Friend
- You've Got It
- You're my Sugar Pie, Gum Drop, Lollipop Kid

PREGNANCY

- 9 Months and Counting
- A wrinkled up forehead and a cute button nose.
- Somersaults and Hiccups
- Before you were born I loved you. Before you were conceived I wanted you.
- Countdown to Baby
- False Alarm
- Hey! It's really cramped in here.
- I hear your voice Mommy - I can't wait to see you.
- I hope you are happy as an only child because I'M NOT DOING THIS EVER AGAIN
- It's so small in here I have to step outside to change my mind.
- My Pregnancy
- My skin's going to pop
- Ten tiny fingers & ten tiny toes
- The Big Day
- There is a great joy coming
- There is no friendship, no love, like that of a mother for her child.
- Will you look like Daddy or me?

PREGNANCY

- A Time to be Born
- 9 Months and Counting
- A Womb with a View
- About to Pop
- Anticipation
- Are you doing somersaults in there?
- Are you done yet?
- Before you were born I loved you
- Before you were conceived I wanted you
- Countdown to Baby
- False Alarm
- Getting Bigger Inch by Inch
- Great Expectations
- Hey! It's really cramped in here.
- Hip, Hip, Pooh-Ray, There's a Baby on the Way!
- I hear your voice Mommy - I can't wait to see you.
- Labor and Delivery
- Labor Day
- Labor of Love
- Lady in Waiting
- My Pregnancy
- Ready or not, here I grow!
- Room to Grow
- POP goes the Momma!
- Special Delivery

- No language can express the power and beauty and heroism of a mother's love. -Chapin
- The Big Day
- The Miracle of Life!
- There Is a Great Joy Coming
- What a Belly!
- Will you look like Daddy or me?
- Ten little fingers and ten little toes, sweet cheeks, too and a button nose
- There is no friendship, no love, like that of a mother for her child
- My skin just can not stretch any more!

PREGNANCY/ULTRASOUND

- A Bun in the Oven
- A sneak peek at baby
- A Womb with a View
- Baby's First Photo
- Beyond Conception
- Coming Attraction
- Peek-a-Boo
- Sneak Preview
- Ultra-Special
- Under Construction
- Pregnant pause
- Your heart beats for me
- Momma's little heartbreaker
- I can feel your heartbeat
- Womb with a View

PRETTY

- A thing of beauty is a joy forever -Keats
- Anyone who keeps the ability to see beauty never grows old. -Franz Kafka
- As we grow old, the beauty steals inward. -Emerson
- Beauty seen is never lost, God's colors all are fast. -John Greenleaf Whittier
- Far away in the sunshine are my highest inspirations. I may not reach them, but I can look up and see the beauty, believe in them and try to follow where they lead. -Louisa May Alcott
- Pretty Baby
- Pretty in Pink
- Pretty is as Pretty does
- Pretty Woman

PROFESSIONS

- Born to party, forced to work
- Carpenters don't get board!
- Choose a job you love, and you will never have to work a day in your life. ~Confucius
- Everyone is in awe of the lion tamer in a cage with wild lions, everyone but a school bus driver.
- Hair today...gone tomorrow
- Hairdressers do it with style.
- Hairstylist are a shear delight

- How old you are is your business...
- I slip from workaholic to bum real easy. -Matthew Broderick
- I'm a beautician...I can tell you stories that will curl your hair
- I'm a beautician...not a magician
- I'm the Dad□No Questions or Arguments
- This is a comb...not a magic wand
- We pretend to work because they pretend to pay us

PROM NIGHT

- Prom King/Queen
- All Dressed Up
- Picture Perfect
- Looking Good!
- Senior Prom
- Junior Prom
- All Decked Out
- The Perfect Day
- Dream Night
- My Prom Gown
- Dancing the night Away
- Pretty as a Princess
- Swept off my feet
- A night to remember
- Memories of High School

PUMPKINS

- The Great Pumpkin
- It's the Great Pumpkin, Charlie Brown!
- It's Pumpkin Time!
- Jack-O-Lantern
- Our Little Punkin
- Pickin' Pumpkins
- Picking the Best Pumpkin
- Pumpkin Patch
- Pumpkin Time

QUIET TIME

- A Place of My Own
- All is Calm
- Alone Again, Naturally
- My Quiet Place
- My Special Spot
- Place of Meditation
- Refreshing the Soul
- Rejuvenation / Time Out
- Desperately Seeking Solitude
- Relaxing and Unwinding
- Rest in the Lord
- Search for Self
- Silence is Golden
- The Sounds of Silence
- There's a Kind of Hush
- Everyone Needs Their Own Spot
- Far from the Madding Crowd
- Be Still and Know that I Am God

QUILT/QUILTER

- A family is a patchwork of love
- A quilt is a blanket of love
- Blessed are the children of piecemakersfor they shall inherit the quilts
- Blessed are the quilters for they shall be called piecemakers
- Families are like quilts - Lives pieced together - Stitched with smiles and tears - Colored with memories and bound by love.
- I am a quilter and my house is in pieces
- I quilt better than I cook
- In the crazy quilt of life, I'm glad you're in my block of friends
- Life is a Patchwork
- May your sorrows be patched and your joys be quilted.
- Old Crafter's never die, they just get more bazaar!
- One who sleeps under a quilt is comforted by love
- Our lives are like quilts - bits and pieces, joy and sorrow, stitched with love
- Quilters are warm people
- Quilters aren't greedy, they're just materialistic
- Quilters come with strings attached
- Quilters lead a piece-ful life

QUILT/QUILTER

- Quilters never cut corners
- Quilting comes from the heart
- Quilting forever--housework whenever!
- Quilting with a friend will keep you in stitches
- Quilts are like friends - a great source of comfort
- When life goes to pieces make quilt
- When life hands you scraps- make quilts
- Quilters make better comforters

RACING

- A Day at the Races
- A Need for Speed
- A Track Record
- Along for the Ride
- And the winner is...
- At the Track
- Away He Goes
- Born to Race
- Breakneck Speed
- Caution - Yellow Flag
- Driving Force
- Enjoying the Ride
- A Day at the Races
- A Need for Speed
- A Track Record
- Along for the Ride
- And the winner is☐
- At the Track

RACING

- Away He Goes
- Born to Race
- Breakneck Speed
- Can't wait to get on the road again
- Caution - Yellow Flag
- Driving Force
- Enjoying the Ride
- Fast, Faster, Fastest
- Final Circuit
- Full Throttle
- Garage Guru
- Gentlemen, Start Your Engines
- GO GO GO!
- Going the Distance
- Good to Go
- Green, Green, Green!
- Hot Wheels
- Little boys grow up to be bigger little boys.
- Loop the Loop
- Mr. Goodwrench
- Not So Fast
- On the Fast Track
- On Track
- One lap to go!
- Ooh! That had to hurt!
- Pit Crew
- Pit Stop
- Portrait of a Winner
- Race to the Finish
- Ready for the Pro-Circuit
- Road Adventures USA

RACING

- Sportsman-like Conduct
- Take it to the Limit
- Taking the Checkered Flag
- Taste of Victory
- The Checkered Flag
- The Driver's Seat
- The Finish Line
- The Green Flag
- The Last Lap
- The Thrill of Victory
- The wheels on my car go round and round
- Thrill Ride
- Tools of the Trade
- Top Speed
- Victory Lap
- Where the Blacktop Ends
- Where the Rubber Meets the Road

RAIN

The best kind of rain, of course, is a cozy rain. This is the kind the anonymous medieval poet makes me remember, the rain that falls on a day when you'd just as soon stay in bed a little longer, write letters or read a good book by the fire, take early tea with hot scones and jam and look out the streaked window with complacency. -Toth

- And the rain, rain, rain, came down, down, down...
- Anyone who thinks only sunshine brings happiness has never danced in the rain.
- Every Cloud Has a Silver Lining
- Gone with the Wind
- I Can See Clearly Now, the Rain is Gone
- I like it when it's foggy and sounding very froggy. I even like it when it rains
- I'm Singin' in the Rain
- Let it rain, rain, rain!
- Listen to the Rhythm of the Falling Rain
- Rain or Shine -- You're a Friend of Mine
- Rain Rain Go Away
- Rainy Day Fun
- Rainy days and Mondays always get me down
- Showers of Blessings
- Some people walk in the rain, others just get wet - Roger Miller
- The Rainbow Connection
- The Sun'll Come Out Tomorrow
- There could be no rainbow without a cloud and a storm.
- Who'll Stop the Rain
- Wishin' for Rain

RAINBOW

- After the Rain
- Everybody needs a rainbow.
- Have a rainbow day.
- Hope your days are filled with rainbows
- It takes both rain and sunshine to make rainbows and flowers
- Just when my life needed a touch of color, you added a whole rainbow.
- Make today a rainbow day
- May your days be filled with rainbows
- My End of the Rainbow
- Never stop searching for rainbows or chasing your dreams
- Over the Rainbow
- Rainbow's End
- Somewhere over the rainbow
- Sunshine, lollipops & rainbows
- The Rainbow Connection
- We all grow better in sunshine and love
- The Full Spectrum
- The Glory Of God
- Rainbow's End
- My End of the Rainbow
- Chasing Rainbows
- So Many Books, So Little Time

READING

An ordinary man can surround himself with books... and thence forward have at least one place in the world in which it is possible to be happy. -Augustine Birrell

- A man is known by the books he reads
- A room without books is like a body without a soul -Cicero
- Adding It All Up
- Adventure is just a page away
- All Booked Up
- Bookworm
- Bored? Read a book
- Do the Math
- Favorite Stories
- Go Figure
- I can read now
- I conceive that a knowledge of books is the basis on which all other knowledge rests.
- I find TV very educating. Every time somebody turns one the set I go into the other room and read a book.
- Once upon a Time
- Our Little Bookworm
- Playing by the Book
- Read me a Story
- Reading Rocks!

READING

- Story Teller
- Story Time
- What I like in a good author is not what he says but what he whispers. Logan Pearsall Smith
- What really knocks me out is a book that, when you're all done reading it, you wish the author that wrote it was a terrific friend of yours and you could call him up on the phone whenever you felt like it. That doesn't happen much, though. J. D. Salinger
- When you reread a classic you do not see more in the book than you did before; you see more in you than was there before. Clifton Fadiman
- Writing does not cause misery, it is born of misery. Montaigne

RELIGIOUS

- A Place of Grace
- Amazing Grace
- As for Me and My House, We Sill Serve the Lord
- Celebration of Faith
- Come as a Child
- Got Jesus?
- WWJD?

- Living Waters
- Jesus Loves Me
- Spiritual Renewal
- Surely the Presence of the Lord Is in This Place
- Thank You Lord
- The Way of the Cross
- Just a Closer Walk with Thee
- Letting Our Lights Shine
- Oh Lord, you are my Lord and I will ever love you
- He Will Hold You in the Palm of His Hand
- Hands to Serve Your Heart to God
- We Believe in Miracles
- Whispering Hope
- Kumbaya, My Lord
- Jesus loves the little children, all the children of the world. Red and yellow, black and white they are precious in His sight.
- How Great Thou Art
- Youth Camp
- Revival
- Going to Church
- Baptism Service
- Baby Dedication
- God's answers are wiser than our prayers
- Give your troubles to God. He'll be up all night anyhow.
- Real men love Jesus

RELIGIOUS

◎ The light in the eyes of him whose heart is joyful, rejoices the heart of others -Prov. 15:30

◎ See God in every person, place, and thing, and all will be well in your world -Louise Hay

◎ Going to church doesn't make you a Christian any more than going to the garage makes you a car.-LJ Peter

◎ God's answers are wiser than our prayers.

◎ Spirit is the real and eternal; matter is the unreal and temporal -Mary Baker Eddy

◎ That "love thy neighbor" thing? I meant it. -God

◎ God promises a safe landing, not a calm passage

◎ We are responsible for the effort, not the outcome

◎ We can never really go where God is not, and where He is, all is well.

◎ The will of God will never take you to where the grace of God will not protect you

◎ The task ahead of us is never as great as the power behind us

◎ Serenity is not freedom from the storm, but peace amid the storm

◎ We set the sail; God makes the wind

■■■■■■■■■■■■■■■■■■■■■■■■■

RETIREMENT

◎ A retired husband is often a wife's full-time job. -Ella Harris

◎ Don't play too much golf. Two rounds a day are plenty. -Harry Vardon

◎ Don't underestimate the value of doing nothing, of just going along, listening to all the things you can't hear, and not bothering. -A.A. Milne

◎ Middle age is when work is a lot less fun and fun is a lot more work.

◎ Retired but not tired!

◎ Retired...Now I have a Life

◎ Retirement is a full-time job

◎ Retirement: Twice as much husband, Half as much $$$

◎ Retirement: When you stop making a living and start making a life.

◎ Retirement: World's longest coffee break.

◎ The Golden Years

◎ The trouble with retirement is that you never get a day off. -Abe Lemons

◎ You are only young once, but you can stay immature indefinitely.

◎ Goodbye Tension! Hello Pension!

◎ Just when a Mother thinks her work is complete....her husband retires.

◎ A retired husband is a wife's Full Time Job

ROMANCE

I f the sky where made of paper and the ocean my ink well; I still would-n't be able to describe how much I love you, and how wonderful you make me feel when I am with you.

◉ There's this place in me where your fingerprints still rest, your kisses still linger, and your whispers softly echo. It's the place where a part of you will forever be a part of me. -Gretchen Kemp

◉ Thou art to me a delicious torment -Emerson

◉ She walks in beauty, Like the night of cloudless climes and starry skies; And all that's best of dark and bright meet in her aspect and her eyes. -Byron

◉ We are each of us angels with only one wing. And we can only fly while embracing each other. - Lucian de Croszonza

◉ What I do and what I dream include thee, as the wine must taste of its own grapes -Elizabeth Barrett Browning

◉ Your words are my food, your breath my wine. You are everything to me. - Sarah Bernhardt

◉ A love song is just a caress set to music. -Romberg

◉ All that you are, all that I owe to you, justifies my love. -Marquis de Lafayette

◉ First love is a little foolish and a lot of curiosity.- George Bernard Shaw

ROMANCE

A Book of Verses underneath the Bough, A Jug of Wine, a Loaf of Bread - and Thou Beside me singing in the Wilderness- Oh, Wilderness were Paradise now! -Omar Khayyam

◉ I cannot exist without you. I am forgetful of everything but seeing you again. My life seems to stop there, I see no further. You have absorb'd me. I have a sensation at the present moment as though I were dissolving. I have been astonished that men could die martyrs for religion...I have shudder'd at it...I shudder no more. I could be martyr'd for my religion: Love is my religion. I could die for that. I could die for you. My creed is love, and you are its only tenet. You have ravish'd me away by a power I cannot resist. -Keats

◉ I am my beloved, and my beloved is me -Song of Solomon

◉ Love is the enchanted dawn of every heart -de la Martine

◉ You're nothing short of my everything. -Block

◉ You & me against the world

◉ I Can't Give You Anything But Love

◉ I love her and that's the beginning of everything - F. Scott Fitzgerald

◉ Love is friendship set on fire

ROMANCE

When I think of romance my thoughts flow to quiet times, tender kisses, smiling eyes, sexy legs, swinging on the tree, chocolate chip cookies, champagne from the valley, roses, sunsets, the ocean, diving for abalone, sweet embraces, love on the roof-top, walks in the vineyards, cool nights on the beach, paradise, soft caresses, sun-rise, tranquil music, summer breezes, warmin' by the fire, rainbows over the volcano, blue skies, starry nights...

When I think of romance I think of you.

Describe your thoughts and memories about the one you Love. Just let your mind wander back over the years and write. Your simple words will evoke such wonderful memories in you and in others. Happy journaling.

- If I could reach up and hold a star for every time you've made me smile, I would be holding the entire evening sky in the palm of my hand

ROMANCE

- Always
- April In Paris
- As Time Goes By
- Babes in Arms
- Baby, It's You
- Be My Love
- Calendar Girl
- Castle of Dreams
- Cheek To Cheek
- Cuddle up a Little Closer
- Dream Lover
- Drop Me a Line
- Embraceable You
- Falling in Love
- Fascination
- Fly Me To The Moon
- Follow Your Heart
- I Only Have Eyes For You
- I'm In The Mood For Love
- In The Still Of The Night
- Isn't It Romantic
- It Had To Be You
- It was Written in the Stars
- Love Is Here To Stay
- Love Letters
- Love Letters In The Sand

ROMANCE

◉ I love thee, I love but thee, with a love that shall not die till the sun grows cold and the stars grow old. -Shakespeare

◉ I pare this pippin round and round again, My sweetheart's name to flourish on the plain; I fling the unbroken paring o'er my head. A perfect L upon the ground is read. -John Gay

◉ I tell you I love you every day for fear that tomorrow isn't another

◉ I wished for nothing beyond her smile, and to walk with her thus, hand in hand, along a sun-warmed, flower-bordered path. -Andre Gide

◉ Love is an act of endless forgiveness, a tender look which becomes a habit. -Peter Ustinov

◉ We never forget those who make us blush. -De La Harpe

◉ If I know what love is, it is because of you. -Herman Hesse

◉ Kiss me and you will see stars; love me and I will give them to you

◉ Love consists in this, that two solitudes protect and touch and greet each other. -Rainer Maria Rilke

◉ Love is like a violin. The music may stop now and then, but the strings remain forever

◉ Love is the irresistible desire to be irresistibly desired. -Mark Twain

◉ Love is the master key that opens the gates of happiness -Oliver Wendell Holmes

◉ I've Got My Love To Keep Me Warm

◉ Maybe love is like luck. You have to go all the way to find it. -Robert Mitchum

◉ My love for you is a journey; starting at forever, and ending at never

◉ With My Eyes Wide Open I'm Dreaming

◉ Seduce my mind and you can have my body, find my soul and I'm yours forever.

ROMANCE

- My One and Only
- My Own Best Friend
- Night And Day
- P.S. I Love You
- Poetry In Motion
- Shall We Dance?
- Some Enchanted Evening
- Sunrise, Sunset
- The Man I Love
- The Nearness Of You
- The Song Is You
- The Way You Look Tonight
- Too Marvelous For Words
- You Look Wonderful Tonight
- Unforgettable
- When I Fall In Love
- On The Street Where You Live
- To love is to receive a glimpse of heaven. -Karen Sunde
- The most precious possession that ever comes to a man in this world is a woman's heart. -JG Holland
- There is only one happiness in life, to love and be loved. -George Sands
- To be in love is merely to be in a state of perceptual anesthesia. -H.L. Mencken
- Once in awhile, right in the middle of an ordinary life, Love gives us a fairy tale
- O, my Love is like the melody, that's sweetly played in tune
- Only love let's us see normal things in an extraordinary way.
- Oh, thou art fairer than the evening air clad in the beauty of a thousand stars - Marlowe
- There is always some madness in love. But there is also always some reason in madness. -Nietzsche
- You have lifted my very soul up into the light of your soul, and I am not ever likely to mistake it for the common daylight. -Elizabeth Barrett Browning
- As fair thou art, my bonnie lass, so deep in love am I: and I will love thee still, my dear, till all the seas go dry. - Robert Burns
- Paradise is always where love dwells. -Jean Paul F. Richter
- The fairest flower of them all, I give to you as we part. For you it is a Red Rose, for me it is my heart
- Gather the rose of love whilst yet is time. -Edmund Spenser

ROMANCE

To love oneself is the beginning of a lifelong romance -
Oscar Wilde

It is never too late to fall in love -Sandy Wilson

If music be the food of love, play on -Shakespeare

Oh, thou art fairer than the evening air clad in the beauty of a thousand stars -
Christopher Marlowe

I love thee, I love but thee With a love that shall not die. Till the sun grows cold and the stars grow old -
Willam Shakespeare

The most eloquent silence; that of two mouths meeting in a kiss.

Harmony is pure love, for love is a concerto -Lope de Vega

Here are fruits, flowers, leaves, and branches, And here is my heart which beats only for you -Paul Verlaine

The hours I spend with you I look upon as sort of a perfumed garden, a dim twilight, and a fountain signing to it...you and you alone make me feel that I am alive...Other men, it is said, have seen angels, but I have seen thee and thou art enough -George Moore

ROSES

La Vie En Rose

A rose is a rose is a rose.

Everything's Coming Up Roses

The rose speaks of love silently, in a language known only to the heart

What's in a name? That which we call a rose by any other name would smell as sweet. -Shakespeare

If love were what the rose is, And I were like the leaf, Our lives would grow together In sad or singing weather. -AG Swinburne

Roses whisper what words cannot say

O, my love is like a red, red rose, that's newly sprung in June

You are the prize of all roses. Delicate and painted with a whisper of love from above. -
LaTourelle

267

RUBBERSTAMPING

- ⊚ A day without rubberstamping is a day without sunshine
- ⊚ Addictive Rubber Stamp Material Enclosed
- ⊚ Born to stamp!
- ⊚ Camp Stamp-A-Lot!
- ⊚ CAUTION! Rubber Stamping is contagious! Proceed at your own risk!
- ⊚ Caution: Confetti Enclosed!
- ⊚ Cover me, I'm stamping!
- ⊚ Stamp Till You Drop
- ⊚ Emboss till you drop
- ⊚ Give me stamps
- ⊚ Gone Stamping
- ⊚ Hand over all your stamps and no one gets hurt!
- ⊚ Hand stamped original
- ⊚ Happy Stamping
- ⊚ I only stamp on days that end with Y
- ⊚ I suffer from OSD-Obsessive Stamping Disorder
- ⊚ Just Stamp It
- ⊚ My husband gave me permission to buy all the stamps I can hide in the back of the closet and under the bed!
- ⊚ My husband said it was him or the stamps. I'll miss him
- ⊚ PMS=Purchase More Stamps
- ⊚ Rubber Rules

RUBBERSTAMPING

- ◎ Stamping is my life
- ◎ Stamp by your man.
- ◎ Stamped with Love
- ◎ Stamper at heart
- ◎ Stamping Addict
- ◎ Stamping away
- ◎ Stamps R Us
- ◎ There are no mistakes in stamping-only embellishment opportunities.
- ◎ When life hands you stamps, make cards
- ◎ Will work for stamps
- ◎ You can tell a stamper by the ink on her hands and everywhere else
- ◎ Your friendship is stamped in my heart!
- ◎ Rubber & Chocolate - Who could ask for anything more?
- ◎ Stamping is cheap therapy
- ◎ Sorry it's late, but I'm stamping as fast as I can

ST. PATRICK'S DAY

- ◎ Erin Go Bragh-Ireland Forever
- ◎ Feelin' Green
- ◎ I'm Looking Over A Four Leaf Clover
- ◎ Kiss the blarney stone
- ◎ Luck 'o the Irish
- ◎ My Wild Irish Rose
- ◎ St. Patty's Day
- ◎ When Irish eyes are smiling

SANTA

- Baking for Santa
- Cookies for Santa
- Cooking for Santa
- Dear Mr. Santa...
- Dear Santa, I want it all and I want it now
- Dear Santa, I've been soooo good
- Desperately Seeking Santa
- Down the Chimney He Came
- Here Comes Santa Claus
- HO, HO, HO
- I believe in Santa
- I Believe!
- I break for reindeer
- I saw Mommy kissing Santa
- Jolly Old Elf
- Jolly Old Saint Nick
- Just for Santa
- Mrs. Claus
- Must Be Santa
- Saint Nick
- Santa and the Mrs.
- Where's Rudolph
- Santa Claus Is Coming to Town
- Santa Collector
- Down through the chimney
- 'Twas the night before...
- Santa Express
- Santa Loves Me
- On Dasher, On Dancer☐
- Santa Was Here
- Santa's Elves
- Sleigh rides here
- Santa's Workshop
- Secret Santa
- Silly for Santa
- Up on the rooftop...
- We believe in Santa!
- Who needs Santa when you have Grandma!
- Yes, _____, there is a Santa Claus
- Fat guy in the red suit
- Must be Santa
- Which way did he go?
- North Pole–Help Wanted
- S is for Santa Claus
- Right Jolly Old Elf
- Milk and Cookies
- I Love Santa
- Santa Rocks
- Sleigh Bells Ring
- Naughty and Nice
- Waitin' for Santa

SARCASM

- Any connection between your reality and mine is purely co-incidental

- Blessed are they who can laugh at themselves for they shall never cease to be amused

- Deadline for all complaints was yesterday.

- Don't try to get on my good side - I don't have one.

- Good morning, let the stress begin

- Having a bad hair day?

- He isn't on his way anywhere, hasn't been for years

- Historical marker: In this room on May 1, 1950, argument was won by the man of this house

- I can only please one person a day & this is not your day.

- I don't do mornings

- I don't repeat gossip, so listen closely the first time!

- I had some words with my wife—she had some paragraphs with me!

- I love to give homemade gifts... umm, which one of the kids would you like?

- Working hard, or hardly working?

- You can agree with me or you can be wrong!

- I read this article that said the typical symptoms of stress are; eating too much, impulse buying, and driving too fast. Are they kidding? That is my idea of a perfect day.

- I started out with nothing, and I still have most of it.

- I only have one nerve left, and you're getting on it!

- If you are grouchy, irritable, or just plain mean, there will be a $50. fee to put up with you

- If You Expect Breakfast in Bed, Go Sleep in the Kitchen

- I'm Right! He's Wrong! End of Story!

- Organized people are just too lazy to look for things.

- Some cause happiness wherever they go; others, whenever they go. -Oscar Wilde

- Some people are so narrow-minded their ears rub together.

- Thank you. We're all refreshed and challenged by your unique point of view.

- The man who can smile when things go wrong, probably's thought of someone to blame

- The trouble with women is that they get all excited about nothing and then marry him.

- Was your head with you all day today? -Bill Cosby

■■■■■■■■■■■■■■■■■■■■■■■■

SAY "I LOVE YOU"

Albanian... Une Te Dua

Chinese... Wo Ai Ni

English... I Love You

Eskimo... Nagligivaget

Finnish... Mina Rakkastan Sinua

French... Je T'aime

German... Ich Liebe Dich

Greek... S'Agapo

Hawaiian... Aloha Wau la Oe

Hebrew... Ani Ohev Otakh

Hungarian... Se Ret Lay

Irish... Thaim In Grabh Leat

Italian... Ti Amo

Japanese... Ai Shite Imasu

Persian... Du Stet Daram

Russian... Ya Lyublyu Tyebya

Spanish... Te Amo

Swedish... Jag Alskar Dig

Turkish... Seni Seviyorum

Sometimes a greeting or an expression written in another language can add a unique embellishment to your page or project. The variations of simple sayings such as "I Love You" and "Merry Christmas" are each beautiful in their own right. If you know anyone who speaks one of these languages, what a special blessing for them to receive a greeting in their native language. Sure to bring a smile!

SAY "MERRY CHRISTMAS"

Afrikander-Een Plesierige Kerfees

Chinese-Saint Dan Fai Lok

Danish - Gl☐delig Jul

English - Merry Christmas

Filipino-Maligayang Pasko

French - Joyeux No

German - Froehliche Weihnachten

Greek - Kala Christouyenna

Hawaiian - Mele Kalikimaka

Hebrew-Mo'adim Lesimkha

Irish - Nollaig Shona Dhuit

Italian - Buone Feste Natalizie

Japanese - Shinnen omedeto

Navajo - Merry Keshmish

Norwegian - God Jul

Portuguese - Feliz Natal Boas Festas

Spanish - Feliz Navidad

Vietnamese-Chuc Mung Giang Sinh

Welsh - Nadolig Llawen

Yugoslavian - Cestitamo Bozic

SCHOOL DAYS

- "Sporting' School Attire
- A Kid with Class
- A No-Brainer
- A Second Chance
- A Touch of Class
- A Year to Remember
- ABC-123
- Adding It All Up
- After School Special
- All Booked Up
- All I Need to Know I Learned in Kindergarten
- Anyone Can Drive A Car, But It Takes Someone Special To Drive A School Bus
- Artificial intelligence is no match for natural stupidity.
- Back to Class
- Back to School
- Back to School Night
- Be curious always! For knowledge will not acquire you; you must acquire it. -Sudie Back
- Be True to Your School
- Big Man on Campus
- Book Buddies
- Brain Overload
- Bus Stop
- Caught Thinking
- Zany Brainy

- Discovery is seeing what everybody else has seen but thinking what nobody else has thought. -S. Breathnach
- Education is not filling a bucket, but lighting a fire.-William Yeats
- Education means developing the mind, not stuffing the memory.
- Elementary School Days
- Fall School Days
- First Day of School
- School Days, Rule Days
- Grad Night
- Graduation Day
- Head of the Class
- High School Sweethearts
- Homework makes you ugly
- Honor Student
- I have no special talents. I am only passionately curious. -Albert Einstein
- I think, at a child's birth, if a mother could ask a fairy godmother to endow it with the most useful gift, that gift should be curiosity. -Eleanor Roosevelt
- If Stupidity got us into this mess, why can't it get us out?
- Imagination is more important than knowledge. -Albert Einstein
- Kudos and Distinctions

■■■■■■■■■■■■■■■■■■■■■■■■■■■■

SCHOOL DAYS

- In a Class of His Own
- It's as Easy as 1-2-3
- Learning Curve
- Making the Grade
- Me and My Big Ideas
- Class Mates
- My Classmates
- My favorite subject is...
- My Favorite Teacher
- My First Day of School
- My Old School
- Our Little Bookworm
- Readin', Writin' & 'Rithmetic
- Reading Rocks!
- Ready for School
- Report Card
- Rock 'n Roll High
- School Clothes shopping
- School Days
- School Daze
- School is Cool
- School is Out!
- School Photos
- School Rules
- School Snapshots
- Schoolhouse Rock
- Smart as a Whip
- Student of the Month

- Super Kid
- Teacher's Pet
- The Dean's List
- The harder you work the easier it looks
- The Nutty Professor
- The Wheels on the Bus
- There are no mistakes, only lessons.
- We are an intelligent species and the use of our intelligence quite properly gives us pleasure...Understanding is joyous. -Carl Sagan
- We Love School
- Welcome Back
- You Can Count on Me
- You can tell whether a man is clever by his answers. You can tell whether a man is wise by his questions. -Naguib Mahfouz

SCRAPBOOKING

- A Complete Scrap Attack
- A Walk Down Memory Lane
- Building Special Memories
- Camp Crop-A-Lot!
- Crop Till You Drop
- Croppin' 4 Fun
- Caught On Film!

SCRAPBOOKING

◎ A Complete Scrap Attack

◎ A day without scrapbooking is a day without sunshine.

◎ After you tell your husband where you'd like to go on your vacation he asks: "Why, is there a scrapbook store there?"

◎ Assembling, Scissor Cutting, Acid Free Testing, Supply

◎ Beware, scrapper on duty

◎ Camp Crop-A-Lot!

◎ Caution: Scrapbooker Ahead

◎ Cream of the Crop

◎ Crop till you drop

◎ Croppin' 4 Fun

◎ Don't just stand there. Scrap something

◎ Every page I scrap is a tiny little piece of history.

◎ Good to the Last Crop

◎ I am a Page Planning, Sticker Art Making, Punch Art Assembling, Scissor Cutting, Acid Free Testing, Supply Shopping Fool

◎ I could have scrapped all night

◎ I scrap therefore I am...broke

◎ I'd Rather be Scrapping

◎ I'm a little punchie

◎ Scrapbooking is cheaper than a psychiatrist

SCRAPBOOKING

- Just Scrap It

- Life is simple....Eat, Sleep and Scrap

- Memories are forever

- My husband let's me have all the scrappin' (stampin') supplies I can hide.

- My name is _____ and I'm a scrapaholic

- Old Scrappers never die, they just punch out!

- Queen of the Crop

- Roses are red, Voilets are blue. I love cropping, How about you?

- Scrap Your Heart Out

- Scrapbook Addict

- Scrapbook Adventures

- Scrapbooking is life☐ the rest is details

- Scrapbooking = Memories

- Scrapper at heart

- Stop, Crop, and Roll

- The only place housework comes before scrapbooking is in the dictionary!

- Visa. It's everywhere my scrapbook wants to be.

- When life hands you scraps, make scrapbooks

- You know you're a scrapper if you can't find your kitchen table

SAND, SUN & SURF

- A Day at the Beach
- A whale of a time (Sea world)
- Ahoy Mateys
- All Aboard
- All Wet
- Attack of the Crab Monsters
- Back to the beach
- Bathing Beauty
- Beach Ball Babes
- Beach Blanket Barbeque
- Beach Blanket Nap
- Beach Bum
- Castle Crashers
- Castles of Sand
- Catchin' some waves
- Come sail away...
- Dive Right In
- Don't Rock the Boat
- Down By The Bay
- Down By the Sea
- Escape to the Cape
- Fun in the sun
- Getting Their Feet Wet
- Hang Ten
- Happiness is... A Day at the Beach
- Happy as Clams

SAND, SUN & SURF

- Having a Sand-sational Time
- Heaven seems a little closer when your house is near the water.
- In the Swim of Things
- Island Paradise
- Itsy Bitsy Teeny Weeny Yellow Polka Dot Bikini
- I've got my toes in the sand
- Junior Lifeguard
- Let's go surfin' now - everybody's learnin' how. - Beach Boys
- Let's Sail Away
- Life is the Beach
- Making a Splash!
- Making Waves
- Mr. Sandman
- Ocean Adventures
- Ocean Fun
- Ocean Waves Here I Come
- On the Boardwalk
- Our Little Fish
- Our little Mermaid
- Paradise
- Pool Party
- Poolside Pals
- Ride the Wave
- Sand castles

SAND, SUN & SURF

- Sand Everywhere
- Sandcastles
- Sand-Tastic
- Sea, sand and surf
- Seashells by the Seashore
- Shell Seekers
- Snorkeling Fun
- Splash Dance
- Splashin' Good Fun
- Splat!
- Splish Splash
- Staying Cool in the Pool
- Summer at the Shore
- Sun & Fun
- Surfer Girl/Boy
- Surfin' Safari - Beach Boys
- Surfin' U.S.A
- Testing the Waters
- The Little Mermaid
- The Ride of your Life
- Treasures from the Sea
- Under the Boardwalk
- Under the Sea
- Underwater Fun
- Water Fight
- We Love the Beach
- Where the ocean meets the sky
- You're all wet

SEASONS

- I loved you when love was Spring, and May, Loved you when summer deepened into June, and now when autumn yellows all the leaves -V West
- To everything there is a season-A time to keep and a time to let go. -Ecclesiastes 3:1
- People come into your life for a reason, a season or a lifetime. When you figure out which it is, you know exactly what to do -Michelle Ventor
- Sing a song of seasons! Something bright in all! Flowers in the summer, Fires in the fall! -Stevenson
- I've watched the Seasons passing slow, so slow, In the fields -Robert Graves
- The flowery Spring leads sunny Summer, The yellow Autumn presses near; then in his turn comes gloomy Winter, Till smiling Spring again appear: Thus seasons dancing, life advancing, Old Time and Nature their changes tell -Robert Burns
- It was the best of times, it was the worst of times, it was the age of wisdom, it was the age of foolishness –it was the spring of hope, it was the winter of despair–in short, the period was so far like the present period . . . . - Charles Dickens

SEASONS–AUTUMN

- Ain't nothing like Mama's holiday cookin' to make a body warm. -LaTourelle
- Carving out memories, one pumpkin at a time -LaTourelle
- Cornucopia of Harvest Blessings
- Costumes and Pumpkins and Candy Corn, Oh My!
- For our country extending from sea unto sea
- The land that is known as the Land of the Free
- Thanksgiving! Thanksgiving!
- I walked on paths of crisp, dry leaves after, that flamed with color and crackled with laughter
- Mama's in the kitchen, cookin' up a storm, Daddy's on the sofa keepin' it warm
- Pumpkin pie and cranberry bread color the table with love
- Real men eat pumpkin pie - LaTourelle
- The Great Pumpkin Adventure
- The vineyards are blazing with the blush of fall, this harvest has been the most blessed of all. -LaTourelle
- Turkey Tunes and Holiday Wishes
- Bewitched, Bothered & Bewildered
- One season following another

- Autumn is a second spring, where every leaf's a flower. -Albert Camus
- Come said the wind to the leaves one day, Come o're the meadows and we will play. Put on your dresses scarlet and gold, For summer is gone and the days grow cold. -A Children's Song of the 1880's
- Delicious autumn! My very soul is wedded to it, and if I were a bird I would fly about the earth seeking the successive autumns. -George Eliot
- For everything there is a season
- Four seasons
- Have patience. All things change in due time. Wishing cannot bring autumn glory or cause winter to cease
- In heaven it is always autumn, His mercies are ever in their maturity. -John Donne
- Indian summer
- No spring nor summer beauty hath such grace as I have seen in one autumnal face -John Donne
- The October day is a dream, bright and beautiful as the rainbow, and as brief and fugitive. -Gibson

■■■■■■■■■■■■■■■■■■■■■■■■■■■■■

SEASONS–WINTER

◉ Now is the winter of our discontent. Made glorious summer by this sun of York -Shakespeare

◉ Life's autumn past, I stand on winter's verge. -Wordsworth

◉ Because the haven was not commodious to winter in, the more part advised to depart thence -Acts 27:12

◉ Yellow leaves lay rustling on the ground, bleak winds went whistling through the naked trees, and cold, white winter snow fell softly down -Lousia May Alcott

◉ If we had no winter, the spring would not be so pleasant -Anne Bradstreet

◉ Let us love winter, for it is the spring of genius. -Pietro Aretino

◉ Winter is an etching, spring a watercolor, summer an oil painting and autumn a mosaic of them all -Stanley Horowitz

◉ Adversity draws men together and produces beauty and harmony in life's relationships, just as the cold of winter produces ice-flowers on the window-panes, which vanish with the warmth - Soren Kierkegaard

◉ Be like the sun and meadow, which are not in the least concerned about the coming winter -George Bernard Shaw

◉ O, Wind, if winter comes, can Spring be far behind? - Percy Bysshe Shelley

◉ What fire could ever equal the sunshine of a winter's day? -Thoreau

◉ Winter is on my head, but eternal spring is in my heart -Victor Hugo

◉ Winter, etches on the windowpanes, finger paints in white. Sculptures strange soft shapes of snow, that glistens in the night

◉ There's no time like SNOW time!

◉ God gave us memories so we might have roses in the deep cold of winter

◉ Summer fading, winter comes– Frosty mornings, tingling thumbs window robins, winter rooks -Stevenson

◉ Snowflakes are God's voice in a whisper, escorted to earth by angels.

◉ Baby It's Cold Outside

◉ Cold Days-Warm Memories

◉ Frosty Nights

SEASONS–SPRING

◉ I love spring anywhere, but if I could choose I would always greet it in a garden - Ruth Stout

◉ Only in dreams of spring shall I ever see again the flowering of my cherry trees -Frances Hodgson Burnett

◉ Science has never drummed up quite as effective a tranquilizing agent as a sunny spring day -W. Earl Hall

◉ No matter how long the winter, spring is sure to follow

◉ And Spring arose on the garden fair, Like the Spirit of Love felt everywhere; And each flower and herb on Earth's dark breast rose from the dreams of its wintry rest. -Percy Bysshe Shelley

◉ April Showers Bring May Flowers & Bugs, too!

◉ Cinco de Mayo

◉ Happy Spring

◉ Spring Flowers bring new life

◉ Spring makes its own statement, so loud and clear that the gardener seems to be only one of the instruments, not the composer -Charlesworth

◉ Spring unlocks the flowers to paint the laughing soil -Heber

◉ Spring shows what God can do with a drab and dirty world -Virgil A. Kraft

◉ Spring would not be spring without bird songs. -Francis M. Chapman

◉ Thinking of you is like the Spring, You bring love and joy to everything

◉ Winter is on my head, but eternal spring is in my heart -Victor Hugo

◉ Daffodils & Daisies Delight Me

◉ Spring has sprung

◉ Tiptoe thru the tulips

◉ The hills are alive with...

◉ Spring hath put a spirit of youth in every thing. - Shakespeare

◉ Flowers are sunshine to the soul

◉ SPRING, the sweet Spring, is the year's pleasant king; Then blooms each thing, then maids dance in a ring, Cold doth not sting, the pretty birds do sing–Cuckoo, jug-jug, pu-we, to-witta-woo! -Thomas Nashe

◉ The fields breathe sweet, the daisies kiss our feet, Young lovers meet, old wives a-sunning sit, In every street these tunes our ears do greet– Cuckoo, jug-jug, pu-we, to-witta-woo! Spring, the sweet Spring! -Thomas Nashe

SEASONS–SUMMER

I know I am but summer to your heart, and not the full four seasons of the year.

Love is to the heart what the summer is to the farmer's year. It brings to harvest all the loveliest flowers of the soul. -Billy Graham

Summer's lease hath all too short a date. -William Shakespeare

In winter I get up at night And dress by yellow candlelight. In summer quite the other way I have to go to bed by day. -Robert Louis Stevenson

Dirty hands, iced tea, garden fragrances thick in the air and a blanket of color before me, who could ask for more? -Bev Adams

Shall I compare thee to a summer's day? -William Shakespeare

I know I am but summer to your heart, and not the full four seasons of the year. -Edna St. Vincent Millay

The Queen of Hearts, she made some tarts, all on a summer day: The Knave of Hearts, he stole those tarts, and took them quite away! -Lewis Carroll

Summer afternoon - summer afternoon; to me those have always been the two most beautiful words in the English language -Henry James

Rest is not idleness, and to lie sometimes on the grass on a summer day listening to the murmur of water, or watching the clouds float across the sky, is hardly a waste of time. - John Lubbock

Ah, summer, what power you have to make us suffer and like it -Russel Baker A perfect summer day is when the sun is shining, the breeze is blowing, the birds are singing, and the lawn mower is broken. -James Dent

No price is set on the lavish summer; June may be had by the poorest come -James Russell Lowell

Summer afternoon - summer afternoon; to me those have always been the two most beautiful words in the English language -Henry James

To see the Summer Sky Is Poetry -Dickinson Emily

SEWING

- A Designer Day - stitch your day with kindness, sew in love and hem it with prayer
- A Stitch in Time is Rarely Possible
- As ye sew, so shall ye rip
- Blessed are the children of the piecemakers . . . for they shall inherit the quilts
- Buttons and patches and the cold wind blowing, the days pass quickly when I am sewing
- Creative minds are rarely tidy
- Don't lie...just embellish
- I love sewing & have a plenty of material witnesses
- If I stitch fast enough does it count as an aerobic exercise ?
- I'm a material girl - want to see my fabric collection ?
- Memories are stitched with love
- My husband lets me have all the fabric I can hide!
- My husband said if I buy any more fabric he would leave me—I'll miss him
- My soul is fed...By my needle and thread
- Sewing Mends the Soul
- So Much Fabric, So Little Time
- Old Crafter's never die, they just get more bazaar!
- One sewing project, like one cookie, is never enough !
- Put your treadle to the metal.
- Sewing and crafts fill my days , not to mention the living room, bedroom and closets.
- Stitch your stress away
- I got a sewing machine for my husband! Good trade, huh?
- Any day spent sewing, is a good day!
- Anytime is stitchin' time.
- Asking a seamstress to mend, is like asking Picasso to paint your garage!
- Caution: Enter this Sewing Room at your own Risk
- Don't Needle the Seamstress!
- Friendships are sewn one stitch at a time.
- Hi Ho, Hi Ho, it's off to sew we go!
- Hug Your Sewing Machine
- I love sewing and have plenty of material witnesses.
- I Think Sew!
- When I learned to sew, I forgot how to cook!

SEWING

- Love is the thread that binds us
- May your bobbin always be full!
- My Husband is a Human Pincushion!
- Old seamstresses never go crazy, they just stay on pins and needles!
- Sewing forever, housework whenever!
- Slow Moving Seamstress: Fast Moving Thread & Needle!
- The love of sewing is our common thread.
- Warning: This Vehicle Stops at all Fabric Shops
- LOST: Husband, dog, and sewing machine. Reward offered for sewing machine!

SHADOW

- I have a little shadow that goes in and out with me, and what can be the use of him is more than I can see. - Stephenson
- Keep your face to the sunshine and you cannot see the shadow -Helen Keller
- Man stands in his own shadow and wonders why it is dark
- Worry often gives a small thing a big shadow

SHOES

- 1 pair, 2 pairs, 3 pairs–20 pairs, 50 pairs–still counting
- Born to buy shoes
- Be weary of a woman with only one pair of shoes
- Don't worry Mom, I can walk in these just fine
- Have shoes–will travel!
- If the shoe fits–wear it!
- Sassy and lovin' it!
- Shoes or Food that is the question?
- Shoes were made for walking, so take a hike!
- Shoesy Cute
- To err is unforgivable. To buy new shoes is divine.
- Whoever said diamonds are a girl's best friend, never owned a pair of high heels!
- Act your age, not your shoe size
- If the shoe fits, wear it
- The old woman who lived in a shoe
- This is no shoe...it's my glass slipper
- Ruby Red Slippers
- Before you criticize someone, walk a mile in his shoes

SHOES

- The Shoe Freak
- Princess Fussy Foot
- Miss Goody Two Shoes
- Baby needs a new pair of shoes
- If I want to hear the pitter patter of little feet, I'll put shoes on my cat
- Shoe be do be do!
- These shoes are made for dancing
- The Red Shoes
- Shoes & purses & shoes oh, my!
- When I get tired of shopping, I sit down and try on shoes
- I can deal with anything as long as I have the right shoes
- If the shoe fits - buy one in every color

SHOPPING

- CHARGE...
- Collector of useless, worthless, can't-find-a-place-for-it, don't-need-it bargain finds! And proud of it!
- I came, I went, I shopped
- I can't be overdrawn, I still have checks
- I never met a mall I didn't like
- I shop at one store at a time, I do it very well, and then I move on
- If I'm not at the mall at least twice a week, they send me a Get Well Soon card
- I'm out of money, I can go home now
- She would buy an Elephant if it were ON SALE!
- Shop til you drop
- Shopping is my life, my hobby, and my love
- Shopping is the fine art buying things you don't need with money you don't have
- Simply Irresistible
- The Mall Crawl
- The mall has given me my very own parking space

Journal about your favorite places to shop. Write about your favorite shopping trip. Was it for a day? Was it with girlfriends? What was your biggest splurge? Most memorable purchase? Most money you ever spent at one time? Who is your favorite shopping partner? Did you ever go on any wild shopping sprees?

SIBLINGS

◎ To the outside world we all grow old. But not to brothers and sisters. We know each other as we always were. We know each other's hearts. We share private family jokes. We remember family feuds and secrets, family griefs and joys. We live outside the touch of time. -Clara Ortega

◎ A sibling may be the keeper of one's identity, the only person with the keys to one's unfettered, more fundamental self. -Marian Sandmaier

◎ Best Buddies

◎ Birds of a Feather

◎ Brothers and sisters are as close as hands and feet

◎ Giggles, Secrets, and Sometimes Tears

◎ How do people make it through life without a sibling?

◎ I don't believe an accident of birth makes people sisters or brothers. It makes them siblings, gives them mutuality of parentage. Sisterhood and brotherhood is a condition people have to work at. -Maya Angelou

◎ Sibling relationships... outlast marriages, survive the death of parents, resurface after quarrels that would sink any friendship. They flourish in a thousand incarnations of closeness and distance, warmth, loyalty and distrust. -Erica E. Goode

◎ I, who have no sisters or brothers, look with some degree of innocent envy on those who may be said to be born to friends. -James Boswell

SIBLINGS

◎ Siblings are the people we practice on, the people who teach us about fairness and cooperation and kindness and caring - quite often the hard way. -
Pamela Dugdale

◎ Siblings may share the same mother and father but appear to come from different families

◎ Siblings share the scent and smells of days gone by

◎ Two of a Kind

◎ We acquire friends and we make enemies, but our siblings come with the territory

◎ We are more than just acquaintances—it's as if we are cut from the same fabric.

◎ We know one another's faults, virtues, catastrophes, mortifications, triumphs, rivalries, desires, and how long we can each hang by our hands to a bar. We have been banded together under pack codes and tribal laws. -Rose Macaulay

◎ We may look old and wise to the outside world. But to each other, we are still in junior school. -Charlotte Gray

◎ We share a history

◎ Siblings for life, friends forever

◎ Siblings by chance...Friends by choice

◎ Your siblings are the only people in the world who know what it's like to have been brought up the way you were -Betsy Cohen

SIBLINGS

◉ You remember where I've been, respect who I've become and encourage me where I'm going.

◉ Oh, what secrets my siblings could tell

◉ Siblings–Can't live with 'em, can't live without 'em

◉ The best friends I've ever had are my siblings

◉ When everyone else walks out, my sister and brother will walk in

◉ When I get big, I'll get even

◉ Like branches on a tree we grow in different directions yet our roots remain as one.

◉ Our siblings push buttons that cast us in roles we felt sure we had let go of long ago - the baby, the peacekeeper, the caretaker, the avoider. . . It doesn't seem to matter how much time has elapsed or how far we've traveled. -Jane Mersky Leder

◉ Our siblings. They resemble us just enough to make all their differences confusing, and no matter what we choose to make of this, we are cast in relation to them our whole lives long. -Merrell

◉ Peas in a Pod

◉ Sibling Harmony

◉ Sibling Rivalry

Sisters are a blessing to cherish. When you need a friend you know they are there. My sister's and I haven't lived near each other most of our adult lives and it's been interesting to discover as the years go by that we have similar likes and dislikes. Little things mean a lot when it comes to sisters. They are the ones who probably know us best. If you have a sister, give her a call, write her a letter, send some pictures, an e-mail, a smile or a hug. Take the time to treasure the moments shared throughout your life together. One way you can do this is through scrapbooking and cards and journaling. It's fun to reminisce about the memories you've shared and even the ones you didn't . It's a great way to keep in touch with life now. May you be as blessed as I am with the love you share as sisters! -Linda LaTourelle

SISTERS

- #1 Sister
- A Sister is a forever friend
- Always My Sister
- Baby Sister
- Being Sisters is something special
- Big Sis
- Celebrating Sisterhood
- Chance made us sisters, hearts made us friends
- Giggles, Secrets, and Sometimes Tears
- Help one another, is part of the religion of sisterhood. -Louisa May Alcott
- How do people make it through life without a sister? -Sara Corpening
- I love my little sister, I'm proud to be her brother, but when she has dirty pants, I bring her to my mother
- I love my Sister
- I'm the Big Sister
- I'm the Little Sister
- In thee my soul shall own combined the sister and the friend. -Catherine Killigrew
- Is solace anywhere more comforting than in the arms of a sister. -Alice Walker

■ ■ ■ ■ ■ ■ ■ ■ ■ ■ ■ ■ ■ ■ ■ ■ ■ ■ ■ ■

SISTERS

- Just Like Big Sister
- Lil Sis'
- My Sister, My Friend
- She is your mirror, shining back at you with a world of possibilities, she sees you at your worst and best, and loves you anyway. -Barbara Alpert
- She's My Sister
- Sister act
- Sister and Friend - two words that mean the same
- Sister by Chance, Friends by choice
- Sisterhood
- Sisters - Gotta Love 'Em!
- Sisters & Sisters together
- Sisters annoy, interfere, criticize. Borrow. Hog the bathroom. But when trouble comes, sisters are there.
- Sisters know when you are smiling, even in the dark
- When sisters stand shoulder to shoulder, who stands a chance against us? -Pam Brown
- You can kid the world. But not your sister. -Charlotte Gray
- When My Sister and I are Old We shall wear Purple!

- Sisters are a work of heart
- Sisters are Blossoms in the garden of life
- Sisters are Forever
- Sisters are Special - Especially Mine
- Sisters are the Best Kind of Friends
- Sisters are tied together with heartstrings
- Sisters are two different flowers from the same garden
- Sisters by Chance, Friends because Mom Said So!
- Sisters from the start, Friends from the heart
- Sisters make the best friends
- Sisters share a special friendship that lasts a lifetime
- Sisters/Brothers are a Special Hug From God!
- Sweet is the voice of a sister in the season of sorrow. - Benjamin Disraeli
- Sweet Sisters
- The best thing about having a sister was that I always had a friend -Cali Rae Turner
- When I get big, I'll get even
- My sister is the one I turn to always

■■■■■■■■■■■■■■■■■■■■■■■

Sisters are for sharing laughter and wiping tears. How do people make it through life without a sister?-Sara Corpening

◉ The desire to be and have a sister is a primitive and profound one that may have everything or nothing to do with the family a woman is born to. It is a desire to know and be known by someone who shares blood and body, history and dreams -Elizabeth Fishel

◉ My sisters have taught me how to live. -George Wasserstein

◉ Sisters share the scent and smells... the feel of a common childhood -Pam Brown

◉ Sisters is probably the most competitive relationship within the family, but once sisters are grown, it becomes the strongest relationship.-Margaret Meed

◉ Having a sister is like having a best friend you can't get rid of. You know whatever you do, they'll still be there.-Amy Li

◉ A sister smiles when one tells one's stories... for she knows where the decoration has been added. -Chris Montaigne

◉ A sister is both your mirror &your opposite. -Elizabeth Fishel

◉ Both within the family and without, our sisters hold up our mirrors: our images of who we are and of who we can dare to become. -E Fishel

◉ Sisters touch your heart in ways no other could. Sisters share... their hopes, their fears, their love, everything they have. Real friendship springs from their special bonds. -Carrie Bagwell

◉ If sisters were free to express how they really feel, parents would hear this: Give me all the attention and all the toys and send Rebecca to live with Grandma -Linda Sunshine

◉ There's a special kind of freedom sisters enjoy. Freedom to share innermost thoughts, to ask a favor, to show their true feelings. The freedom to simply be themselves.

◉ If you don't understand how a woman could both love her sister dearly and want to wring her neck at the same time, then you were probably an only child. -Linda Sunshine

◉ Is solace anywhere more comforting than that in the arms of a sister?-Alice Walker

◉ The best thing about having a sister was that I always had a friend -Cali Rae Turner

SISTERS

Sisters share that unique & special relationship that combines friends and family-a bond that is at the same time supportive and enduring. The woman who shares her life with a sister is blessed.

☺ Be kind to thy sister. Not many may know the depths of true sisterly love. - Margaret Courtney

☺ The bond between sisters is sometimes tightly woven, sometimes loosely held, but never broken.

☺ Sister you are close to my heart. So many dreams we've shared all the laughter and love. You tell me your secrets, I tell you mine. We'll always be together in our dreams. Our hearts will stay side by side

☺ With you as my sister, the icicles tasted colder, the fireflies twinkled brighter, and the stars didn't seem so far away -Ludwig

☺ Best friends are we, my sister and me

☺ Sisters make the best friends

☺ My sister shares a part of me...that no one else shall ever see. And when the days and miles divide us... the bond we have will live inside us. Together sharing dreams, love and laughter–My sister for always, my friend forever

☺ Sisters by chance–Friends by choice

☺ Sisters are special
From young ones to old.
God gave me a sister
More precious than gold.

☺ Sisters share a closeness no one else can understand...
A sister's always there to give a hug or lend a hand
Sisters are the best friends in the whole wide world, it's true–and that friendship is a blessing that lasts a lifetime through

☺ We shared many secrets, the same mom and dad,
We shared lots of good times, don't think of the bad. Our memories we'll cherish, with love without end, I'm glad you're my sister, I'm glad you're my friend.

SLEEP/SLEEPING

- A Dream is a Wish Your Heart Makes
- A Lullaby Moment
- A New Day Is Dawning
- All I Have To Do Is Dream
- All Tucked In
- Beautiful Dreamer
- Boy, am I pooped
- Caught Napping
- Close your little sleepy eyes . . .
- Dream On Little Dreamer
- Dream Sweet Dreams
- Early Riser
- Getting ready for Bed
- Good Morning, Merry Sunshine
- Good night Sweetheart
- Good night, sleep tight, don't let the bed bugs bite.
- Having a child fall asleep in your arms is one of the most peaceful feelings in the world.
- Hush Little Baby
- I Don't Do Mornings
- I told you I was tired

- If I'm not sleeping, nobody's sleeping.
- Tired? Who Me?
- I'm Still Sleepy
- Life is But a Dream
- Lights Out!
- Lullaby and Good night
- Mr. Sandman, Bring Me a Dream
- Mr. Sandman
- Night, Night little one
- Now I lay me down to sleep, I pray the Lord my soul to keep. Good protect me all night long, and angels guard my bed.
- Oh, How I Hate to Get Up in the Morning

SLEEP/SLEEPING

- Our Little Sleeping Angel
- Pajama Party
- Shhh…Baby is dreaming
- Shhh…Baby Sleeping
- Sleep Over
- Sleep Sweetly Precious baby, Angels watch over you… Mama is near
- Sleepless in Seattle (your town)
- Slumber Party
- Sweet Dreams
- The Gift of Slumber
- There is nothing so precious as a sleeping baby
- Things that Go Bump in the Night
- Time for a Nap!
- Time for Bed, Sleepy Head
- To sleep, perchance to dream
- Wake Up Little _____
- When in doubt, take a nap.
- With a butterfly kiss and a ladybug hug, sleep tight little one, like a bug in a rug
- You're Never Too Old For Slumber Parties
- Zonked out

SLEEPOVER

- Over-Nighter
- Pajama Party
- Pillow Fight
- Sleep Over
- Sleepy Sillies
- Up all night

■■■■■■■■■■■■■■■■■■■■■■■■■

SMILES

- A Wink and a Smile
- Big Grin
- Dimples Galore
- Every tear has a smile behind it.
- Grins and Giggles
- Miles of Smiles
- Mona Lisa Smile
- A Smile as Sweet as Spring
- Smiles—the next best thing to halos
- Sweet, Sweet Smile
- When Irish Eyes are Smiling
- Who Could Resist That Smile
- Wrinkles are just antique smiles
- Everyone smiles in the same language
- You Would Smile Too if it Happened to You
- Smile when you feel like crying
- Laugh and the whole world laughs with you
- Laughter is the best medicine
- Smile your heart out

SNOW

- Ice Wars
- It's Snowtime!
- First Snowfall
- Our Snow Angel
- Snow Adventure
- Snow Bunny
- Snow Day
- Snow Fun
- Snow Wonder
- Snow, Snow, Snow
- Snow Is Glistening
- Snow Much Fun
- Fun in the Snow
- Glisten and Glide
- Snowball Fight
- Northern Exposure
- The Polar Express
- Michelangelo of Snow
- South for the Winter
- Snow Princess/Prince
- Have Snow, Will Shovel
- First Snowball of the Season
- The snow fell softly all the night
- There's a Chill in the Air

SNOW

- There's No Business Like Snow Business
- Walking in a winter wonderland
- Keeping Warm bundled up or by the fireplace
- Let it Snow, Let it Snow, Let it Snow
- A blanket of white...
- It made a blanket soft and white
- In the Lane, Snow is Glistening
- But it didn't make a single sound!
- Oh the weather outside is frightful
- Snowflakes Are Angel Kisses
- Jack Frost nipping at your nose
- It's A Hot Chocolate Day
- Wanted: Magic Hat
- Abominable Snowman

SNOWMAN

I'm a little snowman white and fat I can wear a scarf or even a hat My eyes are shiny and my nose may be too long However they make me really isn't wrong. I love to stand and glisten in the sun But when it gets too hot, oh, no, I'll be gone.
-LaTourelle

- Snowmen are the Coolest
- Wearing white is always appropriate.
- Frosty and Friends
- In the meadow, we can build a snowman
- Shaped from the cold by the warmth of young hearts
- Snowball Fight Tonight
- Snowflakes are kisses from heaven...
- Snowmen melt, but memories last
- Star Light, Star Bright, Please don't let me melt tonight!

SNUGGLE

- Snuggable You
- I want to hold your hand
- Cuddle Bugs
- Snuggly, Wuggly
- Snuggle Bug Baby
- Let's Cuddle
- Snuggle Me

SOCCER

- Backyard Soccer
- Goal!
- Having a Ball
- I Get a Kick Out of Soccer
- In a league all your own
- Kick back and have a great time!
- My goal is to play soccer
- Ready, set, goal!
- Soccer Dad
- Soccer is a kick
- Soccer Mom and Proud of It
- Soccer Season
- Soccer's a Ball!
- What a kick!
- Goalie Dude
- Go Team Go!

SOLITUDE

- A creation of importance can only be produced when its author isolates himself, it is a child of solitude. -Von Goethe
- Everybody needs beauty as well as bread, places to play in and pray in, where nature may heal and give strength to body and soul. -John Muir
- I owe my solitude to other people. -Alan Watts
- Never be afraid to sit awhile and think. -Lorraine Hansberry
- Nowhere can man find a quieter or more untroubled retreat than in his own soul. -Marcus Aurelius
- The happiest of all lives is a busy solitude. -Voltaire
- To feel themselves in the presence of true greatness many find it necessary only to be alone. -Tom Masson

True silence is the rest of the mind, and is to the spirit what sleep is to the body nourishment and refreshment.
-WilliamPenn

SONS

- 100% Stupendous Son
- A son is a son until he becomes a dad
- I am so very proud of you
- In all the things you've said and done.
- Like Father, Like Son
- My son you are a treasure
- Our Little Man
- Papa's Little Sonshine
- Simply because you are my son
- Son Flowers
- Sons are so sweet
- Sons are the delight of their mother
- Sons are the light of their father's eyes
- You don't raise heros, you raise sons. And if you treat them like sons, they'll turn out to be heros, even if it's just in your own eyes.
- Ah'm fixin ta do that.
- Cute as a sack full of puppies
- Well, butter my butt and call me a biscuit
- He's as country as cornflakes

SOUTHERN SAYINGS

- Ain't seen you in a coon's age
- As ugly as the north end of a south bound mule.
- Bless your pea pickin' heart.
- Crazier than a run over dog
- Either fish or cut bait.
- Fair to mid-lin
- Faster than greased lightning
- GRITS
- I onst went to...
- If the good Lord's willin' and the creek don't rise.
- In a New York minute
- Meaner 'an junk yard dog
- Nervous as a cat on a hot tin roof
- Plumb tuckered out
- Quicker an' a duck on a June bug
- Scarce as hen's teeth
- She's as ill as a sore tailed cat
- She's dumb as the day is long
- So poor he'd have to borrow money to buy water to cry with
- Well hush my mouth
- So kiss my grits

SPIRITUAL

◎ Physical strength is measured by what we can carry; spiritual by what we can bear

◎ You don't have a soul. You are a Soul. You have a body. -C.S. Lewis

◎ Begin to see yourself as a soul with a body rather than a body with a soul -Wayne Dyer

◎ We are not human beings on a spiritual journey. We are spiritual beings on a human journey -Stephen Covey

◎ The clearest way into the Universe is through a forest of wilderness. -John Muir

◎ No one, nothing is telling you how to feel or who to be

◎ We may explore the universe and find ourselves, or we may explore ourselves and find the universe. It matters not which of these paths we choose.-Diana Robinson

◎ Everything that slows us down and forces patience, every thing that sets us back into the slow circles of nature, is a help.

◎ Everybody needs beauty as well as bread, places to play in and pray in, where nature may heal and give strength to body and soul. -John Muir

◎ Wisdom is oftentimes nearer when we stoop than when we soar.-William Wordsworth

◎ What is life? It is the flash of a firefly in the night. It is the breath of a buffalo in the wintertime. It is the little shadow, which runs across the grass and loses itself in the sunset. -Crowfoot

◎ Wisdom is oftentimes nearer when we stoop than when we soar.-William Wordsworth

◎ To see a world in a grain of sand and a heaven in a wild flower, hold infinity in the palm of your hand and eternity in an hour -William Blake

◎ The garden is a metaphor for life, and gardening is a symbol of the spiritual path.-Larry Dossey

◎ Every natural fact is a symbol of some spiritual fact. -Ralph Waldo Emerson

◎ He does not believe that does not live according to his belief -Thomas Fuller

◎ Do not the most moving moments of our lives find us without words? - Marcel Marceau

◎ Until you know that life is interesting and find it so, you haven't found your soul -Geoffrey Fisher

SPORTS-MISCELLANEOUS

- bad day of golf is better than a good day at work
- Batter Up
- Caddy shack
- FORE
- Get ready to rumble!
- Go for the gold!
- Go for the whole nine yards!
- Go, Team, Go
- GOALS
- GOLF
- Golf Fore Ever
- Golf is a game in which you yell FORE, shoot six, and write down five.
- Golf is a good walk spoiled
- Grand Slam
- Have a field day
- Having a ball
- Hey-batter-batter
- Homerun!
- Hoop Heaven
- Hoop-La
- In a League of your Own
- Kick back and have a great time!

- Makin' Tracks
- Nothing but net
- Old archers never die, they just bow and quiver.
- Old skateboarders never die, they just lose their bearings.
- On Your mark, get set, go
- Play Ball
- Running like the wind
- Score!
- Skateboarders
- Slam Dunk
- Smash Hit
- Soccer's a Ball!
- Step up to the plate for the Grand Slam of the day!
- Super Star
- Take me out to the ballgame
- Tennis! You gotta 'lub' it!
- There's No Time like "Tee Time"
- Time to tackle another year
- To Golf or Not to Golf? What a silly question
- Touchdown
- What a kick!
- When's tee Time?

SPORTS-MISCELLANEOUS

- Above the belt please
- Alive and Kicking
- And in this corner
- Are you Game?
- Armchair Athlete!!
- Back on Track
- Batter UP!
- Be Calm, Be Cool, and Be Collected Hey Hey!
- Birdie
- Born to Ride
- Bowlers never die they just end up in the gutter.
- Breaking Away
- Bump! Set! Spike!
- Bunny Hill Drop Outs
- Buy me some peanuts and cracker jacks. I don't care if I ever get back.
- Call the Ball and Mine.
- Cheer My Way Through
- Cheer them to a WIN!
- Chip Shot
- Court Side
- Dishin' and Swishin'
- Don't Argue With The Line Judge!

- Field of Dreams
- First and Ten
- Floor EX-traordinairy
- Football fan
- Football fun
- Football star
- Have a Ball
- Hay, Batter Batter
- Heaven seems a little closer when your house is near the bowling ally.
- HI MOM!
- High Hopes in High Jump
- Hitting the Lanes
- Hoooop, There it is!
- Hoop It Up
- H-O-R-S-E
- Hot Shots
- If only I could swing like I do in practice.
- If you can't win, make the one ahead of you break the record - Jan McKeithin
- In the Paint
- Instant Replay!
- Iron Man
- It ain't over til it's over. - Yogi Berra

SPRING

When Spring arrives the robin doth rejoice as she feeds her newborn babes. The frosts of winter now quench the thirsty flowers pushing through a drably painted landscape. Soon our Creator will refresh the earth with a magnificent palette of living color. The fragrance of that beauty captures our souls and we delight once again in this awesome cycle of life. -Linda LaTourelle

- I thought that spring must last forevermore for I was young and loved, and it was May -Vera Brittain

- Imagination is the highest kite that one can fly - Bacall

- Nothing is so beautiful as spring

SPRING

- A day in May
- Spring Fever
- Spring Fling
- S is for Spring
- Enchanted April
- Celebrate Spring
- Spring is in the Air
- Spring is Just Ducky
- First Signs of Spring
- Hurrah for Spring
- A very "buzzy" Spring
- As Fresh as Springtime
- In the Merry Month of May
- Springtime is the Best Time
- Somewhere over the rainbow
- Spring is bustin' out all over
- Spring comes: the flowers learn their colored shapes-Maria Konopnicka

- And the Green Grass Grows All Around, All Around
- April showers bring May flowers
- Out like a lion, in like a lamb

Spring's greatest joy beyond a doubt is when it brings the children out -Edgar Guest

STARS

- I named a star for you

- As your bright and tiny glow lights the traveler in the dark, though I know not what you are, twinkle little star

- Catch a Falling Star

- If I could reach up and hold a star for every time you've made me smile, the entire evening sky would be in the palm of my hand

- It was written in the stars

- Star crossed lovers

- Keeper of the Stars

- Reach for the Moon. If you fall short–You may land on a star.

- Reach for the stars, even if you have to stand on a cactus -Susan Longacre

- Stardust Memories

- Starlight, Starbright

- The Stars are Brightly Shining

- The stars are God's dreams, thoughts remembered in the silence of the night -Thoreau

Twinkle, twinkle, little star. Do you know how loved you are?

- Under the Stars

- When the blazing sun is gone, when he nothing shines upon, then you show your little light, Twinkle, twinkle, all the night. Twinkle, twinkle, little star, How I wonder what you are!

- When You Wish Upon a Star

- Wish Upon a Star

- You may not be a star but you need not be a cloud

- Don't let the stars get in your eyes

- You are the star of your life

- Starry, Starry Night

- Starlight makes you glow

- Stars in your eyes

- Stars and Stripes Forever

- May the stars light your journey as you reach for the moon

- I saw a star slide down the sky, blind the north as it went by, too burning and too quick to hold, too lovely to be bought or sold, good only to make wishes on and then forever to be gone.

- I painted a star on my window so bright so I could wish for you on cloudless nights

SUCCESS

◎ A hundred years from now it will not matter what my bank account was, the sort of house I lived in, or the kind of car I drove—but the world may be different because I was important in the life of a child.

◎ A wise man will make more opportunities than he finds. -Francis Bacon

◎ All labor that uplifts humanity has dignity and importance and should be undertaken with painstaking excellence -Dr. Martin Luther King Jr.

◎ Do a little more each day than you think you possibly can -Lowell Thomas

◎ Do not let what you cannot do interfere with what you can do -John Wooden

◎ Don't be afraid to take a big step if one is indicated; you can't cross a chasm in two small jumps. -David Lloyd George

◎ Don't waste time learning the tricks of the trade. Instead, learn the trade -H. Jackson Brown, Jr.

◎ Expect people to be better than they are; it helps them to become better.

◎ Far better it is to dare mighty things, to win glorious triumphs even though checkered by failure, than to rank with those timid spirits who neither enjoy nor suffer much because they live in the gray twilight that knows neither victory nor defeat. -Theodore Roosevelt

◎ Great spirits have always encountered violent opposition from mediocre minds -Albert Einstein

◎ Use what talents you possess: the woods would be very silent if no bird sang there except those that sang best -Henry Van Dyke

■■■■■■■■■■■■■■■■■■■■■■■■■■■

SUCCESS

◎ Guard well your spare moments. They are like uncut diamonds. Discard them and their value will never be known.
Improve them and they will become the brightest gems in a
useful life. -Ralph Waldo Emerson

◎ I am only one, but I am one. I can't do everything, but I can
do something. The something I ought to do, I can do. And
by the grace of God, I will. -Edward Everett Hale

◎ I couldn't wait for success--so I went ahead without it -
Jonathan Winters

◎ I hope that my achievements in life shall be these - that I will
have fought for what was right and fair, that I will have
risked for that which mattered, and that I will have given
help to those who were in need that I will have left the earth
a better place for what I've done and who I've been. -C. Hoppe

◎ If at first you don't succeed, do it like your mother told you.

◎ If opportunity doesn't knock, build a door. -Milton Berle

◎ If you have built castles in the air, your work need not be
lost; that is where they should be. Now put the foundations
under them -Henry David Thoreau

◎ If you hear a voice within you say 'you cannot paint,' then
by all means paint, and that voice will be silenced -Van Gogh

◎ In any moment of decision the best thing you can do is the
right thing, the next best thing is the wrong thing, and the
worst thing you can do is nothing -Theodore Roosevelt

◎ It is one of the most beautiful compensations of this life that
no man can sincerely try to help another without helping
himself -Ralph Waldo Emerson

◎ Whenever it is possible, a boy should choose some occupa-
tion which he should do even if he did not need the money. -
William Lyon Phelps

Success

◎ It is the greatest of all mistakes to do nothing because you can do only a little. Do what you can. -Sydney Smith

◎ It takes as much stress to be a success as it does to be a failure -Emilio James Trujillo

◎ It's nice to be important, but it's important to be nice -Hahn

◎ Make a plan, work the plan

◎ Man's mind, once stretched by a new idea, never regains its original dimensions -Oliver Wendell Holmes, Jr

◎ My alphabet starts with this letter called *yuzz*. It's the letter I use to spell *yuzz-a-ma-tuzz*. You'll be sort of surprised what there is to be found once you go beyond 'Z' and start poking around! -Dr. Seuss

◎ My father always told me, Find a job you love and you'll never have to work a day in your life. -Jim Fox

◎ Obstacles are those frightful things you see when you take your eyes off your goal. -Henry Ford

◎ One person with a belief is equal to ninety-nine who have only interests -of value -Albert Einstein

◎ Organization is the key to success

◎ Rank does not confer privilege or give power. It imposes responsibility -Peter Drucker

◎ Satisfaction lies in the effort, not in the attainment; full effort is full victory -Mohandas K. Gandhi

◎ Shoot for the moon. Even if you miss, you'll land among the stars. -Les Brown

◎ Sow a thought, and you reap an act; Sow an act, and you reap a habit; Sow a habit, and you reap a character; Sow a character, and you reap a destiny. -Charles Reade

SUCCESS

◎ Still round the corner there may wait, a new road or a secret gate -J.R.R. Tolkien

◎ Success in any endeavor depends on the degree to which it is an expression of your true self -Ralph Marston

◎ Success is always inside out

◎ Success isn't a result of spontaneous combustion. You must set yourself on fire. -Arnold H. Glasow

◎ Success lies in the journey—not the destination.

◎ The best helping hand that you will ever receive is the one at the end of your own arm. -Fred Dehner

◎ The best way to predict your future is to create it

◎ The higher we are placed, the more humbly we should walk -Cicero

◎ The question for each man to settle is not what he would do if he had the means, time, influence and educational advantages, but what he will do with the things he has -Hamilton Wright Macbee

◎ There are no shortcuts to any place worth going. -Beverly Sills

◎ To laugh often and much; to win the respect of intelligent people and the affection of children; to earn the appreciation of honest critics and endure the betrayal of false friends; to appreciate beauty, to find the best in others; to leave the world a little better; whether by a healthy child, a garden patch or a redeemed social condition; to know even one life has breathed easier because you have lived. This is the meaning of success -Ralph Waldo Emerson

◎ Try not to become a man of success, but rather try to become a man of value -Albert Einstein

◎ Try not. Do or do not. There is no try -Yoda

◎ Whatever your lot in life, build something on it

■■■■■■■■■■■■■■■■■■■■■■■■

SUCCESS

◎ We must sail sometimes with the wind and sometimes against it, but we must sail, and not drift, nor lie at anchor -Oliver Wendell Holmes, Jr.

◎ What we are is God's gift to us. What we become is our gift to God. -Eleanor Powell

◎ Whether you think you can or think you can't you are right -Henry Ford

◎ You are not here merely to make a living. You are here in order to enable the world to live more amply, with greater vision, with a finer spirit of hope and achievement. You are here to enrich the world, and you impoverish yourself if you forget the errand -Woodrow Wilson

◎ You must do the thing you think you cannot do -Eleanor Roosevelt

◎ Your vision will become clear only when you look into your heart. Who looks outside, dreams. Who looks inside, awakens. -Carl Jung

◎ If you do not change what you're doing today, your tomorrow will be no different than yesterday

◎ Each man has his own vocation; his talent is his call. There is one direction in which all space is open to him. -Ralph Waldo Emerson

◎ Some of the world's greatest feats were accomplished by people not smart enough to know they were impossible-Doug Larson

◎ It is in the small decisions you and I make every day that create our destiny -Anthony Robbins

◎ Every achiever I have ever met says, "My life turned around when I began to believe in me" -Robert Schuller

◎ One step - choosing a goal and sticking to it - changes everything. -Scott Reed

◎ Realize that if you have time to whine and complain about something then you have the time to do something about it-Anthony J. D'Angelo

SUMMER

- Sing a Song of Summer

- A Little Taste of Summer

- A perfect summer day is when the sun is shining, the breeze is blowing, the birds are singing, and the lawn mower is broken. -James Dent

- A Place in the Sun

- A Slice of Summer

- A Summer Place

- Ah, summer, what power you have to make us suffer and like it. -Russel Baker

- Backyard Barbecue

- Bathing Beauties

- Diving into Summer

- Do what we can, summer will have its flies. - Ralph Waldo Emerson

- Dog Days of Summer

- Fun in the sun

- HELLLLO Sunshine

- Here are the fireflies Last to remember The end of August And first of September.

- Hot fun in the Summertime

- I know I am but summer to your heart, and not the full four seasons of the year. - Edna St. Vincent Millay

- In the depth of winter, I finally learned that within me there lay an invincible summer. -Albert Camus

- In The Good Ol' Summertime

- It amazes me that most people spend more time planning next summer's vacation than they do planning the rest of their lives.

- Keeping Cool

- Lakeside Adventures

- Lazy days of summer

- Love is to the heart what the summer is to the farmer's year. It brings to harvest all the loveliest flowers of the soul.

- May the Sun Shine Warm Upon Your Face

- School's Out for the Summer

- Seasons in the sun

- Shall I compare thee to a summer's day? -Shakespeare

- Splashing' Good Time

- Summer afternoon - summer afternoon; to me those have always been the two most beautiful words in the English language. -Henry James

- Summer Days & Summer Nights

- Song of Summer

SUMMER

◎ The Sun'll Come Out To-morrow

◎ This bud of love, by summer's ripening breath, May prove a beauteous flower when next we meet - Shakespeare

◎ To see the summer sky is poetry...-Emily Dickinson

◎ Where's the lemonade?

SUN

◎ Fun In The Sun

◎ Walkin' On Sunshine

◎ A New Day Is Dawning

◎ A Place in the Sun

◎ Bring on the sun

◎ I Was Raised on Country Sunshine

◎ If you awake and see the sunrise bathing earth in red and gold, As you gaze you'll somehow find it brings a washing of the soul.

◎ It fills one with anticipation to start the say with such a sight. God is good to give each new day, a gift wrapping so bright.

◎ Just a spoonful of sunshine to help brighten your day - Get Well Soon

SUN

You rose into my life like a promised sunrise, brightening my days with the light in your eyes -Maya Angelou

◎ Keep your face toward the sunshine and the shadows will fall behind you.

◎ Laughter brings sunshine into the home.

◎ Let the Sun Shine In

◎ May the Sun Shine Warm Upon Your Face

◎ May your pathways be full of sunshine, joy and safety as you travel life's journey.

◎ Rise and Shine

◎ Sunrise, Sunset swiftly fly the years...-Fiddler on the Roof

◎ Watching the Sunrise

◎ We all grow better in sunshine and love

◎ We'll Sing In The Sunshine

◎ You are my sunshine

◎ Good Morning Sunshine

◎ Have a funshine day

◎ Let the Sun Shine In

◎ Seasons in the Sun

311

SWIM & SURF

- Belly Flops
- 20,000 _____ Under the Sea
- A Human Cannonball
- A Splashing Good Time
- Bathing Beauty
- Big belly flop!
- Coolin' off in the Pool
- Dive Right In
- Diver Dude
- Diving Board Dare Devil
- Diving Diva
- Diving for _____
- Drenched
- Floatin'
- Getting Their Feet Wet
- Hair-larious
- High Divin' Dare Devil
- In the Swim
- In the Swim of Things
- Junior Lifeguard
- Just Floatin'
- Just keepin' my head above water
- Kerplunk! Kersplash!
- Lifeguard in training!
- Machine' Waves
- Making a splash in the world
- Making a Splash!
- Making fishy faces
- Making Waves
- Our Little Fish
- Our Little Mermaid
- Poolside Pals
- Pooly Wogs
- SINK or SWIM
- Skinny Dipper
- Sliding into Fun
- Soaking Wet
- Spilsh, splash, we're having a blast!
- Splash Dance
- Splash Down
- Splashing the Day Away
- Splat!
- Splish Splash
- Star Swimmer
- Stayin' Afloat
- Sun-bathing Beauty
- Surf City
- Surfer Boy/Girl

TEA

I had a little tea party this afternoon at three. 'Twas very small, three guests in all, Just I, myself and me. Myself ate up the sandwiches, While I drank up the tea. 'Twas also I who ate the pie, And passed the cake to me.

⊚ Life is like a cup of tea, it's all in how you make it

⊚ Sit long, talk much, drink tea with me

⊚ There are few hours in life more agreeable than the hour dedicated to the ceremony known as afternoon tea. - Henry James

⊚ I wish we could sit down together and have a cup of tea, but since we can't, when you have this one I hope you'll think of me.

⊚ Come and share a pot of tea, my home is warm and my friendship's free -Emilie Barnes

⊚ If I could take your troubles, I would toss them in the sea. But since I can't, I'm sending you, my favorite cup of tea.

⊚ My copper kettle whistles merrily and signals that it is time for tea. There is a great deal of poetry and fine sentiment in a chest of tea - Ralph Waldo Emerson

⊚ Come along inside– We'll see if tea and buns can make the world a better place - The Wind in the Willows

⊚ Time for you and time for me, And time yet for a hundred indecisions, And for a hundred visions and revisions, Before the taking of a toast and tea -TS Eliot

⊚ Tea for Two

⊚ I cannot sit and chat with you, the way I'd like to do. So brew yourself a cup of tea, I'll think of you, you think of me

TEACHERS

- Home Sweet Classroom
- A great teacher loves teaching others to love learning.
- A Kid With Class
- A Mark Of Class
- A teacher affects eternity; he can never tell where his influence stops. -Henry Adams
- A teacher gives, a teacher shares, but most of all a teacher cares
- A Teacher Is A Rainbow Between Hope And Achievement.
- A teacher takes a hand, opens a mind, and touches a heart
- A teacher's purpose is not to create students in his own image, but to develop students who can create their own image.
- A Touch Of Class
- Back to Class
- Caution! Learning zone!
- Children are a great deal more apt to follow your lead than the way you point.
- Class of _____

- Teachers Do the Write Thing
- Teachers Have Class
- . Teachers help us to learn from yesterday,
- Teachers love to hear the pitter patter of little feet going out to recess
- Teachers make the grade !!
- Teachers make the little things count...
- Teacher's Motto: When all else fails, pray for a fire drill
- Teacher's Pet
- Teachers Rule
- Teachers that love to teach...Create kids that love to learn
- Teaching creates all other professions.
- Teaching is a work of heart.
- Teaching is to touch a life forever...
- Teaching Today-Touches Tomorrow

TEACHERS

◉ Education is not the filling of a pail. It is the lightening of a fire -Yeats

◉ For every person wishing to teach, there are thirty not wanting to be taught, often in the same classroom

◉ He who can, does. He who cannot, teaches.

◉ He who opens a school door, closes a prison. - Victor Hugo

◉ Head of the Class

◉ How do kids ever learn to read and write? Bat, cat, hat, rat, sat...

◉ I am not a teacher, but an awakener. -Robert Frost

◉ I cannot teach anybody anything, I can only make them think.

◉ I have never let my schooling interfere with my education. -Mark Twain

◉ I like a teacher who gives you something to take home to think about besides homework. -Lily Tomlin

◉ Real learning begins with one good teacher

◉ Read each day—Keep the cobwebs away

◉ If you think education is expensive, try ignorance

◉ I'm just as lucky as I can be cause the world's best teacher is teaching me!

◉ In a Class of His Own

◉ It's what you learn after you know it all that counts.

◉ Learning is a journey, not a destination

◉ Learning is a treasure that will follow its owner everywhere

◉ Learning opens the world to minds ripe for the journey...

◉ Like all great teachers, you let me learn from my own mistakes.

◉ live for today, hope for tomorrow.

◉ Love is the square root of teaching

◉ Many can teach. A special few can reach

◉ No written word nor spoken plea can teach our youth what they should be nor all the books on all the shelves, it's what the teachers are themselves

◉ This Is What a Great Teacher Looks Like

TEACHERS

One hundred years from now, it will not matter What kind of car I drove or what kind of clothes I wore. All that will matter is that I made a difference In the life of a child!

◉ Praise the young and they will bloom.

◉ Preschool teachers enjoy the little things in life

◉ See Jane run. See Jane read. See Jane teach.

◉ I touch the future. I teach.

◉ I went to school to become a wit, but only got half way through!

◉ If you can count your blessings...thank a teacher!

◉ Old teachers never die—they just lose their class

◉ Kindergarten teachers hold their students hands for a short while—their hearts forever

◉ Tell me and I'll forget; show me and I may remember; involve me and I'll understand. - Chinese Proverb

◉ If you can read this....thank a teacher !

◉ None of us got where we are solely by pulling ourselves up by our bootstraps. We got here because somebody - a parent, a teacher, an Ivy League crony or a few nuns - bent down and helped us pick up our boots. - Thurgood Marshall

◉ Often, when I am reading a good book, I stop and thank my teacher. That is, I used to, until she got an unlisted number.

◉ Leading a child to learning's treasures—gives a teacher untold pleasures

◉ Life Lessons you can learn from your children: Play more. Be curious. Get all wrapped up in what you're doing. Even the littlest things can bring you pleasure.

◉ Here's to the kids who are different, the kids with the mischievous streak. For when they have grown, as history has shown, it's their difference that makes them unique.

TEDDY BEARS

Teddy Bear, Teddy Bear, torn and tattered, you were my friend when it really mattered. Here sits my teddy bear, all tattered and torn. Everybody loves him even though he's so worn. His body is floppy--His hair is a mess. But I love him dearly and he loves me best.

- Beariffic
- Ted E. Bear
- Beary Cute
- Beary special
- Bear with me
- Grin and bear it
- Beary Precious
- Bearly dressed
- Beary Best Buddies
- Beary Best Friends
- Life is Beary Precious
- Little hearts never fear when Teddy bear is near
- Love Bears All Things
- Love bears all things
- I can "bearly" wait!
- I Love Bear Hugs
- It Bears Repeating
- I love you beary much
- Me and My Teddy Bear
- A Beary Special Boy/Girl
- Don't be a bear...smile!
- Everyone has a soft spot
- Have a Beary Happy Day
- Beauty is in the eyes of the bear-holder
- Everyone needs someone to hold on to
- Everything in life I'll share, except my Teddy Bear
- A true friend can bear your faults
- Bear hugs and back rubs welcome
- Bear hugs make the friendliest greetings
- Bear hugs welcome here

TEDDY BEARS

- Friends make life Bearable

- Guardian Teddy Bear on Duty

- Happiness is a Beary big hug

- Happiness is always found in the "bear necessities"

- I wish I were a Teddy Bear, the more worn out you get, the more valuable you become

- It's OK to let your stuffing show now and then

- Learn to forgive like a Teddy Bear with heart open not caring who is right

- Learn to listen like a Teddy Bear, with ears open and mouth closed tight.

- Learn to love like a Teddy Bear, with arms open and imperfect eyesight.

- Love a bear and he will follow you anywhere.

- Lions and Tigers and Bears, Oh My!

- Listening is as important as talking

- Love is supposed to wear out your fur a little

- I Love Bears

- Love me--Love my Teddy Bear!

- Momma Bear, Poppa Bear and Baby Bear

- My Teddy, my best friend

- Never too old to play with Teddy Bears.

- One good cuddle can change a grumpy day

- Someone's got to keep their eyes open all the time

- Teddy and me, we welcome thee

- Teddy Bear Collector: trained in warm hugs and story telling.

- Teddy Bear! Teddy Bear!

- Teddy Bears are for cuddlin' and luvin'

- Teddy bears are stuffed with dreams and memories.

- Teddy bears are wonderful reminders for us to have soft edges

- Teddy bears are wonderful reminders for us to have soft edges, be full of love and trust,and always ready for a hug.

- The nicest dreams that will ever be are the dreams shared by my teddy and me

318

TEDDY BEARS

- The Teddy Bears' Picnic
- This is a home for Bears
- We all need a little tender loving bear.
- We bearly caught anything
- We can't bear to see you go
- Love is supposed to wear out your fur a little.
- There's nothing like a "warm fuzzy".
- One good cuddle can change a grumpy day.
- Bear hugs make the friendliest greetings.
- It's OK to let your stuffing show now and then.
- Someone's got to keep their eyes open all the time.
- Happiness is always found in the "bear necessities"
- Nobody cares if they're fat, and the older they get, the more they're worth!
- Teddy Bears are for cuddlin' and luvin'
- Teddy bears are stuffed with dreams and memories
- It's OK to let your stuffing show now and then

TEEN

- A child is someone who passes through your life, and then disappears into an adult.
- Adventures in Babysitting
- And this is my room!
- Awesome!
- Bottomless Pit
- Buff Boys
- But I need my own car
- But mom, everyone is wearing them
- Caught thinking
- Cool Chic
- First Date
- Freedom is a driver's license
- Generation Gap
- Grounded again
- Growing up means knowing when common sense must be applied and when it should be flouted in a few cases, in favor of uncommon sense

TEEN

◎ Hangin' Out

◎ Hey Nineteen

◎ Hip To Be Square

◎ How I spent my summer vacation

◎ If you want to recapture your youth, cut off his allowance -Bernstein

◎ I'm So Cool

◎ Is this Cool, or What?

◎ It's a Teen Thing

◎ It's not an Empty Nest until they get their stuff out of the basement.

◎ I've spent a fortune on my kid's education and a fortune on their teeth. The difference is, they use their teeth.

◎ My parents, my problem

◎ My telephone is my life

◎ The Dating Game

◎ Say What!?

◎ Shopping is my life

◎ Sixteen is the worst age to be. All the things you want most and all the things you can't have are exactly the same.

◎ Sweet Sixteen

◎ Talk to the Hand

◎ Teen Digest

◎ Teen Fling

◎ Teen Scene

◎ Teenage children are quick to correct the deficiencies of their mother and fathers so that those parents, in their old age, will be able to get along on their own.

◎ Teenagers complain there's nothing to do, then stay out all night doing it. -Bob Phillips

◎ Teens Just Wanna Have Fun

◎ Teens Rule!

◎ Telling a teenager the facts of life is like giving a fish a bath. -Arnold H. Glasow

◎ The best substitute for experience is being sixteen. -Raymond Duncan

◎ Where the Boys Are

TEETH

- Bless this Food
- Bless those gathered in this place, with thankful hearts and gifts of grace.
- Bunch of Turkeys
- Bushel Of Blessings
- Canning Our Bounty
- Cornucopia of Blessings
- Count your blessings
- A Day of Thanks
- Family & Turkey & Football... Oh My!
- Family and Food
- Family Traditions
- The Feast
- Feast with the Pilgrims
- Friends, Family, Food, and FOOTBALL!
- Give thanks
- Giving Thanks
- Gobble! Gobble!
- God is Great... God is Good
- A Happy Heart Is A Thankful Heart
- Harvest Delight
- Horn of Plenty

TEETH

- I Am Thankful
- I Can't believe I ate the whole thing
- I'm thankful for...
- In Everything Give Thanks
- It's Turkey Time!
- Let's Get Stuffed
- Let us Give Thanks
- May the bounty of the season fill your heart and your home
- Nap Time
- O, the Lord's been good to me
- On Thanksgiving Day all over America, families sit down to dinner at the same moment--halftime!
- Over the River and Through the Woods
- Pilgrims and Indians Remembered
- Pilgrim's Pride
- Pilgrim's Progress
- Praise God from whom all blessings flow...
- Pumpkin Pie
- Sharing the Food
- Sharing the Harvest

TENNIS

- 40 - Love
- Clear the net! / Over the net!
- Don't Argue With The Line Judge!
- I can't really play - I just love the outfits.
- I Love Tennis
- Love Tennis!
- Point-Set-Match
- Tennis - It's Not Just A Game
- Tennis Anyone?
- Tennis Bum
- Tennis is my Racquet

THANKFULNESS

- Were there no God, we would be in this glorious world with grateful hearts: and no one to thank - Christina Rossetti
- A contented mind is the greatest blessing a man can enjoy in this world - Joseph Addison
- As we express our gratitude, we must never forget that the highest appreciation is not to utter words, but to live by them. -JFK
- No duty is more urgent than that of returning thanks

THANKFULNESS

- Gratitude is the heart's memory
- He who can give thanks for little will always find he has enough.
- If you can't be content with what you have received, be thankful for what you have escaped.
- O Lord, that lends me life, lend me a heart replete with thankfulness -Shakespeare
- One act of thanksgiving made when things go wrong is worth a thousand when things go well.
- Thank you for just being you
- Thank you for touching my life
- Gratitude is not only the greatest of virtues, but the parent of all the others - Cicero
- Gratitude is the fairest blossom which springs from the soul -Henry Ward Beecher
- There is a calmness to a life lived in Gratitude, a quiet joy -Blum
- To speak gratitude is courteous and pleasant, to enact gratitude is generous and noble, but to live gratitude is to touch Heaven -Gaertner

■■■■■■■■■■■■■■■■■■■■■■

THANKSGIVING

◎ So much to be thankful for

◎ Take time to be thankful

◎ Thankful Hearts

◎ Thanks for the Giving

◎ Pilgrims and Indians

◎ Thanksgiving Bounty

◎ Thanksgiving Day

◎ Thanksgiving is for all creatures great and small

◎ Thanksgiving Traditions

◎ There shall be showers of blessings.

◎ A Time for Giving Thanks

◎ Tons of Turkey

◎ True Family Gathering

◎ The Turkeys Play On Thanksgiving Day

◎ Turkey and Dressing

◎ Turkey & Family Trimmings

◎ Turkey Day!

◎ Turkey, dressing & pumpkin pie

◎ Turkey in the Straw

◎ Turkey Time

◎ Turkey Tunes and Holiday Wishes

◎ We Are Gathered Here...

◎ We are thankful...

◎ We are Thankful For...

◎ We Gather Together

◎ We gather together to ask the Lord's blessings.

◎ We Give Thanks

◎ What a Bunch of Turkeys!

◎ We Are Thankful For...

◎ Merrily sing the harvest home -LaTourelle

◎ For our country extending from sea unto sea, The land that is known as the "Land of the Free"-Thanksgiving! Thanksgiving!

◎ The Turkey is a funny bird, His head goes wobble wobble. But all that he can ever say, is Gobble, Gobble, Gobble.

◎ Forever on Thanksgiving Day the heart will find the pathway home -Roger North

◎ Come, ye thankful people

◎ Raise the song of Harvest home! -H. Alford

◎ Turkey, dressing and pumpkin pie

◎ Turkey in the Straw

◎ Thank you God for everything

323

THEME PARKS

- ◎ A Pirate's Voyage
- ◎ Ahoy there Matey
- ◎ Your dreams can come true
- ◎ Animals, Animals, Animals
- ◎ Argh- Matey
- ◎ Bouncy, bouncy, bouncy
- ◎ Can you feel the love?
- ◎ Ducky Love
- ◎ Everyone Smiles
- ◎ Fairy Tales Do come true
- ◎ Feel the Magic
- ◎ I just can't wait to be King!
- ◎ I Won't Grow Up!
- ◎ It's a Jungle out there!
- ◎ Let the Adventure Begin
- ◎ Magical Moments
- ◎ My Goofy Kids
- ◎ Oh, Bother
- ◎ On the right Track
- ◎ Quack Attack
- ◎ Shiver Me Timbers

THEME PARKS

- ◎ The Happiest Place I've Been
- ◎ The Mad Hatter
- ◎ Under the sea
- ◎ We survived the Mountain
- ◎ When you wish upon a Star
- ◎ Woody's round up
- ◎ You Quack Me Up
- ◎ Family grows one smile at a time

TIME

- ◎ As Time Goes By
- ◎ Moments in Time
- ◎ Once upon a Time
- ◎ Somewhere in Time
- ◎ Time is Fleeting
- ◎ A Time to Be Born
- ◎ A Time to Remember
- ◎ The Time of My Life
- ◎ Take Things One Day at a Time
- ◎ Time that is not spent loving is wasted
- ◎ It Was the Best of Times

■■■■■■■■■■■■■■■■■■■■■■■

TIME

To everything there is a season, a time for every purpose under the sun. A time to be born and a time to die; a time to plant and a time to pluck up that which is planted; a time to kill and a time to heal ... a time to weep and a time to laugh; a time to mourn and a time to dance ... a time to embrace and a time to refrain from embracing; a time to lose and a time to seek; a time to rend and a time to sew; a time to keep silent and a time to speak; a time to love and a time to hate; a time for war and a time for peace. -Ecc. 3:1-8

◉ A Time and a Place for Everything

◉ Time may be a great healer, but it's a lousy beautician.

◉ Time Flies When You're Having Fun

◉ The sooner you fall behind, the more time you have to catch up

TIME

◉ All the treasures of earth cannot bring back one lost moment

◉ Love is not a matter of counting the years...but making the years count. - Michelle St. Amand

◉ Take time for each other- for nothing else is that important.

◉ Take time to live- to dance for fun to sing for joy to paint or sew or create a beautiful gift.

◉ Take time to watch- the snow swirling outside the windowpane, the flames dancing in the fireplace.

◉ There are not enough hours in a day to see what I'd like to see. There are not enough days in a week to enjoy the things that are free. There are not enough weeks in a year this wonderful world to view. There are not enough years in a lifetime To spend in loving you.

◉ How did it get so late so soon? It's night before it's afternoon. December is here before it's June. My goodness how the time has ewn. How did it get so late so soon? -Dr. Seuss

325

TOO COOL

- Hip To Be Square
- Hot Shots
- The Magnificent Seven
- The Mod Squad
- Rad
- Too Cool
- Totally
- Hot Dude
- Shabby Chic

TOOLS

- Toolman
- Drillman
- More Power!
- My Mr. Fix-It
- Tools of the trade
- Fold flap A into slot B
- I came ,I tooled, I built
- I've got extra pieces left over. Is that good?
- Man of Many Vises
- Measure Twice - Cut Once
- Some assembly required
- Do you know what you're doing?
- Call Me Tool-Man
- Mr. Contractor

TOYS

The Child's Toys and the Old Man's Reasons Are the Fruits of the Two seasons. -Blake

- A Doll's House
- Me and My Teddy Bear
- Me and My Toys
- My Favorite Things
- Puzzle Place
- The Marvelous Toy
- The Teddy Bears' Picnic
- My Toy Story
- Toyland
- Dolly and Me
- Won't you ride in my little red wagon
- When I was sick and lay a-bed, and all my toys beside me lay I had two pillows at my head, to keep me happy all the day-Robert Louis Stevenson
- ...of nature, the sun, and moon, the animals, the water, and stones, which should be their toys. -Ralph Waldo Emerson
- Building Blocks of Love
- I Love Toy Store
- Toys r My Passion

326

■ ■

TRACK

◎ A Day at the Races

◎ A Need for Speed

◎ Back on Track

◎ Camptown Races

◎ Chariots of Fire

◎ Dash of Excitement

◎ Giant Leap

◎ Go the Distance

◎ Going the Distance

◎ Have a Field Day

◎ High Hopes

◎ I Can Go the Distance

◎ In the Running

◎ Life in the Fast Lane

◎ Life in the Slow Lane

◎ Makin' Tracks

◎ Makin' Tracks

◎ On the Fast Track

◎ On Track

◎ On Your Mark, Get Set, Go

◎ On your mark, get set, go!

◎ One Giant Leap for Man

◎ Outpaced

◎ Race to the Finish

◎ Sprint to the Finish

TRAINS

◎ Choo choo

◎ All Aboard

◎ The Little Engine

◎ Caboose

TRAVEL

◎ Adieu, Paris

◎ All roads lead to Rome

◎ Almost Paradise

◎ America the Beautiful

◎ An American in Paris

◎ Are we there yet?

◎ Austin City Limits

◎ Bahama Mama

◎ Bon Voyage

◎ Bonnie Scotland

◎ California Girls

◎ A Dutch Treat

◎ Carribean Cruising

◎ Down in old Mexico

◎ Enchanted Journey

◎ Escape to the Cape

◎ From Here to Eternity

◎ Here Today-Gone to Maui

◎ I Love Paris or wherever

◎ I'm Leaving on a Jet Plane

◎ In Old Chicago

◎ Just Another Day in Paradise

◎ Merrie Old England

◎ Moon Over Miami

◎ New York, New York

◎ Oh, Canada

■ ■

TRAVEL

◉ Oh, the places you'll go!

◉ On The Road Again

◉ Tourist Trap

◉ Two Tickets to Paradise

◉ Way Down South

◉ Windmills and Tulips

◉ Wish You Were Here

◉ Wining Tasting in Napa

◉ Paris in the Spring

◉ Parisian Love Affair

◉ Sweet Home_____

◉ All Aboard the Wine Train

◉ Sweet Aloha

◉ South Pacific

◉ The Big Apple

◉ The Maine Place

◉ The Great Niagara

◉ Westward Hoe

◉ What A Wonderful World

◉ World Traveler

◉ Yankee Country

◉ Yellow Rose of Texas

◉ Gulliver's Travels

◉ No one realizes how beautiful it is to travel until he comes home and rests his head on his old familiar pillow. -Lin yutang

◉ Take only memories. Leave nothing but footprints. -Chief Seattle

◉ The joy is in the journey, not at the journey's end.

◉ There are two kinds of travel - first class and with children.

◉ From the Mountains to the Prairies

◉ Once you have traveled, the voyage never ends, but is played out over and over again in the quietest chambers-the mind can never break off from the journey.

◉ The Spa Treatment

◉ Home Sweet Hotel

◉ The most important trip you may take in life is meeting people halfway. -Henry Boye

◉ Way Down South in Dixie

TRUE LOVE

- Ahhhhh!
- Loverboy
- Baby Love
- Boys Rule
- Calendar Girl
- Dream Girl
- Dream Lover
- Dreamboat
- Goin' Steady
- Sweethearts
- Love You 4-ever
- Love of my Life
- Young Lovers
- My Funny Valentine
- Always and Forever
- Boys just wanna have fun
- Love Letters In The Sand
- High School Sweethearts
- Hold Me, Thrill Me, Kiss Me
- I Only Have Eyes For You
- It's Only Make Believe
- It's Only Puppy-Love
- Heart And Soul
- Baby CakeWhat a Babe!
- Wild and Crazy

Love makes the world go round.

- And they lived happily ever after.
- Seduce my mind and you can have my body, find my soul and I'm yours forever.
- Kiss me and you will see stars, love me and I will give them to you
- For me you have rendered all other men dull and all other lives uninteresting. -de Montherlant

TWINS & TRIPLETS

- 2 Times Terrible Two
- A Double Blessing
- A Winter Twin-derland
- And then there were two/three
- Double the Fun
- Double Trouble
- Father of twins-twice the man
- Friends forever, twins for life
- Got Twins? Got Triplets?
- Happiness is being the mother/Father/Mother of Twins
- I'm twin, but I'm one of a kind!
- If you think I'm cute, you should see my twin!
- Experience Wildlife-Raise Twins
- It's So Much Better With Two
- Me and my Womb-mate
- Mommy's Miracles
- Teeny Bopper Twins
- Terrific Triplets
- Three of a Kind
- Toothless Twins
- Triple Treasure
- Trouble Times Two
- Twice as Nice
- It Takes Two
- Twice the Blessing
- Twinkle, Twinkle Tiny Twins
- Twins are SNOW much fun
- Twins in our Tribe
- Twins in Training
- Twins Rule!
- Two by Two
- Two heads are better than one
- Two of a Kind
- Two Peas in a Pod
- Two Times the Love
- Two to Tango

ULTRASOUND

- My First Photographs
- Our Growing Family
- Under Construction
- Womb with a view
- In my womb I loved you
- Developing in the dark room

UNCLE

- Undenialbly
- Naturally
- Charismatic
- Loving
- Everyday
- Uncles are Awesome

VACATION

- Ahh! Relaxation
- Automobile Adventure's
- Come Sail Away
- Beach Bums
- Graceland: The King's Castle
- Have a Maui, Maui Christmas
- Here Today..Gone to Maui
- Hittin' the Slopes
- Two Tickets to Paradise
- The Last Time I Saw Paris
- The rainy days a man saves for usually seem to arrive during his vacation
- Those that say you can't take it with you never saw a car packed for a vacation trip.
- A vacation is having nothing to do and all day to do it in.
- What I Did On My Summer Vacation
- Vacation: When you spend thousands of dollars to see what rain looks like in different parts of the world
- Are we there yet?
- Road Trip
- On the Road Again
- Almost Paradise
- Family Vacation
- Goin' To Grandma's
- Bed & Breakfast Blessings
- Picture Postcards
- Bon Voyage
- We'll Sing in the Sunshine
- Gone to the Mountains
- Summer Vacation
- Life's A Beach
- Fun in the Sun
- Makin' Memories
- Wave Chaser
- Adventure Time
- Dream Vacation
- Romantic Vacation
- Going Places
- Just Plane Fun
- Our Getaway
- Room with a View
- We're off
- Summer Fling

VALENTINE'S DAY

- 1st Valentine
- 2 Hot 2 Handle
- Be Mine
- Be My Love
- Bee My Valentine
- Candy Hearts
- Caught By Cupid's Arrow
- First Love
- Funny Face, I Love You
- Grandmas' Little Heart throbs
- Happy Valentine's Day
- Heart of my Heart
- Hearts and Kisses
- Heartthrob!
- Kiss Me
- Let It Be Me
- Let Me Call You Sweetheart
- Love Letters
- Love Me Tender
- My Funny Valentine
- My heat leaps for you
- Sealed with a Kiss
- Some Bunny Loves You
- Sweetest Heart
- Sweets for the Sweet
- The Glory Of Love
- The Key to My Heart
- The Sweetest Days
- True Love
- Will You Be My Valentine?
- World's Best Kisser
- XOXOXOXOX
- You Send Me
- There's always time for chocolates and flowers
- Flowers, and Candy and Hearts, Oh my
- Love is in the air
- Loverboy

Roses are Red
Violets are Blue
Flowers are Nice
But Chocolate is Too!

Embrace me, my sweet embraceable you. -Gershwin

L ove looks not with the eyes, but with the mind; And therefore is winged Cupid painted blind. -Shakespeare

VEGGIES & FRUIT

- Two peas in a pod
- Never enough thyme
- Cool as a cucumber
- Hot Potato
- Sweet Tomato
- Apple of My Eye

VOLLEY BALL

- Bump! Set! Spike!
- Dig It
- Net Attack
- Net Force
- Queens of the Court
- Side Out
- Volley Girls
- What a Dig!
- What a Volley!
- Win the Rally
- It's a Net Thing

VOLUNTEERS

◉ Destiny is not necessarily what we get out of life, but rather, what we give. -Cary Grant

◉ How wonderful that no one need wait a single moment to improve the world. -Anne Frank

◉ It is not how much you do, but how much love you put in the doing. -Mother Theresa

◉ It is one of the beautiful compensations of this life that no one can sincerely try to help another without helping himself. -Ralph Waldo Emerson

◉ May I never get too busy in my own affairs that I fail to respond to the needs of others with kindness and compassion. -Thomas Jefferson

◉ No act of kindness, no matter how small, is ever wasted. -Aesop

◉ 'No joy can equal the joy serving others.' -Sai Baba

◉ One is not born into the world to do everything but to do something-Thoreau

◉ The best way to find yourself, is to lose yourself in the service of others. -Ghandi

◉ Those who can do more....volunteer.

◉ Volunteers are special folks

◉ Volunteers do not necessarily have the time; they just have heart

◉ Volunteers-Giving time today, to make life better tomorrow.

◉ You make a living by what you get. You make a life by what you give.

■■■■■■■■■■■■■■■■■■■■■■■■■■■■■

WALKING

- ◎ I Saw Her Standing There
- ◎ I'm Walkin' on Sunshine
- ◎ Just a Closer Walk with Thee
- ◎ Practice makes perfect
- ◎ The Journey Begins with a Single Step
- ◎ These Boots Are Made for Walking
- ◎ These Feet Were Made for Walkin'
- ◎ Walk On By
- ◎ You'll Never Walk Alone

WATER, SEA & OCEAN

- ◎ Crazy about Kayaking
- ◎ Hand in hand, through the sand
- ◎ On the Waterfront
- ◎ Red Sails in the Sunset
- ◎ Row, Row, Row Your Boat
- ◎ Sailing Away
- ◎ Still Waters Run Deep
- ◎ The Big Wave
- ◎ Whatever Floats Your Boat
- ◎ Where the ocean meets the sky, I'll be Sailing
- ◎ If the sky where made of paper and the ocean my ink well; I still wouldn't be able to describe how much I love you, and how wonderful you make me feel when I am with you.
- ◎ As the ocean is never full of water, so is the heart never full of love.
- ◎ If love was water, I'd give you the sea

WATERMELON

◎ When one has tasted watermelon, one knows what angels eat -Mark Twain

◎ A sittin' and a slurpin' and spittin' and a thinkin' watermelon

◎ Watermelon, it's a good fruit. You eat, you drink, you wash your face. -Enrico Caruso

WEAVING

◎ Handspinners put their own twist on things...

◎ Just another fiber artist, bobbin and weavin'...

◎ Look at the weaver, looming in the corner.

◎ Spent so much time on the loom, I've got nothing left

WEDDING

◎ I Thee Wed

◎ Circle of Love

◎ A Time for Us

◎ Kiss the Bride

◎ Dearly Beloved

◎ Cake in the Face

WEDDING

◎ I Do, Love You

◎ Always and Forever

◎ An Everlasting Love

◎ And the story begins

◎ Fairy tales do come true

◎ Father of the Bride

◎ From This Day Forward

◎ Getting Hitched

◎ Here Comes the Bride

◎ Honeymoon Heaven

◎ A kiss to build a dream on

◎ Hopelessly Devoted to You

◎ I'll Love You For Always

◎ Two Shall Become One

◎ I'm my Beloved's and he is mine

◎ In the Chapel in the Moonlight

◎ Little Band of Gold

◎ Together Forever

◎ Tying the Knot

◎ Wedding Bells Ring

◎ We've Only Just Begun

◎ Pretty in White

◎ Magnificent Bride

WEDDING

- Match made in Heaven
- Matchmaker
- Mother of the Bride
- Much Ado About Something
- My Best Friend's Wedding
- One Heart, One Mind
- Our Love Story Begins...
- Rules of Engagement
- Sealed With A Kiss
- Taking the Big Leap
- The Greatest of These is Love
- This Diamond Ring
- This Guy's In Love with You
- To Have and to Hold
- Today, I marry my best friend
- Will You Marry Me
- With This Ring
- Goin' to the Chapel
- Pretty maids all in a row
- Pre-wedding jitters
- Man of the Hour
- You look wonderful tonight
- They Live Happily Ever After
- You & Me Against The World
- Something Old New Borrowed Blue
- When I fall in love, it will be forever

■■■■■■■■■■■■■■■■■■■■■■■■■

Love is patient, love is kind. It does not envy, it does not boast, it is not proud. It is not rude, it is not self-seeking, it is not easily angered, it keeps no record of wrongs. Love does not delight in evil but rejoices with the truth. It always protects, always trusts, always hopes, always perseveres. Love never fails. -1 Cor. 13:4-8

◎ Love is you and me

◎ Swift the measured sands may run; Love like this is

never done- Dorothy Parker

◎ Love is patient; love is kind; love never ends.

◎ Can I have this dance for the rest of my life

◎ How sweet it is to be loved by you. -Eddie Holland

◎ When I give my heart, It will be completely

◎ Love and marriage, love and marriage, go together like a horse and carriage

◎ I cross my heart and promise to give all I've got to give to make all your dreams come true. -George Strait

◎ The road is bright before us, as hand in had we start. We'll travel on together, one mind, one soul, one heart

◎ You have to kiss a lot of frogs before you find your prince

WEEKDAYS

◎ Monday's child is fair of face; Tuesday's child is full of grace; Wednesday's child is full of woe; Thursday's child has far to go. Friday's child is loving and giving; Saturday's child works hard for its living; but the child that is born on the Sabbath day is fair and wise and good and gay.

◎ TGIF

◎ Sunday Brunch

◎ Sunday Funnies

◎ Monday, Monday

◎ Saturday Matinee

◎ Saturday Night Live

◎ Rainy Days and Mondays

◎ Saturday Morning Cartoons

WESTERN

◎ Tally Ho!

◎ Barrel Jumpin

◎ Country Girl

◎ Wild Wild West

◎ Bless this Barn

◎ The OK Corral

◎ Cowtown Cuties

◎ Lasso the moon

◎ Little Cowpoke

◎ Wild Wild West

◎ Just Horsin' Around

◎ Ye Old Homestead

◎ At Home on the Range

◎ How the West Was Fun

◎ Thank God I'm a Country Boy

◎ Rodeo Queen/King

◎ Hitch yer wagon to a star - Emerson

◎ Mamas don't let your babies grow up to be cowboys

WIFE

◎ A wife of noble character who can find? She is worth far more than rubies. -Prov. 31:10

◎ Spoiled rotten wife lives here.

◎ My name is not "Martha"

◎ If ever two were one, then surely we. If ever man were lov'd by wife, then thee. If ever wife was happy in a man, Compare with me, ye women, if you can. I prize thy love more than whole Mines of gold Or all the riches that the East doth hold. My love is such that Rivers cannot quench, Nor ought but love from thee give recompense. Thy love is such I can no way repay. The heavens reward thee manifold, I pray. Then while we live, in love let's so persever That when we live no more, we may live ever. - Anne Bradstreet

◎ Wives submit to your husbands as you submit to the Lord. -Gen.3:16

◎ wife: bride, apron, better half, bride, chauffeur, cook, dame, headache, helpmate, helpmeet, housecleaner, housewife, lady, little woman, madam, maid, mama, mat, mate, matron, mistress, Mrs., old lady, other half, partner, rib, roommate, sex godess, spouse, squaw, wifey

■■■■■■■■■■■■■■■■■■■■■■■■■■■■

WINTER

- All Bundled Up
- Arctic Blast
- Baby It's Cold Outside
- Brrrrr... It's Cold
- Bunkered in for the Blizzard
- Chill Out!
- Chilly Weather
- Cold Hands, Warm Heart
- Dashing Through the Snow
- Digging Out
- Eskimo Kisses
- First Snowball of the Season
- First Snowfall
- Fun in the Snow
- Give Me Hot Chocolate Any Day
- Have Snow, Will Shovel
- Snow is Glistening
- Jack Frost nipping at your nose
- Jingle Bells, Jingle Bells
- Mitten Weather
- Northern Exposure
- Our Snow Angel
- Our Snow Day
- Sleigh Ride
- Snow Angels
- Snow Bunny
- Snow Diggin'
- Snow Is Glistening
- Snow Much Fun
- Snow Play
- Snow Queen
- Snow Wonderful
- Snow, Snow, Snow
- Snowflakes Are Angel Kisses sent with Love
- The snow fell softly all the night It made a blanket soft and white. It covered houses, flowers and ground, But it didn't make a single sound!
- Snowflakes fall from Heaven's land softly and tenderly out of God's hand covering the earth with color so white creating beauty so pretty and bright. -LaTourelle
- The birds are gone, The ground is white, The winds are wild, They chill and bite. The ground is thick with slush and sleet, and I barely feel my feet.
- Smooth and clean and frosty white The world looks good enough to bite That's the season to be young Catching snowflakes on your tongue. -Ogden Nash

WINTER

◉ Snowball Fight
◉ Snow cones for Sale
◉ Snowed In
◉ Snowy Day
◉ South for the Winter
◉ Splendor in the Snow
◉ Sub-Zero
◉ The Chill Factor
◉ The Fire is So Delightful
◉ The Ice Man Cometh
◉ The Polar Express
◉ The Weather Outside is Frightful
◉ There's a Chill in the Air
◉ There's No Business Like Snow Business
◉ There's No People Like Snow People
◉ There's Snow Place like Home
◉ Walking in a winter wonderland
◉ Warm and Cozy bundled up or by the fire
◉ Warm toes and tummies
◉ Warm Woolen Mittens
◉ Winter is "Snow" Much Fun!
◉ Winter White

WINTER SPORTS

◉ Hitting The Ice
◉ Gliding Light
◉ Ski Bum
◉ Sledding Buddies
◉ Slip and Slide
◉ Smooth as Ice
◉ Future Olympian
◉ Skating Sweetly

WISDOM

I believe in the sun even though it is slow in rising. I believe in you without realizing. I believe in rain though there are no clouds in the sky. I believe in truth even though people lie. I believe in peace though sometimes I am violent. I believe in God even though he is silent

◎ Reach high, for stars lie hidden in your soul. Dream deep, for every dream precedes its goal.

◎ Yesterday is already a dream, And tomorrow is only a vision, But today well lived makes every yesterday a dream of happiness and every tomorrow a vision of hope.

◎ Accept me as I am, so I may learn what I can become.

◎ Let us be silent that we may hear the whisper of God.

◎ Let your life lightly dance on the edges of Time like dew on the tip of a leaf. -Tagore

◎ Love is that condition in which the happiness of another person Is essential to your own. -R.A. Heinlein

◎ The best feelings are those that Have no words to describe them.

◎ Whatever you are, be a good one. -Abraham Lincoln

WISDOM

What lies behind us, and what lies before us are tiny matters compared to what lies within us. -Ralph Waldo Emerson

◉ The greatest strength is gentleness. -Iroquois

◉ This is the day that the Lord hath made-be glad and rejoice in it

◉ To touch the soul of another human being is to walk on holy ground. -Stephen Covey

◉ Write it on your heart that every day is the best day in the year. -Ralph Waldo Emerson

◉ You may only be one person to the world, but you may also be the world to one person.

◉ From the moment of birth until our last breath our life is a unique story unfolding. Tales of faith, hope and trials; of miracles, adventures and romance; of joys, sorrows and love, blend harmoniously together to reveal the wonder of God's purpose in bestowing upon us this incredible gift of life. Yea, we are fearfully and wonderfully made and what we do with this blessing called life is our gift to God. Moment by moment our life's journey is a distinctively unique narrative illuminating our Creator's awesome love for us. -Linda LaTourelle

WISDOM FOR CHILDREN

- ◉ Dream Big
- ◉ Don't Worry
- ◉ Lighten up
- ◉ Look for the Fun
- ◉ Express yourself
- ◉ Dress how you like
- ◉ If you want it, ask for it
- ◉ Keep asking why 'til you get it
- ◉ You can color outside the line
- ◉ Don't waste time on nonsense
- ◉ Make up your own rules
- ◉ Share with your friends
- ◉ Use your imagination
- ◉ You gotta cry a little
- ◉ You gotta laugh a little
- ◉ Don't sweat the junk
- ◉ Believe in the impossible

WISHES

- ◉ Even the wishes of an ant reach heaven.
- ◉ When you wish upon a star
- ◉ Wishes really do come true
- ◉ I painted a star on my window, so I could wish on cloudy nights.

WOMEN

- Damsel in Distress
- Exclusively Feminine
- Ladies Night
- Modern Woman
- The Lady in Red
- Woman of the Year
- I am a woman in love
- My Wife, My Life

Lady Godiva
Ladies First
Little Women
Pretty Woman
Who's that Lady?
Wanted: Good Woman
Sexy Lady

- And God created Woman

- I am Woman hear me roar

- My Woman, My Woman, My Wife

- Earth's noblest thing, -a woman perfected

- Mirror Mirror on the Wall, I've my mother after all

- Some Women Are Dripping With Diamonds

- Woman was created from the rib of man. She was not made from his head to top him, nor out of his feet to be trampled upon, but out of his side, to be equal to him; under his arm, to be protected; and near his heart, to be loved.

- Women are like stars, there are millions of them out there, but only one can make your dreams come true

- Women still remember the first kiss after men have forgotten the last

WOMEN

◉ Inside some of us is a thin person struggling to get out, but they can usually be sedated with a few pieces of chocolate cake

◉ THREE wise men - are you serious?

◉ I keep trying to lose weight-but it keeps finding me

◉ Sure God created man before woman. But then you always make a rough draft before the final masterpiece

◉ Men are like a fine wine. They start out like grapes, and it's our job to stomp on them and keep them in the dark until they mature into something you'd like to have dinner with

◉ Stressed spelled backwards is desserts. Coincidence? I think not!

◉ Behind every successful woman... is a substantial amount of coffee. ~Stephanie Piro

◉ Who ever thought up the word "Mammogram"? Every time I hear it, I think I'm supposed to put my breast in an envelope and send it to someone. ~Jan King

◉ I've been on a constant diet for the last two decades. I've lost a total of 789 pounds. By all accounts, I should be hanging from a charm bracelet. ~Erma Bombeck

◉ The old theory was "Marry an older man, because they're more mature." But the new theory is: "Men don't mature. Marry a younger one." ~Rita Rudner

WOOD

◎ A chip off the old block

◎ Knock on wood

◎ Love is a many splintered thing

◎ Shiver me timber

WORK

◎ God put me on earth to accomplish a certain number of tasks. As of today I am so far behind, I need to live forever.

◎ I do my work at the same time each day ... the last minute!

◎ Women don't work as long and hard as men ... they do it right the first time.

WORTHINESS

We do not believe in ourselves until someone reveals that deep inside us is valuable, worth listening to, worthy of our trust, sacred to our touch. Once we believe in ourselves we can risk curiosity, wonder, spontaneous delight or any experience that reveals the human spirit.
                                            - e.e. cummings

WRITING

◎ The pen is mightier than the sword. -Bulwer-Lytton

◎ Written on My Heart

◎ Write your heart out!

◎ Writing is the only thing that, when I do it, I don't feel I should be doing something else. -Steinham

YOU KNOW YOU'RE A MOM WHEN:

Your favorite television show is a cartoon
Your kid throws up and you catch it
You hide in the bathroom to be alone
You spend an entire week wearing sweats
Spit is your number one cleaning agent
You buy cereal just for the marshmallows
You automatically double-knot everything you tie
You hate the thought of his wife even more
You stop criticizing the way your mother raised you
You have time to shave only one leg at a time
Your idea of a good day is the kids taking a long nap
You grocery shop at 1:00 a.m. at the 24 hour supermarket
You can't bear to give away baby clothes - it's so final
You're up each night until 11 PM vacuuming, dusting, wiping,
You can't bear the thought of your son's first girlfriend
You hope ketchup is a veggie, since it's the only one your child eats
When you automatically reach over and cut up the food on
your husband's plate at dinner time
When the kids are fighting, you threaten to ground them for the
rest of their life if they don't stop immediately
You count the sprinkles on each cupcake to make sure they're equal
You use cute little cookie cutters to make sandwiches for
your husband's lunch, along with a sippy cup
Your feet stick to jelly on the kitchen floor, there's cookie
crumbs in your bed...and you don't care
You know all the latest kiddie songs and sing them while
cooking dinner or washing the dishes
You're so desperate for adult conversation that you corner
the UPS driver for a chat
You know you're a mom when you actually start to like the
smell of strained carrots mixed with applesauce
You're willing to kiss your child's boo-boo, regardless of
what body part it happens to be on
You hear your mother's voice coming out of your mouth
when you say, "Not in your good clothes!"

YARDSALES

- Born to Garage Sale!
- Garage Sale Goddess
- Garage Sale Junkie
- Junkyard Junkies
- Pack Rat to the Max
- Trash to Treasure
- White Sales at Dawn
- Yardsale Queen
- What a Find!
- Buy of the Century
- What a Bargain!
- Collector of useless, worthless, can't-find-a-place-for, don't-need-it, bargain finds! And proud of it!
- So many garage sales –so little time

ZOO TIME

- A zoo-perific day
- African Safari
- I Work for Peanuts
- In the Jungle
- Monkey see-Monkey Do
- Peanut Gallery
- Suburban Safari
- Talk to the animals
- The lion sleeps tonight
- The Reptile House
- This Place is a Zoo
- Under the Big Top
- Zoo-ped-i-doo-da
- Zoo'pendous time
- Zoorassic Park
- Watch out zoo, here we come
- Please Don't Feed the Animals

FAVORITE QUOTES

_____

_____

_____

_____

_____

_____

_____

_____

_____

These are some of my favorite links:

www.creatingkeepsakes.com: Creating Keepsakes is a totally wonderful magazine. Interesting, fun, they even an e-mail newsletter that is packed full of news. Check out the great products they sell. The typestyle used throughout my book is one of their many products. You'll love their website and their other media.

www.scraptalk.com: Scraptalk.com is the place to talk about scrapbooking. Good place for reviews of products, too. Fun and catchy site! Go there and check out the new and upcoming products.

www.platinumheart.com: Strikingly beautiful cards designed with vintage penmanship and fine art. The items are absolutely magnificent...a treasure you'll keep forever. Camilla Smith is an amazing artist. You will love her cards and artwork. Truly unique creations some on handmade paper. Truly charming!

www.arnoldgrummer.com: If you have never tried your hand at papermaking, you are in for a blessing. You can make elegant, unique, funky or beautiful paper in just minutes with the kits offered by Arnold Grummer's. Whether you're young or old—the process is so simple. Handmade paper is so beautiful and enchanting, once you've made some you will be hooked.

Do you want to really add some pizzazz to your scrapbooking, stamping or artwork? Then you must try this fun and easy craft. The one-of-a-kind results will amaze and delight you and your friends. You'll never buy a card again, with all the gorgeous paper you can create for those special occasions. All your friends will be in awe of your new-found talent! I have personally met the owners, they are charming people. You'll love their down home help. Check them out for a great selection of all the supplies, molds and kits you'll need to make awesome looking handmade paper.

Celebrating Memories Scrapbook Store: If you live near the Napa Valley in Northern California, this store is a must to check out. It is stocked full of all the latest and best scrapbooking supplies. They also hold crops and special happenings quite regularly. They're not online, but they have a newsletter. Give them a call or stop on in for some very friendly service. **3158 Jefferson Street, Napa, CA Tel. (270) 254.7399**

www.inspiregraphics.com Looking for great fonts and clips for scrapbooking? Check these guys out. I have all their fonts and they're great!

For additional copies of our book
perhaps for a friend or a family member
or
visit our website to order
www. service@theultimateword.com
service@theultimateword.com

More ideas

Paper Projects:
Announcements
All Occasion Cards
Birthday Cards
Calendars
Christmas Cards
Envelopes
Invitations
Gift Bags
Gift Wrap
Letters
Journals
Newsletters
Photo Mats
Postcards
Posters
Signs

Handmade Projects:
Ceramics
Crafts
Gifts
Sewing
T-shirts
Needlework

Food Projects:
Labels for goodies
Decorating a cake

Other Decorating:
Windows
Door Hangings
Outdoor items
Holidays

- ◉ **Endless Uses**
- ◉ **Use pen, marker or brush**
- ◉ **Personalized for special touch**
- ◉ **Save money on gift**
- ◉ **Says "I Love You"**

■■■■■■■■■■■■■■■■■■■■■■■■■■■ ■ ■ ■

Need another book?

Are you looking at your friends book right now?
Order extra copies below or go to our website at:
www.theultimateword.com
Send us an E-mail:
service@theultimateword.com

MAIL ORDER FORM

Please send _____ copy/s of:
The ULTIMATE Guide to the Perfect Word

Name: _____

Address: _____

City: _____State_____Zip: _____

E-mail: _____Phone: _____

Please include $19.84 plus $1.95 s/h (per book)
(KY add 6% tax)

Blue Grass Publishing
PO Box 634
Mayfield, KY 42066
Tel. 270.251.3600

If you're looking for a gift that will be
well-loved and used regularly order now...

The ULTIMATE Guide to the Perfect Word

Available at your local scrapbook retailer, too.

If you love this book–
We know you'll be delighted
with our brand new collection of

Fabulously Fun Books

@

Scrappin' Expressions
Volumes 1 – 8
Designed to help transform your scrapbook pages,
stamping projects or handmade cards
into a work of art showcasing
your creative genius

Be looking for
more books coming soon by
Linda LaTourelle

BLUE GRASS
publishing
Mayfield, KY